H. G. Wells's Literary Criticism

H. G. Wells's Literary Criticism

EDITED BY

Patrick Parrinder
Reader in English,
Department of English, University of Reading

and

Robert M. Philmus
Professor
Department of English, Concordia University

THE HARVESTER PRESS · SUSSEX
BARNES & NOBLE BOOKS · NEW JERSEY

First published in Great Britain in 1980 by
THE HARVESTER PRESS LIMITED
Publishers: John Spiers and Margaret A. Boden
16, Ship Street, Brighton, Sussex

and in the USA by
BARNES & NOBLE BOOKS
81 Adams Drive, Totowa, New Jersey 07512

© 1980 by The Estate of H. G. Wells
Introductions and notes © 1980 by Patrick Parrinder and Robert M. Philmus

British Library Cataloguing in Publication Data
Wells, Herbert George
   H. G. Wells's literary criticism.
   1. English literature—History and criticism
   I. Parrinder, Patrick
   II. Philmus, Robert Michael
   820'.9   PR401
   ISBN 0–85527–768–8

Barnes & Noble Books
ISBN 0-389-20035-2

Text set in 11/12 pt Linotron 202 Bembo, printed and bound in Great Britain at The Pitman Press, Bath

All rights reserved

For David Hughes, Dale Mullen, and David Smith

Contents

Preface and Acknowledgements   ix
Table of Abbreviations   xiii
Introduction   1
H. G. Wells as Drama Critic for the *Pall Mall Gazette*   19
    An Ideal Husband, 24; The Importance of Being Earnest, 27; The Notorious Mrs Ebbsmith, 32; Delia Harding, 36; 'The Pose Novel,' 40; 'A Sawdust Doll,' 44.

Literary Criticism for the *Saturday Review*   48
    'Joan Haste,' 55; 'Mr Grant Allen's New Novel,' 59; 'The Method of Mr George Meredith,' 63; 'The Novel of Types,' 67; The Three Impostors, 72; 'Popular Writers and Press Critics,' 74; 'Jude the Obscure,' 79; On Lang and Buchan, 83; 'An Outcast of the Islands,'88; 'The Simple Art of Popular Pathos,' 94; More Haggard, 98; 'The Lost Stevenson,'99; 'A Servants' Hall Vision,' 104; 'The Well at the World's End,' 111; 'A Slum Novel,' 115; 'An Adelphi Romance,' 119; 'The Lost Quest,' 124; 'Flickers of Imagination and a Flare,' 129.

Gissing, Crane, and Joyce   134
    'The Paying Guest,' 141; 'The Novels of Mr George Gissing,' 144; 'The New American Novelists,' 156; 'Stephen Crane. From An English Standpoint,' 161; 'James Joyce,' 171; Experimental Science vs. Experimental Art, 176.

H. G. Wells and Henry James   178
    'Three *Yellow-Book* Story-Tellers,' 189; from 'The Contemporary Novel,'192; 'Of Art, of Literature, of Mr Henry James,' 207; 'The Novel of Ideas,' 216.

On Science Fiction, Utopian Fiction, and Fantasy   222
    On Max Pemberton, 230; On George MacDonald,

Contents

232; 'About Sir Thomas More,' 234; Preface to *The Sleeper Awakes*, 238; Preface to *The Scientific Romances,* 240; 'Fiction about the Future,' 246.

Bibliography   252

Index   253

Preface and Acknowledgements

Recognition of Wells's standing as a literary critic has been long delayed. The oversight is not surprising: he published the great majority of his reviews anonymously, at the beginning of his literary career, and infrequently spent his mature energies on this kind of exercise of his literary judgement. It is nevertheless regrettable that his fame in other roles has largely eclipsed any memory of him as a literary journalist. His progress through the literary world of his contemporaries profoundly affected his conception of himself as a social commentator, 'novelist of ideas', educationalist, and twentieth-century prophet; and his literary criticism, often witty and penetrating, provides a detailed chronicle of that journey. It also serves to correct a prevalent misunderstanding about his attitude towards literature. The controversies surrounding him during the years in which he quarrelled with Henry James, and afterwards, have left the impression that Wells was antagonistic to all established literary virtues. At times he himself seemed to join his detractors in encouraging some such idea. But his stance was never that simple. Placed beside his early critical writings, his later pronouncements reveal a similar commitment to literature, and a similar ambivalence about that commitment. The present selection from the best of those writings, early and late, is intended to permit a balanced and accurate assessment of the issues that he addresses and of his position regarding them.

Everything that Wells published in the way of literary criticism would fill a volume at least four to five times the size of this anthology. He wrote notices of more than 285 books for the *Saturday Review* alone. Many of these reviews concern authors and books now deservedly forgotten. The same can be said—not so inevitably—of the prefaces that he contributed to books by other writers. Yet even in speaking about authors whom the modern reader would not think of as meriting attention, Wells often has engaging things to say. It has therefore not always been easy to decide which of his

H. G. Wells's Literary Criticism

critical writings to exclude. In choosing among them, the editors have given priority to those dealing with novelists of established reputation—such as Meredith, Hardy, and James—and others, equally notable, whom Wells was instrumental in 'discovering'—chiefly, Conrad, Crane, and Joyce. Special consideration has also been accorded to reviews that most fully enunciate Wells's critical principles, particularly his strictures against the popular fiction of the day, and to his self-criticism and criticism of fiction cognate to his own 'scientific romances'.

Almost all of the items selected are not readily available elsewhere. Most have never been reprinted: among them, the reviews of Conrad, Crane, Haggard, Morrison, Stevenson, Turgenev, Wilde, and eighteen other writers. 'Fiction about the Future', an important statement on the art of 'prophecy', is printed here for the first time. A few of the remaining texts in this volume have been reprinted at various times, but often in unjustifiably truncated form, or in contexts that did not make it clear why Wells should have written them, or—on occasion—by scholars ignorant of their authorship. These texts, accompanied by the kind of introduction and annotative comments necessary for appreciating their significance, have been reprinted again here mainly for the sake of doing justice to Wells's views.

The items included in this anthology have been parcelled out under five headings and within each section usually appear in chronological order. (Exceptions to this rule occur in the case of 'The Pose Novel,' which for the purpose of continuity has been placed after Wells's drama criticism, and in the arrangement of his writings on Gissing and Crane). Why and how these divisions have been determined on should be evident from the introductory essays that precede each group of selections. In two instances, however, the disposition of texts may require an explanation. Wells's remarks about *The British Barbarians* and *The Well at the World's End* have little bearing on the generic content of the books in question, but do touch upon matters pertinent to the standpoint of much of his early criticism. For those reasons, his reviews of Grant Allen and William Morris have been grouped with other articles originally published in the

Preface

Saturday Review rather than with the material 'on science fiction, utopian fiction, and fantasy'.

Where more than one authorized version of a text exists, the editors have adopted the latest (or in the case of one preface, the most complete), but have noted any textual variants that might be meaningful. To regularize matters of spelling, it has occasionally been necessary to substitute 'z' for 's'. This is the only kind of editorial intervention not indicated in some way. The original title of any selection—when it may have been composed by Wells himself—appears within inverted commas; on the other hand, titles like '"An Ideal Husband," at the Haymarket,' or 'Fiction' or 'Preface,' have been replaced by others less awkwardly utilitarian, or more to the point. Various sorts of information, mostly concerning books that Wells cites or quotes from, have usually been interpolated in brackets instead of being consigned to footnotes. Quotations from each book discussed by Wells have been located with reference to the first English edition, by chapter and page—and if necessary, by the next largest division of the work (eg, [i:6:26] = part 1, ch 6, p 26; '0' = preface or introduction). Wherever it has been practicable to do so, brackets have been used also to correct misspelled names or to restore words omitted from quotations. When, by reflex or deliberately, Wells has reworded the text quoted, and when the rewording is not extensive, the original word or phrase has been bracketed after it, *in italics*.

Most of the selections have been reproduced in their entirety. But in order to include as many texts as possible, the editors have had to make cuts in nine of them. The precise nature and extent of these cuts have been noted whenever they occur. In five cases, the material left out consists of long quotations from books that Wells is reviewing, and in three others, of passages irrelevant to the context in which the item appears. A few pages of illustrative but inessential historical discussion have likewise been omitted from 'The Contemporary Novel'.

To avoid a proliferation of footnotes, references to various sources have been abbreviated. Those most frequently cited can be found in the table at the front of this volume.

H. G. Wells's Literary Criticism

Secondary works listed in the bibliographical appendix have elsewhere been designated only by author or editor. In a few instances, the reader may have to consult the index to discover the page on which full bibliographical data appear.

Our first acknowledgement must be to the various scholars whose labours in establishing the canon of Wells's literary criticism have made the present anthology possible. The essential articles on which a knowledge of Wells's reviewing activities is based, together with some other items that were especially useful to us, can be found in the bibliography at the end of this volume.

Permission to reprint Wells's writings has been granted by the Wells Estate through the good offices of A. P. Watt & Son, and in particular of Mr Michael Horniman. Items from the Wells Collection are reproduced by kind permission of the custodians of the University of Illinois Library at Urbana–Champaign.

The Dedication records our debt to three fellow-Wellsians whose advice and encouragement have immeasurably assisted us in putting together this anthology. In addition, we are grateful to Mary Ceibert, Assistant Librarian of the Rare Book Room at Urbana, and Joan Selby and Ann Yandle in Special Collections at the University of British Columbia Library, for indispensable aid, beyond the call of duty; to Gerald Auchinachie, Roger Bowen, Louise Clubb, C. H. Hill, Robert K. Martin, Patrick McCarthy, Alan Munton, Darko Suvin, and Stanley Tick for sharing with us their expertise in various matters, often going out of their way to do so; to Mariette Pilon for her patience and care in helping us assemble our final typescript; and, of course, to Ewa Parrinder and Maria Philmus for their sympathetic attention and support. On Patrick Parrinder's behalf, we would also like to thank the Research Board of the University of Reading for financial assistance, and the Department of English at the University of Illinois and the Central Bureau for Educational Visits and Exchanges for making it possible for him to complete his part of this book at Urbana–Champaign.

P. P.
R. M. P.

Table of Abbreviations

CH   H. G. Wells: The Critical Heritage, ed. Patrick Parrinder, (Routledge & Kegan Paul, London & Boston, 1972).
E&R   Henry James and H. G. Wells, ed. Leon Edel & Gordon N. Ray, (Hart–Davis, London and University of Illinois Press, Urbana, 1958).
EW   H. G. Wells: Early Writings in Science and Science Fiction, ed. Robert M. Philmus & David Y. Hughes, (University of California Press, Berkeley, Los Angeles, & London, 1975).
ExA   H. G. Wells, Experiment in Autobiography, (Gollancz & Cresset Press, London, and Macmillan, New York, 1934). Note: because the pagination of the American edition differs from that of the English, this work is referred to by chapter: section.
PMG   Pall Mall Gazette
SR   Saturday Review
West   Geoffrey West, H. G. Wells: A Sketch for a Portrait (Gerald Howe, London, 1930).

1 Introduction

H. G. Wells was not primarily a literary critic. The essays and reviews collected in this book added very little in his lifetime to the impact that he made as novelist, scientific romancer, educationalist, and prophet of man's future. Although he worked hard as drama critic of the *Pall Mall Gazette* (January–May 1895) and as chief fiction reviewer for the *Saturday Review* (March 1895–April 1897), his influence on public taste cannot be compared with that of his friends Arnold Bennett and Bernard Shaw. Most of his early reviews were published anonymously, and in the years of his fame he returned only very occasionally to literary criticism. More than that, he has been widely—but misleadingly—accused of 'turning his back' on literature altogether.

But Wells's criticism holds much greater interest than is suggested by this bare statement of the facts. His early reviewing—largely forgotten until Gordon N. Ray and others began to publicize the results of their research into the Wells Collection at the University of Illinois in the late 1950s—provides a week by week record of a remarkable period in English fiction and drama, seen through the eyes of a young writer whose advent was itself one of the major literary events of the time. The spring of 1895 saw first performances of Henry James's *Guy Domville* and of Wilde's *The Importance of Being Earnest*. Wells was present on both occasions, and as he came away from the fiasco of *Guy Domville* he first made the acquaintance of Bernard Shaw. The new novels of 1895–97 included Hardy's *Jude the Obscure*, Stevenson's *Weir of Hermiston*, Meredith's *The Amazing Marriage*, Morrison's *A Child of the Jago*, Gissing's *The Whirlpool*, Constance Garnett's translation of Turgenev's *Fathers and Children*, and first appearances by novelists such as Joseph Conrad, John Buchan, and Stephen Crane. In the same period Wells himself, previously known only as an author of biology text-books, produced *The Time Machine*, *The Island of Dr Moreau*, and *The Invisible Man*.

H. G. Wells's Literary Criticism

Wells's literary ambitions went well beyond the scientific romance, as is evident from his observations on the aims and techniques of those novelists who most captured his attention. At the same time he was sharp, witty, and frequently merciless in his dealings with the ballast of sentimental fiction and romantic fantasy which made up the major proportion of the literary diet of the 1890s. No other reviewer of his time was so consistently successful in sifting the good from the bad and in recognizing new talent.

Although Wells gave up regular reviewing in 1897, he continued to produce occasional literary essays and reviews for the rest of his life. Among these are seminal essays on George Gissing and Stephen Crane, a historic review of James Joyce's *A Portrait of the Artist as a Young Man*, and a large number of prefaces and introductions, both to his own books and to those of others. The latter category affords many instances of his generosity towards his fellow-writers, since he took pains to promote not only major 'discoveries' such as Joyce and Conrad, but minor writers such as Frank Swinnerton, W. N. P. Barbellion, and even the Folkestone bath-chairman George Meek.[1] Nevertheless, the best-known of Wells's later writings on the art of fiction are, inevitably, those surrounding his quarrel with Henry James—a quarrel which has long been recognized as one of the literary *causes célèbres* of the twentieth century. Wells's side of this aesthetic argument is still frequently slighted and misunderstood, mainly as a result of his outburst in *Boon* against the Master of Rye, and of his own subsequent carelessness about his literary reputation. Unable to sympathize with the lemon-squeezing literary formalism of James and his admirers, Wells preferred to declare himself an outcast from the 'hierarchy of conscious and deliberate writers' (West, p 13). To call for a reassessment of the Wells–James quarrel is not to deny the older man's achievements as novelist and critic. Wells himself paid many tributes to James. Yet Wells's critical writings, together with his fiction, stand as a reminder that James was not the only possible kind of novelist, and that the Novel, as refined by him, could not claim to monopolize the whole of prose fiction. Wells's declaration that 'To you literature like paint-

Introduction

ing is an end, to me literature like architecture is a means, it has a use' (E&R, p 264) makes him the fit antagonist of James in a conflict which has re-emerged in different forms and guises whenever the respective merits of artistic formalism versus social commitment have been debated in this century. In this respect, James and Wells are the two crucial, if antithetical, precursors of the modern man of letters.

1

Wells (1866–1946) learned to read and write in his mother's basement kitchen in Bromley, Kent. A shopkeeper's son, he was sent between the ages of seven and thirteen to the Commercial Academy of Thomas Morley, a master more concerned with preparing his pupils for the world of book-keeping than for the world of literature. Thanks to the lucky accident of a broken leg, Wells had already become a voracious reader by the time that he entered Mr Morley's school. *The Desert Daisy*, a high-spirited comic tale that he wrote and illustrated during the years 1878–80, provides what evidence there is of his early literary ambitions. Among the preliminary matter to this book (modelled, in all probability, on *Struwwelpeter*), Wells included a page of 'Notices of the Press' ('Beats Paradise Lost into eternal smash! Will be read when Shakespear is forgotten—but not before')[2]—juvenile comments which reveal not simply precociousness but the basic irreverence which was to be one of his most vital creative assets.

Only determination and good fortune could have permitted Wells's literary ambitions to survive the next phase of his development, his two-year apprenticeship (1881–83) as a shop assistant at Hyde's Drapery Emporium in Southsea. Forced into the drapery trade by his father's insolvency, Wells saw that the only way to escape from this position was to suppress his creativity and to acquire Useful Knowledge. He made a rule which he kept for several years, 'never to read a work of fiction or play a game' (*ExA* 4:2). Such free time as he had he devoted to reading popular science and to the usual adolescent self-questioning about religion. Later, when he had persuaded his mother to part with her meagre

H. G. Wells's Literary Criticism

savings in order to send him to Midhurst Grammar School, he occupied himself single-mindedly with passing the examinations that eventually won him a scholarship to the Normal School of Science at South Kensington in 1884. Another sporadic but crucial influence during these years was that of his brief holidays at Uppark, the country mansion to which his mother had returned as a domestic servant. The tenant of the house was an elderly lady who allowed her housekeeper's son freedom of a library which included *Gulliver's Travels, Vathek, Rasselas,* the works of Voltaire and Tom Paine, and, above all, Plato's *Republic.* Uppark was the perfect seeding ground for a future atheist, republican, and social critic.

The opportunities that Wells discovered for himself both at Uppark and at South Kensington—where he became a pupil of the great biologist and social thinker T. H. Huxley—may be said to have determined the whole course of his intellectual life. Though Wells derived his lifelong commitment to the scientific world-view from Huxley's teaching, in his second and third years at the Normal School he neglected his scientific studies to the point where he failed his final examination in geology. Much of his time was spent in the adjacent museums and libraries, where he first read the major romantic writers, from Blake and Shelley to Tennyson and Carlyle. He became a prominent figure in the college Debating Society, he wrote for and edited the *Science Schools Journal,* and he bought a blood-red tie to announce his conversion to socialism. Wells's writings of this time (produced, in all probability, while he was playing truant from Professor Judd's geology classes) are Carlylean in tone and express a self-conscious revolt against both the evangelical Christianity of his family and the utilitarianism of the Normal School. His essay on 'Socrates' in the *Science Schools Journal* for December 1886 is an earnest defence of the Athenian philosopher against the Philistine assault of Macaulay's essay on Bacon—the classic Victorian expression of the gospel of scientific progress to which many of Wells's fellow-pupils at the Normal School subscribed. Socrates's clarification of the intellectual conceptions of mankind, Wells argues, was quite as valuable as the technological

Introduction

benefits produced by post-Renaissance science. Wells's early identification with Plato and Socrates is of great significance. Although he himself was to become a prophet of technological progress, he never saw the achievement of material perfection as a substitute for a Utopia based upon adequate conceptions of the beautiful and the good.

Wells's most substantial contribution to the *Science Schools Journal* was a very different work, 'The Chronic Argonauts', the first of a series of drafts of the story which eventually became *The Time Machine*. Between 1887 and 1893 he earned his living by teaching science, and filled up his spare time with his efforts to become a writer. After a brief and terrifying encounter in 1891 with Frank Harris, editor of the prestigious *Fortnightly Review* (see ExA 6:6), he drifted into regular journalism for two obscure educational papers, the *Educational Times* and the *University Correspondent*. His breakthrough into full-time writing and journalism came in 1893, after a near-fatal lung haemorrhage. Wells's talents were recognized first by Harry Cust of the *Pall Mall Gazette*, then by W. E. Henley of the *National Observer* and by Frank Harris, now editor of the drastically reorganized *Saturday Review*. With the appearance of *The Time Machine* in book form in 1895, he became known not only as an up-and-coming journalist but as a young writer of genius. Literary London lay open before him.

2

'The literary life', Wells wrote in 1909, 'is one of the modern forms of adventure'.[3] In these years of the middle '90s he was working with immense creative energy to establish himself as a writer, and, together with his second wife Jane, he was also enjoying the adventure to the full. The romances and short stories which made his reputation he privately regarded as young man's work, and as a means of realizing his true vocation, which lay in realistic fiction. Wells's tendency to play down his achievement in the 'scientific romances' was, in large measure, a testimony to the awe in which the 'classical' nineteenth-century novelists, notably Dickens, Thackeray, George Eliot, and Balzac, were

H. G. Wells's Literary Criticism

held by his generation. At the same time, their informality of method was being challenged by the new doctrines of realism, from Zola's 'scientific' naturalism to James's concern with the refinement of narrative method. As a reviewer, Wells took a conscientious interest in the new doctrines, but finally rejected them as putting unnecessary restraints on the artist's freedom of self-expression. Though a natural writer of fiction, he was never at ease with the discussions of the formal properties of the novel that preoccupied his contemporaries. Wells was not yet a convert to the propaganda novel or novel of ideas; he was particularly scornful of Grant Allen's attempts, in *The British Barbarians* and *The Woman Who Did*, to deck out a moral message in fictional clothing. But he clearly preferred novels which combined a vigorous narrative tone, such as that which Dickens and Thackeray had used, with a pungent and wide-ranging exploration of contemporary problems.

Wells's discovery of literary London began when, at thirty-six hours' notice, he became the *Pall Mall Gazette*'s drama critic. He had no evening clothes and had scarcely visited a London theatre. Yet, within eighteen months, he was venturing into the company of Meredith and Hardy and making the acquaintance of Gissing at an Omar Khayyam Club dinner; and soon he and Jane Wells began to practise a literary hospitality which was to become legendary. In her novel *Pilgrimage,* one of their friends, Dorothy Richardson, portrays an early Wells party, held in their villa at Worcester Park, Surrey; the date must be 1896 or 1897. The atmosphere is one of 'clever literary people trying to say things well . . . they would despise everybody who was living an ordinary life, or earning a living in anything but something to do with books'.[4] The host, thinly disguised as 'Hypo Wilson', is looked upon by everyone as 'a coming great man; the great new "critic"; a new kind of critic'. Wilson believes that 'the business of the writer [is] imagination, not romantic imagination, but realism, fine realism, the truth about "the savage", about all the past and present' (*Pilgrimage*, II, 132, 122). He looks to science as the only source of enlightenment, and takes it for granted that literature will have been transformed beyond recognition in fifty years' time.

If Wells in his Worcester Park period suspected that there

Introduction

might be a fundamental conflict between the literary and the scientific outlooks, his early reviews do not reveal it. Influenced by Darwin's Theory of Evolution, with its stress on variation and development in species, he had rejected scientific positivism for a philosophy of pragmatism and 'experiment' based on the metaphysical notion that 'nothing is strictly like anything else'. This concept of the 'unique', put forward as a fundamental norm in his paper 'The Rediscovery of the Unique' (1891), is also an underlying principle of his early literary criticism. 'There are', he says, 'no rules for the greater factors' that differentiate the best in literature from mediocrity: 'Every writer who is worth reading is a law unto himself'.[5] Accordingly, he eschews the kind of academicism which values each new literary work in proportion to its imitativeness of the 'classics'. The primary function of the critic, as Wells sees it, flatly contradicts the assumptions of such an approach. His job should be 'to appreciate essentials, to understand the bearing of structural expedients upon design, to get at an author through his workmanship, to analyse a work as though it stood alone in the world'; and toward that end he must above all possess 'a vast breadth of sympathy to understand the various standpoints, the various aims of fiction'.[6] Prizing 'uniqueness' as the paramount literary value, he seizes on every opportunity to hold up its opposite, the meretricious posturing of best-selling fiction, to ridicule.

Uniqueness, for Wells, does not imply autonomy. The purpose of the variation is to advance the species to which it belongs. He takes it for granted that fiction is a mode of social communication, and that the value of individuality in literature can only be ascertained through its bearing on the 'typical'. Clearly, he thought of his reviews as having an educative function; he was simultaneously instructing and entertaining the *Saturday Review* readership with his articles popularizing science. His fiction reviews express a fellow-craftsman's respect for the technical command of novelists such as Meredith and Stephen Crane, on the one hand, and a prevailing belief that fiction should be a rational and sociologically useful art on the other. He criticizes Morrison for omitting the broader social context in his portrayal of the

H. G. Wells's Literary Criticism

London slums in *A Child of the Jago*, and hails *Jude the Obscure* for its introduction of the 'voice of the educated proletarian' into English literature. His insight into Gissing's achievement as a novelist was tempered by a somewhat naive faith in his friend's power to correct the flaws in his work under rational critical guidance. Although Wells's rationalism contrasts with the prevailing mood of the 'aesthetic 'nineties', it is likely that he would have remained nothing more than an antagonistic voice in the literary world of his time, had it not been for his contacts with scientists and, increasingly, with Fabian socialists. As it was, his critical disagreements with his fellow-writers turned gradually into disaffection with certain qualities of the modern literary imagination as such. It is for this reason that he was not tempted in his years of fame to set up as an arbiter of popular literary taste, in the way that his friend Arnold Bennett was to do. Wells's ambitions, unlike Bennett's, were not to be satisfied by success and influence within the 'world of books'.

The Worcester Park period recorded by Dorothy Richardson was succeeded by Wells's move in 1898 to a very different milieu, that of Sandgate in Kent, where he found himself on regular visiting terms with Henry James, Joseph Conrad, and Ford Madox Hueffer (later Ford). George Gissing was a frequent visitor, and Stephen Crane and his wife Cora were brief but unforgettable tenants of the nearby mansion of Brede Place. From the account given in his *Autobiography*, it seems evident that Wells tried hard to impress his social and scientific ideas on these men, while they contrived to engage him—and sometimes to infuriate him—with the minutiae of artistic technique. Wells was accepted as a literary genius in the Sandgate circle, but the mutual respect among its members—witnessed, for example, in Conrad's dedication of *The Secret Agent* to Wells in 1907—was ultimately to develop into a settled intellectual enmity. His growing negligence in matters of detail and carelessness about the exact artistic 'impression' became increasingly painful to Conrad and James. Wells, for his part, concludes the series of coldly brilliant character-sketches of his fellow-artists in *Experiment in Autobiography* with the

Introduction

judgement that, by the standards of his scientific training, they all had 'uneducated' minds. For all their sensitivity and openness to impressions, they were deficient in the analytic and systematizing habits that were nourished by sociological or scientific studies. Wells came to view the artistic temperament as 'impulsive, uncoordinated, wilful', in contrast to the trained, scientific intelligence which was the only guarantee of salvation for modern man (see *ExA* 8:5).

In Conrad and James, Wells had encountered not only two major writers, but two writers who were convinced of the special mission of the artist to an exceptional degree. It is clear that one does not need such a conviction in order to become a great novelist. Wells, dedicated to an ideal of broadening culture transformed by scientific thinking, was unable to agree that literature should become more theoretical and erudite in its concerns; at best, he could only concede that the Jamesian and Conradian complexities of narrative technique and point of view might have the status accorded to esoteric experiments within a scientific field. His own conception of knowledge was one which saw the synthetic overview and the broad generalization as the climax of cognitive endeavour. He went on trying for many years to find a role which he could play within the 'literary world' while roaming at large outside it; for example, in his association with Ford Madox Hueffer in the launching of the *English Review* in 1908–9, and (much later) in his championship of free expression as President of the International P.E.N. Clubs in the 1930s. But Wells's antagonism to the aesthetic specialism he had met with in Conrad and James came increasingly to mark his pronouncements on art in general.

3

'. . . all these books, in fifty years' time, burnt up by the air; he did not seem to think it an awful idea' (*Pilgrimage*, II, 130). Like Hypo Wilson in *Pilgrimage*, Wells's revolutionary views of culture and society were calculated to cause unease among his fellow-writers of the late Victorian and Edwardian period. He was not convinced that the techniques of art mattered supremely, because he was comparatively unmoved by the traditional belief in the permanence of art; the belief, expressed in Shakespeare's sonnets and implicit in the heroic self-dedication of so many of the great post-romantic artists, that it is given to the poet and to him alone to transcend the ravages of time. In Wells's view, the writer was always the creature of his time and place, and his responsibility lay towards his contemporaries. While his sense of the expendability of past literature is by no means unprecedented, it runs counter to the general consecration of the literary tradition which has taken place in the last two hundred years. One of Wells's favourite fictional strategies was to 'modernize' an older work; thus More's *Utopia* became *A Modern Utopia* (1905), Machiavelli's *The Prince* became *The New Machiavelli* (1911), the Book of Job became *The Undying Fire* (1919), and Burton's *Anatomy of Melancholy* became *The Anatomy of Frustration* (1936). He would not have claimed that these works were 'better' than their originals, only that they had more immediate relevance to contemporary readers. He likewise suggests that modern historiography and biography may come in time to replace realistic fiction such as that of Bennett and Galsworthy, and confesses to doubting whether his own creations Kipps and Mr Polly have 'that sort of vitality that endures into new social phases' (*ExA* 8:5). It may be asked whether his beliefs as to the unprecedented situation of twentieth-century man, and the obsolescence of the literary tradition, do not align him—despite appearances—with certain aspects of the modernist movement in literature and the arts? Wells's literary attitudes, however, are not those of modernism, partly because of his predilection for the relatively informal narrative methods of the earlier novelists such as Swift, Sterne, and Thackeray, and partly because of his commitment to science. For all their obsession with science and technology, such movements as Italian Futurism were really characterized by an extreme aestheticism. The Futurists worshipped the most violent manifestations of science while utterly rejecting the constraints of scientific method, which—as Wells's example shows—are closely related to the ideals of nineteenth-century liberalism. Scientific method assigns ab-

Introduction

solute value to freedom of thought and publication, clarity of expression, and the need for independent confirmation and correction of all aspects of a theory. Modern art, on the other hand, tends to assert the privileged insight of the artist and his right to use a personal language which defies immediate or widespread comprehension. The artist, defined in this way, is simply an anomaly in Wells's view of culture.

That view is systematically outlined in *Mankind in the Making* (1903), the second of the books of sociological essays (the first was *Anticipations*, published two years previously) with which he made his reputation as social thinker and prophet of the new century. In *Mankind in the Making* he deals with all aspects of the future cultivation of the individual, from conception and birth to adult participation in the life of the state which Wells (referring to Plato, rather than to W. H. Mallock's book with that title) calls the 'New Republic'. If the community is to realize its maximum potential, participation in its intellectual life must be open to everyone. Interestingly enough, several of Wells's specific proposals in the area of education and cultural life anticipate the objectives of the New Criticism which emerged in England and America in the 1920s. He advocates the formation of an English Language Society to improve the quality of English teaching in schools. (The English Association, dedicated to these ends, was founded in 1906.) At a higher level, there should be university 'lectureships and readerships in which questions of style and method could be illustrated by quotation (not necessarily of a flattering sort) from contemporary work'. Without such criticism of contemporary writing, he adds, 'the criticism and circulation of the classics is quite manifestly vain'. If these statements look back to his practice as a reviewer, with his use of quotations to expose best-selling bathos and to assert basic standards of literary sanity, they might also be said to anticipate the 'practical criticism' later championed by I. A. Richards, F. R. Leavis, and others. In the same way, his plea for the establishment of a critical review, and his later involvement with Ford Madox Hueffer's *English Review*, look forward to such seminal critical journals of the 1920s and '30s as the *Criterion*, the *Calendar of Modern Letters*, and *Scrutiny*.

Though he refers (perhaps inconsistently) to criticism as the

H. G. Wells's Literary Criticism

'mineralogy of literature and art' (pp 367–68), Wells in *Mankind in the Making* suggests a broader function for criticism 'at the present time' than even Matthew Arnold had done in his famous essay of 1865. Unlike Arnold, Wells does not accord imaginative writing any degree of implicit priority in intellectual life; his view of culture is, in large part, a synthesis of Arnoldian ideas with those of Arnold's Victorian antagonists, such as J. H. Newman, J. S. Mill, and T. H. Huxley. Perhaps remembering Carlyle, Wells defines 'literature' in the widest terms possible, so as to include

all that is good in journalism; all untechnical speculative and philosophical writing; all that is true and new in the drama, in poetry, fiction, or any other distinctly literary form; and all scientific publication that is not purely a matter of recording or technical working out, all scientific publication, that is, that deals with general ideas. (p 341)

'Literature' in this sense is synonymous with 'thought', and the penultimate chapter of *Mankind in the Making* is devoted to 'Thought in the Modern State'. In modern usage one perhaps needs an artificial term such as 'social discourse' to cover a comparable range of meaning. Wells's idea of social discourse is one of cognitive communication on the model of a scientific congress; in *Boon* (1915), his attack on Henry James is part of a comprehensive satire (itself a modernization of W. H. Mallock's satire *The New Republic*, written a generation earlier) on the contemporary literary world for its failure to achieve any sort of collaborative advancement of knowledge or clarification of concepts. The true ideal of criticism, Wells implies, should be the process of discussion and independent verification to which scientific papers are subjected. However, it would be wrong to conclude from Wells's 'scientific' model of social discourse that he believed that certainty could be attained in aesthetic judgements. His relativistic attitude to literary values is consistent not only with his biological evolutionism, but with his rejection of scientific positivism in favour of the pragmatist epistemology outlined in his essay 'Scepticism of the Instrument' (1905). He argues in that essay that the classifications the scientist imposes on phenomena have no final objective reality, being determined by the schemata of the human brain. The same must be true of the 'mineralogy' of literary criticism.

Introduction

What of the institutional setting of literature in the 'New Republic'? In accordance with the general principles of the welfare state that he outlines in *Mankind in the Making*, Wells recommends that a system of public endowments should be paid to writers. One of the bodies administering these is to be an elective Guild of Authors, with some of the functions and privileges of a literary academy. Wells's somewhat ambivalent response to the idea of an academy is significant, revealing both his uneasy hostility to the literary establishment and the conflict in his mind between anarchism and Fabian collectivism. The many alterations in the machinery of social life that he proposes in *Mankind in the Making* are typical of what he would later denounce as 'bureaucratic socialism'. In the same year as this book appeared, he wrote in the magazine *Young Man* that an English academy at the present time could be nothing but 'the last refinement of vulgarity'.[8] The idea of an academy nevertheless held considerable attractions for many of Wells's Edwardian contemporaries. The nucleus of the movement was the Academic Committee of the Royal Society of Literature, whose members included Henry James, W. B. Yeats, Joseph Conrad, Bernard Shaw, and Edmund Gosse, as well as many lesser figures. Wells described the Academic Committee in a 1911 article in the *Eye-Witness* as a queer and even sinister body, and suggested somewhat flippantly that its future activities might even extend to the censorship of books.[9] (As he felt he had narrowly escaped censorship with *Ann Veronica* and *The New Machiavelli*, novels which were banned in 1911 by certain public libraries, he was highly sensitive on this point.) After a discreet interval, Gosse and James decided to approach him in early 1912 to invite him to join the Committee. Though at other times in his career he might well have accepted these overtures, Wells refused with a vehement affirmation of the necessary anarchy of the artist's calling, and of his need for freedom from all direction from outside. The position that he now took up, however unpalatable to James, was consistent with his argument in the introduction to *The Country of the Blind, and Other Stories*

H. G. Wells's Literary Criticism

(1911) that creativity depended upon the 'new and variant', rather than upon rigid rules. In an essay putting his own achievements in the short story in the context of the remarkable flowering of that form in the 1890s, he wrote that 'I am all for laxness and variety in this as in every field of art. Insistence upon rigid forms and austere unities seems to me the instinctive reaction of the sterile against the fecund'.[10]

Ironically, Wells had to admit in the same essay that the sources of his inspiration as a short-story writer had now dried up. *The Country of the Blind* was the last of his volumes of short stories, and represented, in large part, a republication of much earlier work. A general view of the fiction that he produced in the decade after *The New Machiavelli* (1911), including such voluminous and turgidly-written novels as *The Research Magnificent* (1915) and *Joan and Peter* (1918), suggests that he was suffering from imaginative exhaustion. His major achievement in this period lay not in the novel but in the *Outline of History* (1920). Nevertheless, when he wrote to James in 1915 that he would rather be called a journalist than an artist, he was referring to his aims as a novelist rather than to his extra-fictional activities. He was now habitually using the novel as a vehicle for communicating his thoughts and opinions to a wide audience, in defiance of the artistic principles that he had championed as a young reviewer.

Wells never renounced the creation of literary fictions. Despite his assessment of his career in *Experiment in Autobiography*, from the age of thirty until his death he can be described as first and foremost a novelist. His fullest statement of his ideal of the novel as social discourse appears in his essay 'The Contemporary Novel' (1911). There he energetically claims new freedoms for the novel-form, which he regards as inherently a powerful means of moral persuasion, and hence as the most effective vehicle for a wide-ranging discussion of ideas and social conventions. By this argument, he justifies his commitment to fiction. What he leaves unexplained, however, is his lifelong preoccupation with fantasy.

Although he never explicitly accounted for that commit-

Introduction

ment, how he would have done so can be inferred from his practice. He uses fantasy primarily as a speculative device, a means of cognitive exploration. Nor is the attitude behind this understanding of fantasy confined to his 'fantasies': it is fundamental to Wells. 'The habitual interest in [the writer's] life is critical anticipation. Of everything he asks: To what will this lead?', he wrote in his last book *Mind At the End of Its Tether* (1945). Speculation is the mainspring of Wells's science fiction, in which—as he says in his preface to the *Scientific Romances* (1933)—he starts from a single more or less fantastic hypothesis, and then seeks to follow out its consequences. Moreover, his realistic novels are also speculative instruments in that they seek to enlarge the reader's understanding of how society works and of the possibilities of individual behaviour within the society. As the figure of George Ponderevo in *Tono-Bungay* shows, such fiction at its best is a genuine experiment in social understanding, the results of which cannot be predicted in advance. 'Social understanding' here should not be confused with positivistic social science, since the Wellsian sociological novel is always a highly personal statement, an expression (as he wrote to Bennett in 1900) of 'a purblind laborious intelligence exploring that cell of Being called Wells' (Wilson, p 47). Insofar as he was able to use the novel as a speculative device in this manner, Wells's vocation as a prophet and his gift for imaginative projection became as one. For prophecy, however much it is cloaked with an air of scientific sobriety, always has an act of fabulation or make-believe as its basis. Thus Wells's post-1915 stance as a social prophet, with its consequent devaluation of merely 'artistic' achievements, was the expression of certain literary choices, of a particular set of responses to the major literary questions of his age. His way of reacting to fame and success says much about the opportunities and temptations that lie before the modern writer. But only from a narrowly dogmatic standpoint can it be described (as James and his followers have described it) as a renunciation of literature.

5

Boon, the satire in which Wells passed judgement on the

H. G. Wells's Literary Criticism

literary world, is a chaotic and yet unforgettable book, and one to which it is impossible to do justice in the present anthology. (It is to be hoped that some publisher will see his way to reissuing it.) Behind the savage comedy of his attack on the Edwardian intelligentsia it is not difficult to discern the despair he felt as the full enormity of the First World War became apparent in England. The individual caricatures of his literary *confrères* (and these are not all hostile—there is a fine tribute to Ford, for example, as the 'Only Uncle of the Gifted Young') are circumscribed by Wells's fear that the intellectual life of his contemporaries is symptomatic, not of progress, but of uncontrollable disintegration. *Boon* was, indeed, written in a state of distress (hinted at in his half-hearted apology to Henry James) comparable to that expressed in *Mind At the End of Its Tether* exactly thirty years later. Wells's first efforts to master his wartime distress resulted in the religiosity of *Mr Britling Sees It Through* (1916), but his more permanent and satisfying answer to the disintegration of the literary milieu he had known was to compile *The Outline of History*. The *Outline* is not only a universal history but a heroic attempt to comprehend and, if possible, reverse the forces of decay in modern civilization.

During the last thirty years of his life, Wells's position in the literary world became steadily more isolated. His reputation was that of a popular writer whose contemporary importance derived from his powers as a social visionary rather than from the quality of his writing. Where artists like James, Conrad, Gissing, and Ford had looked to him as an equal, the leaders of the new generation condescended to him as a writer whose time was past. Wells himself laboured tirelessly to promote his ideas in political and scientific circles, but regarded his imaginative achievements with undue modesty. In his late essay on 'The Novel of Ideas' (1940), for example, he portrays himself as a practitioner of the 'great tradition' of the fictionalized dialogue, but admits that the merits of his own contributions may be 'infinitesimal'. Similarly, in his *Autobiography* he discusses 'Whether I am a Novelist' (7:5). He was, in fact, a novelist who was rapidly and—to some extent—undeservedly losing his public.

Since his death, the memory of Wells's renunciation of the

Introduction

status of a literary artist in the aftermath of his battle with James has continued to give scandal to a proportion of contemporary readers. Alternatively, it has sometimes been suggested that a writer who sacrificed the praise and approval of the *littérateurs* in order to fulfil his sense of a mission towards mankind as a whole might be seen as a kind of spiritual hero.[11] The issues involved are not trivial ones: Wells both as artist and propagandist addressed himself to the most inescapable of twentieth-century anxieties, that concerned with the future survival of civilization itself. But if the word 'prophet' is, together with 'novelist', that which best sums up his multifarious activities, this is not only on account of his preoccupation with the future, but because it draws attention to his affinities with such nineteenth-century forebears as Carlyle, Emerson, Ruskin, and William Morris—writers whose work is equally diverse, and whose literary eminence is equally difficult to justify from a strictly formalist point of view. Like some of his predecessors, Wells's attitude was diametrically opposed to literary academicism, because he saw the future of literature as being, ultimately, of greater moment than either its past or its present. While he came to view the technical refinements of art as luxury products in the present phase of the world's history, he made unbridled artistic activity one of the cornerstones of his portrayal of Utopia. Art, he argues in *The Work, Wealth and Happiness of Mankind* (1931), is an exploration of human possibilities beyond the limits of material necessity. As advancing civilization releases more and more of man's surplus energies, his need to find fulfilment through literature and art will be correspondingly greater. In Utopia, at last, art will take precedence over science, because, while the main product of science is power over nature, 'it is art alone which can find uses for power'.[12] This argument, which is borne out by his portrayals of Utopia in *Men Like Gods* (1923) and elsewhere, is evidence that the Arnoldian strain in Wells's dealings with literature and criticism was never finally extinguished. But there is one fundamental difference from Arnold, and from the disciplines of literary and art criticism as they have developed since Arnold's day—a difference that was already

H. G. Wells's Literary Criticism

perceived by Dorothy Richardson in those early years at Worcester Park. Wells continued to see art as the expression of the perpetual changes in man's consciousness, so that nothing that can be called a tradition has final authority.[13] Though his criticism of other men's writing was usually exemplary in its concreteness, his attitude to the canon of artistic achievements in general was to value it less as a monument to the past than as a vague foreshadowing of what might be to come. Speaking in the visionary role which was so essential a part of his genius, Wells wrote in *The Work, Wealth and Happiness of Mankind* that 'it is absurd to suppose that all that we now call art, the masterpieces, the supreme attainments, is anything more than an intimation of what the surplus energy of mankind may presently achieve' (*ed. cit.*, II, 784).

NOTES

1. See his introductions to Swinnerton's *Nocturne* (1918), to *The Journal of a Disappointed Man* by W.N.P. Barbellion (1919), and to *George Meek, Bath-Chairman, by Himself* (1910).
2. *The Desert Daisy*, with an introduction by Gordon N. Ray (Beta Phi Mu, Urbana, Illinois, 1957), p iv.
3. 'Mr Wells Explains Himself', *T. P.'s Magazine*, December 1911, p 341. (In the postscript [p 343] Wells says that he wrote this piece in 1909).
4. Dorothy Richardson, *Pilgrimage* (Knopf, New York, n.d.), II, pp 116–17.
   Later citations refer to this edition.
5. 'The Secrets of the Short Story', SR 80: 23 November 1895, p 693.
6. 'Certain Critical Opinions', SR 82: 11 July 1896, p 33.
7. *Mankind in the Making* (Chapman & Hall, London, 1903), p 371. Subsequent references in the text are to this edition.
8. 'The Decay of the Novel' (symposium), *Young Man*, 17: January 1903, p 24.
9. 'The Academic Committee', *Eye-Witness*, 28 September 1911, pp 464–5.
10. *The Country of the Blind, and Other Stories* (Nelson, London, n.d.), p vii.
11. For a sceptical view of this matter, see David Lodge, *The Novelist at the Crossroads* (Cornell University Press, Ithaca, N. Y., 1971), p 213.
12. *The Work, Wealth and Happiness of Mankind* (Doubleday, Doran & Co, Garden City, N.Y., 1931), II, p 784.
13. In this, his utopianism resembles that of William Morris in *News from Nowhere* (1891).

2 H. G. Wells as Drama Critic for the Pall Mall Gazette

Harry Cust, the editor of the *Pall Mall Gazette,* engaged H. G. Wells in January of 1895 to review plays for his daily. Although Cust had promised him the first available position, the appointment was somewhat odd in that the candidate seemed to be only minimally qualified for the job. Since publishing textbooks on biology and physiography (in 1893), Wells had been eking out a living as a freelance journalist. He had written a number of articles on pedagogical and scientific subjects for various newspapers and periodicals. Over the eighteen months or so prior to his assuming the duties of drama critic, he had submitted to Cust some light and for the most part ephemeral essays; but while some of these dealt with the literary scene, even the best of them—'The Pose Novel', for example—had been couched in rather general terms. He had had a fair amount of experience reviewing books, both for the *Pall Mall Gazette* and for the *Saturday Review*; but with rare exceptions, the books that Cust and Frank Harris had given him to report on had been scientific texts, popularized accounts of scientific developments, or pseudo-scientific disquisitions.[1] Moreover, his knowledge of the theatre was scant, to say the least. According to his own testimony, he told Cust at the time that 'not counting the Crystal Palace Pantomine and Gilbert and Sullivan, I've been only twice to the theatre' (*ExA* 8:2).

During his five-month stint as a critic of the drama, Wells was in effect competing with George Bernard Shaw. Wells, however, did not have the time or (perhaps as a consequence) the space that Harris put at Shaw's disposal. He had to post his copy to Cust immediately; and, as he himself admits (see *ExA* 8:2; also 'The Notorious Mrs Ebbsmith'), he regularly spent the hours from midnight till two or three in the morning writing down his impressions of the performance that he had just witnessed. Shaw's reviews for the *Saturday Review*, on the other hand, usually appeared a week or more after he had seen the play(s) on which he comments.

Given this difference in working conditions, given also the disparity in their credentials, it might seem absurd to compare the pronouncements of the neophyte with those of the man widely regarded as one of the most perspicacious critics of the stage. And yet, surprisingly enough, Wells does stand up to the comparison. Shaw, of course, clearly has the advantage when it comes to analyzing matters of stagecraft, acting style, and dramatic technique. But where knowledge gives precedence to intelligence and intuitive insight, Wells reveals himself to be Shaw's equal.

Sometimes their judgements conflict. Shaw, for instance, much preferred *An Ideal Husband* to *The Importance of Being Earnest*.[2] Wells did not. Perceiving that as a dramatist 'Oscar Wilde is, so to speak, working his way towards innocence, as others work towards experience', he deemed *Earnest* to be by far the better play. Disagreements of this kind, however, are uncommon. More frequently, the remarks of the two critics complement each other while diverging in emphasis. Thus Shaw, lauding the intent of the author of *A Leader of Men*, concentrates on those aspects of the political meaning of the drama that Charles Ward had to disguise or suppress altogether, and uses the occasion to attack censorship and the institution of Censor. Wells, having likewise bestowed praise on Ward for his 'sincere attempt to be modern and lifelike', devotes his attention principally to the actors, and especially to Mr Fred Terry, whose histrionics in the role of Llewellyn he contemns as typifying 'the old stage method' of Victorian convention.[3]

This latter opinion of Wells's is one that Shaw repeatedly endorses. Nor is it exceptional for them to agree. Their assessments as a rule coincide, and in some cases coincide to an extent that is striking in its particularity. Both, for example, speak of Arthur Wing Pinero's failure of courage in *The Notorious Mrs Ebbsmith*, and both cite the incident which concludes the third act of the play as epitomizing that failure:

H. G. Wells as a Drama Critic

A less sensible and less courageous stage effect I have never witnessed. If Mr Pinero had created for us a woman whose childhood had been made miserable by the gloomy terrorism which vulgar, fanatical parents extract from the Bible, then he might fitly have given some of the public a very wholesome lesson by making the woman [Mrs Ebbsmith] thrust the Bible into the stove and leave it there.... But to introduce a woman ... whose one misfortune—her unhappy marriage—can hardly by any stretch of casuistry be laid to the charge of St Paul's teaching; to make this woman senselessly say that all her misfortunes are due to the Bible; to make her throw it into the stove, and then injure herself horribly in pulling it out again: this, I submit, is a piece of claptrap so gross that it absolves me from all obligation to treat Mr Pinero's art as anything higher than the barest art of theatrical sensation. (Shaw in SR 79:347)

Mrs Thorpe and her brother, ... [i]nstead of presenting us any longer with shocked British respectability, ... suddenly become two noble and sexless souls bent upon saving Mrs Ebbsmith. They poke a Bible at her, which she thrusts into the stove and then burns her arm in attempting to recover. A large number of solid-thinking people will regard that tawdry effect as a fine piece of courage on Mr Pinero's part. (Wells)

Here the point that Shaw makes at length Wells conveys with terse sarcasm. But sometimes the reverse is true. Of *Delia Harding*, for example, Shaw caustically declares: 'Sardou's plan of playwriting is first to invent the action of the piece, and then to carefully keep it off the stage and have it announced merely by letters and telegrams' (SR 79:508). Wells is more circumstantial in his critique. Only after having enumerated the 'documents'—seven in all—does he observe: 'Unless our solicitors take a hand, few of us play out our tragedies with that amount of paper'.

In later years Wells inclined to exaggerate his differences with Shaw. 'Shaw like James and like his still more consciously cultivated disciple, Granville Barker, believed firmly in The Theatre as a finished and definite something demanding devotion; offering great opportunities to the human mind ... I had no such belief' (*ExA* 8:2). This last assertion, however, misrepresents his actual stance as a reviewer. His criticisms of the English stage of the 90s by no means disclose an antipathy to the Shavian Theatre of Ideas. On the contrary, he insistently demands that plays should appeal to the intelligence and consistently denigrates as mindless those which do not. The standpoint from which he condemns Sardou varies from Shaw's solely in its historical perspective. Shaw looked upon 'Sardoodledom' as the culminating *reductio ad absurdum* of the nineteenth-century *pièce bien faite* (SR 79:725–27). Wells, instead, views *Delia Harding* synchronically, as it were, and by his choice of terms of opprobrium allies it with contemporary farce in the worst sense: 'The people are impossible, the development is impossible, and some of the scenic effects even are impossible. And for all this impossibility there is neither emotional effect, nor pervading beauty, nor the literary interests of wit or satire, nor sustained intellectual interest'.

Wells does not categorically object to farce. He admired *Earnest* and found *A Pair of Spectacles* (PMG, 18 January 1895, p 4) amusing. But 'original farcical comedy'—a sardonic and self-contradictory phrase as he deploys it—is for him the type of bad drama. It presents a world that he calls 'Stageland', based upon 'a view of life that is got, we believe, by walking about with the eyes shut, and reading the penny comic papers'.[4] Its situations are impossibly contrived and usually repetitive; its 'jests' 'familiar' and frequently 'coarse'; and above all, its personages are invariably stereotypic. 'It is a play not of characters, [but] of characteristics', he writes of one specimen; and of another: 'not a character . . . is really taken out of life, or has, indeed, the slightest claim to be considered a human being'.[5]

That Wells did not totally dissociate the realm of the drama from that of the novel is evident from 'The Sawdust Doll', where he speaks of the 'conventional' heroine of Victorian fiction as having 'walked the stage a thousand times'. He may have held to the view that the exigencies of theatrical presentation limit the degree of subtlety a playwright can aspire to;[6] but otherwise the criteria expressed or implied in his drama criticism carry over—along with concepts like authorial 'posturing'—into his reviews of fiction for the *Saturday Review*. There the romance occupies a place analogous to that of farce in his work for the *Pall Mall Gazette*. To be sure, he articulates the standards by which he depreciates the Scott tradition in a less rudimentary and less perfunctory fashion than he does in expressing his strictures against 'original farcical comedy'. But his allegiance to

H. G. Wells as a Drama Critic

verisimilitude, wit, and originality as measures of excellence remains constant.

NOTES

1 For a selective bibliography of these writings, see EW, pp 230–44.
2 Compare G.B.S. on *An Ideal Husband*, in 'Two New Plays', SR 79: 12 January 1895, pp 44–45, with his opinion of *Earnest*, in 'A New Play and a New Old One', SR 79: 23 February 1895, p 250.
3 Shaw, 'A Purified Play', SR 79: 16 February 1895, pp 216–18; Wells, '"A Leader of Men", at the Comedy', PMG, 11 February 1895, p 3.
4 'An Original Farcical Comedy at Terry's' (Barton White's *Margate*), PMG, 6 February 1895, p 4.
5 '"The Passport", at Terry's', PMG, 26 April 1895, p 3; '"A Pair of Spectacles", at the Garrick', PMG, 18 January 1895, p 4.
6 'A play written for the stage may very well be compared to a pen-and-ink drawing that is to undergo reproduction by some cheap photographic process. Delicate turns, soft shades, refinements of grey *must* be avoided; bold strokes, black and firm—that is all that is possible': '"Guy Domville", at the St James's', PMG, 7 January 1895, p 3.

H. G. Wells's Literary Criticism

AN IDEAL HUSBAND

An Ideal Husband *was Oscar Wilde's third comedy. Wells's first assignment as drama critic took him to the Haymarket Theatre for its première, on January 3, 1895. His review appeared in the next day's* Pall Mall Gazette *(p 3).*

'Do tell me your conception of the "Ideal Husband"', said Lady Stutfield, in the *Woman of No Importance* [1893]. 'I think it would be so very, very helpful' [Act 2]. Mrs Allonby, you will remember, thought there couldn't be such a thing, and wandered into objectionable flippancy. And Mr Oscar Wilde, having, we more than suspect, a lingering sympathy with Mrs Allonby, has written a whole play to demonstrate this impossibility. In many ways his new production is diverting, and even where the fun is not of the rarest character the play remains interesting. And, among other things, it marks an interesting phase in the dramatic development of its author. Your common man begins in innocence, in his golden youth he wears his heart upon his sleeve; but Oscar Wilde is, so to speak, working his way to innocence, as others work towards experience—is sloughing his epigrams slowly but surely, and discovering to an appreciative world, beneath the attenuated veil of his wit, that he, too, has a heart. In the end the sorely-tried Sir Robert and Lady Chiltern, amidst the applause and emotion of a crowded house, decided that love was the best of life; the engagement of Lord Goring and the altogether charming and always innocent Miss Mabel Chiltern was successfully accomplished, and the villanies of the abominable Mrs Cheveley were—if the adjective is permissible—routed with Adelphian ignominy.[1]

The interest centres around Sir Robert Chiltern. The Woman with a Past is becoming a little commonplace, and here, accordingly, the Man with a Past has his fling. In his youth he was seduced by a wicked financier and the craving for power, and betrayed the Cabinet intentions with regard to the Suez Canal shares. Thereby he made £85,000, and on this capital rose to political eminence and lived a life of

H. G. Wells as a Drama Critic

ostentatious integrity. But his wife—to whom he has been married some years—believes him to be as pure as the driven snow. A wicked woman, Mrs Cheveley—singularly ill dressed, by the way, for a wicked woman—becomes possessed of the letter betraying his secret, and with this she comes to England to machinate. She endeavours to utilize her power to involve him in a discreditable Argentine swindle, and subsequently, out of sheer abominable wickedness, to marry herself to Lord Goring, his confidential friend. Her motive is spite against Lady Chiltern, a sufficiently adequate motive in any woman. But, having stolen a diamond bracelet, and being so unwise as to wear this in society and drop it in Sir Robert Chiltern's house, she is exploded by Lord Goring, who recognizes it. She tells Lady Chiltern the unhappy man's secret in the second act, and Act 3 sees his agony and her own when Lord Goring foils her schemes. Chiltern does the right thing while he still thinks the threat hangs on him, and his wife forgives him his one lapse from blamelessness in Act 4. That is the main story.

Mr Lewis Waller gives us Sir Robert Chiltern in a fine vein of caricature. A more delicious rendering of that distinctive denizen of stageland—the good, pure, emotional man trying to forget his one secret sin, so good that even his wife does not suspect that he falls short of perfection—it would be impossible to imagine. His emotions are terrible, he clenches his fists—one may imagine the nails dug into his palms—opens and shuts his voiceless lips, rolls his eyes, and so lives through four terrible acts of mental torment. He drives along, as he remarks, 'a ship without a rudder in a night without a star' [Act 3]. If anything, we would object that he scarcely avails himself sufficiently of the hand clasped upon the forehead—always a beautiful expression of a strong man's despair. Miss Julia Neilson makes a graceful Lady Chiltern, and keeps her emotions throughout in the key of Mr Waller. Miss Florence West as Mrs Cheveley is most human in the first act; thereafter she follows the imperious mandate of the playwright and becomes an impossible wicked woman in equally impossible costumes. Mr [Charles H.] Hawtrey as Lord Goring plays a double and difficult part; in one aspect he is the honest, noble friend of the main plot, and in another the very delightful wooer of Miss Maud Millett's delightfully fresh Miss Mabel Chiltern. This latter episode is indeed singularly bright and innocent, and from Mr Oscar Wilde unexpected, and the only possible objection is that it has nothing whatever to do with the development of the play.

Miss Fanny Brough as Lady Markby is delightful, her account of the older system of feminine education is an especially bright specimen of tea-table conversation. She has no business in the play except to introduce Mrs Cheveley, yet nevertheless she could be ill spared. But why Lady Basildon, Mrs Marchmont, the Vicomte de Nanjac, or Mr Montfort exist as distinct super-super entities is an absolute mystery. The two ladies speak on the topic of husbands, a matter already sufficiently discussed by Lady Stutfield and Mrs Allonby in a previous play, and having discharged with precision a few characteristic paradoxes—'the seven deadly virtues',[2] for instance—they pass away and we see them no more. Apparently they were forgotten as the dramatist warmed to his work.

So much for the play. It is not excellent; indeed, after *Lady Windermere's Fan* [1892] and [*A*] *Woman of No Importance*, it is decidedly disappointing. But worse have succeeded, and it was at least excellently received. It may be this melodramatic touch, this attempt at commonplace emotions and the falling off in epigram, may be merely a cynical or satirical concession to the public taste. Or it may be something more, an attempt to get free from the purely clever pose, that merely epigrammatic attitude, that has been vulgarized to the level of the punster. But, taking it seriously, and disregarding any possibly imaginary tendency towards a new width of treatment, the play is unquestionably very poor.

NOTES

1 The Adelphi Theatre, from the time it received that name (1819) to the end of the nineteenth century, was known principally for its melodramas.
2 This phrase is actually Mrs Cheveley's (Act 1).

H. G. Wells as a Drama Critic
THE IMPORTANCE OF BEING EARNEST

The Importance of Being Earnest *opened on February 14, 1895 at the St James's Theatre. Directed by the deservedly famous actor-manager George Alexander, who took for himself the role of John Worthing, the play was Wilde's last and best (and might also be thought of, albeit anachronistically, as the last and perhaps the greatest Restoration Comedy of Manners). Wells, in a review (PMG, 16 February 1895, p 4) that clearly indicates his esteem for Wilde's achievement, interprets it from a rather novel perspective: as a satire on Victorian conventions of play-writing.*

It is, we were told last night, 'much harder to listen to nonsense than to talk it';[1] but not if it is good nonsense. And very good nonsense, excellent fooling, is this new play of Mr Oscar Wilde's. It is, indeed, as new a new comedy as we have had this year. Most of the others, after the fashion of Mr John Worthing, J.P., last night, have been simply the old comedies posing as their own imaginary youngest brothers. More humorous dealing with theatrical conventions it would be difficult to imagine. To the dramatic critic especially, who leads a dismal life, it came with a flavour of rare holiday. As for the serious people who populate this city, and to whom it is addressed, how they will take it is another matter. Last night, at any rate, it was a success, and our familiar first-night audience—whose cough, by-the-bye, is much quieter—received it with delight.

You must understand that his John Worthing, J.P., was found in a bag, a very respectable but by no means imposing two-handled black bag, at Victoria Station. He was a baby at the time. Mr Cardrew [sic] took him by mistake, and to save the bother of inquiry adopted him, called him Worthing, after the day's destination, and endowed him with a Manor House. Then, dying without any indecent longevity, he made Cecily Cardrew [sic], his grandchild, ward to John Worthing. In the country John Worthing was a quiet man, in London a blade: and to conceal the scandal from his ward and the vicar, he called himself Ernest Worthing in town, and explained in the country that that was his younger brother. And in town he became enamoured of the Hon. Gwendolen Fairfax, who loved him because his name was Ernest, and his ward in the country, who had never seen her brother Ernest, loved that legend for the splendour of his wickedness. Then Algernon Moncrieffe, cousin to Gwendolen Fairfax, demanding certain explanations from John Worthing (hitherto known to him as Ernest), learns [of] this duplicity—Mr Alexander should make the confession more pathetic—and learns, too, of the existence of the charming ward. And while Mr John Worthing, with that virtue of intention that only the first contemplation of matrimony can give, is resolving that his alias, his brother Ernest, must die, Mr Algernon Moncrieffe is preparing a charming little expedition. He professes to be called away from town by the sickness of a convenient chimera called Bunbury, and rushes down to introduce himself to the charming ward, as the penitent reprobate Ernest. He arrives, meets with the ward and excellent fortune, and disappears into the house with her. She is of altogether Gilbertian artlessness, and explains that she has been relieving the tedium of her existence, under the instruction of Miss Prism, by an imaginary love affair with Ernest, and that they are already engaged. This places things on an easy footing at once. Then—a brilliant situation— —arrives John Worthing, dressed like a hearse, to announce to Miss Prism and the Rev. Chasuble, with infinite pathos, that his brother—his long-lost brother—is dead. Miss Prism, hoping against hope, trusts that 'he'll profit by it' [Act 2]. To whom enter the ward and Algernon Moncrieffe, as the defunct brother.

Then presently arrives Gwendolen Fairfax, in flight from her recalcitrant mother, who objects to a son-in-law with no more family than a handbag; and an amusing but rather too flabby scene follows between Gwendolen and Cecily, the ward. Both imagine they are engaged to the non-existent Ernest. They both attach a magical virtue to the name, and could not possibly love men with any other names. Hence the importance of being Ernest. The scene ends with revelations, four peoples' despair, and the hazardous enterprise of John and Algernon to get christened

H. G. Wells as a Drama Critic

Ernest forthwith. (Afterwards Lady Bracknell thought this talk of christening 'a little premature' [Act 3].)

But it all comes right. It was Miss Prism who lost that bag when she was nursemaid to Mrs Moncrieffe. She had written a three volume novel in her scanty leisure, and, being absent-minded, put that into the perambulator and the baby into a bag, and so it comes out that John Worthing is Ernest after all. Ernest Moncrieffe, Algernon Moncrieffe's brother. 'I always said I had a brother', he remarks in the tone of an ill-used man [Act 3]. Gwendolen's mother—who was worse than a Gorgon, because she was 'a monster and yet not a myth' [Act 1]—is appeased, and the curtain descends on three happy couples. For Mr Oscar Wilde, with a commendable regard for dramatic customs, has supplied the Rev. Canon Chasuble, D.D., for the excellent Miss Prism. It is all very funny, and Mr Oscar Wilde has decorated a humour that is Gilbertian with innumerable spangles of that wit that is all his own. Of the pure and simple truth, for instance, he remarks that 'Truth is never pure and rarely simple'; and the reply, 'Yes, flowers are as common in the country as people are in London', is particularly pretty from the artless country girl to the town-bred Gwendolen.[2]

Now, to act really artistic burlesque is a difficult thing. A more admirable Miss Prism than that of Mrs George Canninge would scarce be possible; and Miss Leclercq, Miss Vanbrugh, and Miss Evelyn Millard all acted with humour, if with a trifle too much naturalness.[3] But the actors scarcely recognized that it was their business to poke fun at conventional play-acting as the author poked fun at conventional play-writing. The most successful among them was Mr [Allan] Aynesworth as Algernon, but he was funny *in* the part rather than at the expense of the part. Mr Alexander might with advantage study Mr Fred Terry's Llewelyn—'tis a pity his own Guy Domville is inaccessible to him.[4] The part of John Worthing, played with the infinite seriousness of common comedy, with frowns and starts at his guilty secret, brow-clasping remorse, and crescendo emotion, would be irresistible. Mr Alexander was best in the third act, and his heartrending cry of 'Mother! mother!'—he fancied for a few terrible moments that Miss Prism was his mother—

was a moving piece of stage pathos. But he would be better if he mouthed his words more, and stamped a little, and glared. Mr [H.H.] Vincent, too, as a sympathetic Canon, threw away an excellent chance of dramatic caricature.

How Serious People—the majority of the population, according to Carlyle—how Serious People will take this Trivial Comedy written for their learning remains to be seen. No doubt seriously. One last night thought that the bag incident was a 'little far-fetched'. Moreover, he could not see how the bag and the baby got to Victoria Station (L.B. and S.C.R. station) while the manuscript and perambulator turned up 'at the summit of Primrose Hill'. Why the summit? Such difficulties, he said, rob a play of 'convincingness'. That is one serious person disposed of, at any rate.

On the last production of a play by Mr Oscar Wilde we said it was fairly bad, and anticipated success.[5] This time we must congratulate him unreservedly on a delightful revival of theatrical satire. *Absit omen.*[6] But we could pray for the play's success, else we fear it may prove the last struggle of its author against the growing seriousness of his dramatic style.

NOTES

1 The line that Wells quotes—or perhaps misquotes—does not appear in the retrenched three-act version of *Earnest* that evolved during rehearsals and that Alexander had published some time after the play closed in May of 1895. But it is to be found at the conclusion of Act 3 in the four-act *Earnest* that Wilde delivered to Alexander in January of 1895:

> *Jack.* Oh, that is nonsense; you are always talking nonsense.
> *Algernon.* It is much cleverer to talk nonsense than to listen to it, my dear fellow. And a much rarer thing, too, in spite of all the public may say.

It thus seems likely that Alexander made a few additional, if minor, cuts in the text following its first performance.

2 Unless the mistake was Aynesworth's, Wells has transposed the adverbs in Algernon's epigram about Truth (Act 1). The line next quoted is not, of course, in reply to it but to Gwendolen's 'I had no idea there were any flowers in the country' (Act 2).

H. G. Wells as a Drama Critic

3 Rose Leclerq, Irene Vanbrugh, and Evelyn Millard acted the parts of Lady Bracknell, Gwendolen Fairfax, and Cecily Cardew, respectively.
4 Henry James's *Guy Domville* had played at the St James's the previous month, with Alexander in the title role. Opening night had been a fiasco, largely (in Wells's view) because Alexander's acting had been inadequate and inappropriate for his part (PMG, 7 January 1895, p 3; see also *ExA* 8:2).

The suggestion that Alexander take a hint from the gallant posturing of Ellen Terry's brother in his role of Llewelyn (see the editors' introduction) is in line with Wells's notion that the meaning of *Earnest* as a travesty on conventional play-writing would be more apparent if 'the actors . . . recognized that it was their business to poke fun at conventional play-acting'.

5 Compare Wells's review of *An Ideal Husband*.
6 Wells's sense of foreboding proved to be unjustified. *Earnest* ran through eighty-one performances and was a box-office success. It even for a time survived the adverse publicity that the (first) trial of its author generated. (When that trial began, in mid-April, Alexander ignominiously had Wilde's name removed from all notices.)

H. G. Wells's Literary Criticism
THE NOTORIOUS MRS EBBSMITH

Sir Arthur Wing Pinero (1855–1934) is said to have invented the 'Problem Play'—a watered-down version of the social drama of Ibsen, and the staple of serious West End theatre in the late Victorian and the Edwardian years. The 1891 London performance of a translation of Ibsen's Ghosts *prompted Pinero to undertake his first essay in this mode,* The Second Mrs Tanqueray *(1893). Surprised and encouraged by its success, he then wrote* The Notorious Mrs Ebbsmith. *Wells, in '"The Notorious Mrs Ebbsmith", at the Garrick' (PMG, 14 March 1895, p 4), deplored the playwright's want of courage. So did the man whose reputation as a 'problem' dramatist was soon to eclipse Pinero's: George Bernard Shaw (see above, pp 25–6).*

Three magnificent acts, splendidly written, splendidly set, and splendidly played; three acts of steady development, of subtle interplay, of absorbing interest; three acts which promised to place this play a head and shoulders above any other play in London—and then a smash. That is the sum of Mr Pinero's new four-act play. It was impossible to be anything but intensely enthusiastic at the end of the second act; so far the play seemed a masterpiece, a play as much greater than the *Second Mrs Tanqueray* as that had been greater than its predecessors among Mr Pinero's works; and at the end of the third act it still appeared a noble work. That is the point at which the intelligent playgoer should leave the theatre. In the fourth act the weakness of the piece declares itself; the disease latent in the first and second, and merely a feverish touch in the third, becomes virulent. The fourth act reflects back upon its predecessors, explains the whole and spoils it all. From the critical point of view the fourth act is the key to the play and to the playwright. It amply justifies the verdict that Mr Pinero comes near to being, and yet beyond all question is *not*, a writer of great plays.

The play will be called a Problem Play. Such it is—if playing with a problem constitutes one. It belongs to that great and growing class of plays and novels in which a

H. G. Wells as a Drama Critic

respectable author sets out, with infinite blowing of trumpets and beating of drums, with pomp and banners, to discuss the question of marriage, and in which, having paraded awhile within a measurable, even it would appear a dangerous, proximity to that threatening question, he presently returns, with nothing won and nothing settled, in a state of *Te Deum*, his respectability intact and his reputation for courage vastly enhanced among the more serious sections of society. From the present play we gather that marriage is a damnable state for women, that all men are brutes, that curates are angels, and that the best thing for poor humanity is to be asexual. This appears to be the essence of what serious people will probably regard as Mr Pinero's 'teaching' as he circles solemnly round and round what some one has called 'the great pre-occupation'. Ibsen and Tolstoi have evidently not lived in vain—so far as Mr Pinero is concerned. Fielding and Smollett, with their frank and wholesome methods, as evidently have.[1]

The 'notorious Mrs Ebbsmith' was the daughter of a Radical agitator, a Hyde Park atheist. She married Ebbsmith, a barrister, and underwent the horrors of marriage for eight years. When she married she was a devout Christian, the result of a natural reaction from the bigoted teaching of her father; but she lost faith, hope, everything, in the disgusting slavery of wifehood. All the women in the play testify vaguely to the unknown infamies of the Husband. It upsets the equanimity of the common man. It sends one home uneasy, asking oneself, am I too a scoundrel? Is this wife of mine, my dear and most trusted friend, really enduring unspeakable things, and holding herself in hand to prevent herself screaming out at me? However, we wander from Mrs Ebbsmith. After her married life she takes to Socialistic agitation, and, when at last she is almost starving, to nursing.

Mr Lucas Cleeve is a young politician of good family, on the brink of dying of his wife. He says she is so 'unsympathetic'. He is nursed back to life by Mrs Ebbsmith, and he falls in love with her. They determine to live together, unmarried, as Mr Grant Allen's couple did[2] to teach the world a lesson; and the play opens with them at the Palazzo Arconate at Venice. This determination involves the sacrifice of Cleeve's political career and the loss of most of his friends. In the first act the effect of the discovery that the so-called Mrs Cleeve is not Mrs Cleeve upon a casual friend, Mrs Thorpe, is admirably developed. 'Adieu to *them*, then, eh?' says Cleeve, beginning to realize what it means to him. An insidious Duke of St Olpherts has been deputed by the Cleeve family to separate the two; and gradually under his hands Cleeve's fine ethical fervour for humanity and freedom undergoes a complete analysis, and of it all only a bare passion for Mrs Ebbsmith remains. At the end of the third act the shrivelling of Lucas Cleeve is complete; he is willing to patch up an outward reconciliation with his wife and save his 'career', on the understanding that Mrs Ebbsmith will act as a *de facto* wife in the suburbs. The scene closes on her despair as she realizes the real nature of her 'influence' upon him.

So far, we say, the play is an extraordinarily powerful one, but at its very climax comes the collapse. Mr Pinero seems to have reached the very limit of his courage. The rest is apology and retraction. Mrs Thorpe and her brother, the curate, reappear in a new light altogether. Instead of presenting us any longer with shocked British respectability, dodging round unclean corners to avoid meeting the Cleeves, they suddenly become two noble and sexless souls bent upon 'saving' Mrs Ebbsmith. They poke a Bible at her, which she thrusts into the stove and burns her arm in attempting to recover. A large number of solid-thinking people will regard that tawdry effect as a fine piece of courage on Mr Pinero's part. Then comes a fantastic scene, in which Mrs Cleeve asks Mrs Ebbsmith to become Cleeve's mistress [in Act 4]. Mr Pinero's experience of life may be peculiar. We certainly never met or heard of a woman behaving at all as he represents Mrs Cleeve doing. There is an absurd entrance and a comic exit of the exploded Cleeve when Mrs Ebbsmith speaks of praying. The Duke flickers out, and the play ends forthwith an unexpected wreck, the curtain descending upon Mrs Ebbsmith ('saved!'), Mrs Thorpe and the curate all rigid and staring hard at nothing in particular, unless it is the grey prospect of life before them in the Yorkshire retreat.

H. G. Wells as a Drama Critic

Now our diagnosis must needs be hasty, written between midnight and three in the morning, but the essence of the trouble seems to be the conflict between the problem and the play. The finer part is the study of human motives and consequences that culminates as we have said. That is the healthy body, the play itself. And the disease, which grows to a head in the fourth act, is the desire to seem to evolve some profound moral principle of general application, after the Ibsen fashion, that shall appeal to serious people.

But if the play is not great it is so like greatness through much of its length, and it is so admirably wrought, that it must inevitably succeed. Mr John Hare, Mrs Patrick Campbell, and Mr Forbes Robertson act—the adverb is deliberately chosen—magnificently. Nothing milder will do for it. Mr Thorne, Mr Carne, Mr Du Maurier, Mr Aubrey Smith, Miss Calhoun, and Miss Jeffreys do excellent work. Either Mr Ian Robertson or his part is a trifle too wooden.[3] And the play is staged as though it had come to stay.

NOTES

1 Wells is no doubt referring to the 'problematic' way in which Ibsen and Tolstoi treat extra-marital affairs (like that between Mrs Ebbsmith and Lucas Cleeve), in contrast to the carefree handling of them in (most of) the novels of Fielding and Smollett.

2 In *The Woman Who Did* (1895): see the headnote to 'Mr Grant Allen's New Novel'.

3 The original cast of *Mrs Ebbsmith* featured John Hare as the Duke of St Olpherts, Mrs Campbell as Agnes Ebbsmith, and actor–manager Johnston Forbes-Robertson as Lucas Cleeve. It also included Fred Thorne as Dr Kirke, Gerald Du Maurier as the servant Fortuné, C. Aubrey Smith as the Rev. Amos Winterfield, Eleanor Calhoun as Sybil Cleeve, Ellis Jeffries as Gertrude Thorpe, and Ian Forbes-Robertson as Sir Sandford Cleeve.

H. G. Wells's Literary Criticism
DELIA HARDING

In April of 1895, Delia Harding began a month-long run at the Comedy Theatre, then under the management of J. W. Comyns Carr (1849–1916). The melodrama was billed as Carr's adaptation[1] from Victorien Sardou (1831–1908), who succeeded Eugène Scribe as the most popular French playwright of the nineteenth century. On Wells, its 'effect . . . was profoundly dispiriting' (PMG, 18 April 1895, p 3).

The new performance at the Comedy has at least one merit from the critical point of view: excepting, perhaps, Mr Cyril Maude and Miss [Rose] Leclercq, the acting and the play go very well together. The actors and actresses act—like actors and actresses; the play holds the mirror up to life, as it is lived in Stageland. The people are impossible, the development is impossible, and some of the scenic effects even are impossible. And for all this impossibility there is neither emotional effect, nor pervading beauty, not the literary interests of wit or satire, nor a sustained intellectual interest. Heaven forbid that we should say that the stage should be limited to the grey realities of life, that the stage should be Gissingized.[2] But assuredly the only excuses for a departure from reality are beauty, laughter, or other emotion, or the concentration of light upon some particular phase of life, to the exclusion of other aspects. And this play has none of these excuses. It avails itself of all the conventions and gives us nothing in return. It is as if it were made by a kind of play-weaving machine constructed to interlace the traditional threads in the traditional manner. Three acts measured off, and there you are! It is the artistic equivalent of the gilt-framed oleographs of the Chalk Farm Road.[3]

There is the traditional immaculate woman, traditionally acted by Miss Marion Terry. She has sworn away her honour to save her brother from a charge of attempted murder. He had shot (but not killed) the villain in a drunken quarrel over cards. It happened at Calcutta, and the villain threatened to die. So the heroine said the villain was her lover, and that on that account her brother had shot him.

H. G. Wells as a Drama Critic

(You are allowed to shoot your sister's lover in Calcutta; he is, indeed, almost the only shooting there). So her brother got off at once. No doubt M Sardou's jury was French, and the thing was credible; shifting the affair to Calcutta and the impossible is probably Mr Comyns Carr's idea. Thence the villain, who loves the heroine, and wants her money, machinates away as hard as he can and brings off the play. Miss Marion Terry is always sweet and always herself, but we do not remember any occasion when she has been so frankly free from the trammels of probability. Arrayed in a beautiful white dress with a train and limelight trimming, she wanders alone by the Lake of Como, admiring a jerky moonrise under just the very sky for a heavy dew, and so drifts into the grounds of an hotel where she has absolutely no business at all. But sentimental occasions were infrequent in her part compared with her previous opportunities, and a certain tragic intensity was required of her—when, for instance, she has to prepare poison for herself (the villain drinks it, of course)—to which she scarcely seemed equal. At that crisis she did not affect us all as being sufficiently broken-hearted—she simply knitted her brows, cast her eyes upward, and appeared to be bothered to death.

Mr Mackintosh had the eyebrows, the teeth, and the laughter of a double-dyed villain: he dressed like a shopman and talked like a parliamentary candidate. The dose of digitalis was well earned. 'I have been poisoned', he said, pointed to the villa, and became insensible. As they could not arrest the villa they arrested the heroine as occupier. Miss Dorothy Dorr, as Mrs Venables, made a beautiful and sinister lady-villain (jealousy). She machinates steadily, occasionally glowing with a special red light like red fire—presumably with the intensity of her machination—and as soon as she heard of the poisoning she came along with the Syndic and entered with an impressive, 'That is Miss Harding!' Whereupon, as the custom of Stageland is, they try the heroine for murder on the spot, the lady-villain conducting the prosecution, the defence being ably handled by the hero, and the witnesses dropping in with letters, and confessions, and so forth, by the balcony and the several doors as they are needed. Things were already clearing up, when a note arrived from the murdered man to explain that he was getting better and had been poisoned by accident. So she was discharged without a stain on her character, and every one was happy—except a few people in the gallery—as the curtain fell.

Documents have, indeed, a remarkably important part in the play. Mrs Venables, the lady-villain, gets a letter (1) about the heroine's past, and so opens her intrigues. There are two letters (2 and 3) from the brother, both of vital importance. The maidservant hands another letter (4) addressed to the heroine to the nearest villain (as the rule is—'Villains take precedence with all letters'), and he machinates vigorously with it. Then an incriminating cheque (5) is found on his poisoned (but presently resuscitated) person. Then, again, there is a confession (6) made by the brother before he dies. Finally, the note (7) above mentioned, to say the villain presents his compliments to the Syndic, and he was poisoned by accident. That is as many as we can recall—one or two others may have slipped our memory for the moment. Anyhow, seven documents in twenty-four hours! M Sardou's experiences must be peculiar. Unless our solicitors take a hand, few of us play out our tragedies with that amount of paper.

Mr Fred Terry is still the same brow-clutching, diaphragm-gripping, manly fellow we have seen so often. With him it is the make-up that varies. Mr Cyril Maude jarred with the other principal characters by behaving like an ordinary human being, his performance of Sir Arthur Studley being indeed the best thing in the play. Plays may come and plays may go, but Miss Leclercq remains loyal to her double eyeglasses, and points all her matronly rudeness with them in her usual charming way. Mrs [Sarah] Brooke was plump and comfortable as the faithful nurse; her Scotch is for those who know that language, we have our doubts. She prefers the scenery of Dumfries[4] to Como, and this is reiterated in a manner that suggests a jocular intention (probably Mr Comyns Carr's). The rest of the cast scarcely calls for remark.

The entire effect of the play upon the critic, at least, was profoundly dispiriting, but his feelings found a vent in the

H. G. Wells as a Drama Critic

opening paragraph. The important and comforting thing is the decided note of dissent at the conclusion of the play. We believe the days of the play written to a formula, and of acting that is merely conventional posturing, are numbered, at least in London, whatever the provinces are still willing to endure.

NOTES

1 The contents of the playbill can be found in William Archer's *The Theatrical 'World' of 1895* (Walter Scott, London, 1896), p 408. In the details of its plot, *Delia Harding* corresponds to Sardou's *A Woman's Silence* (1892; written in English)—which suggests that the two may well have been the same play under different titles.
2 By this time Wells may have read George Gissing's *Eve's Ransom*, whose 'harsh greyness' he protested against in a review titled 'The Depressed School' and printed in SR for 27 April 1895 (79:531).
3 That is, cheap oil paintings used for decorative purposes.
4 In Scotland.

'THE POSE NOVEL'

'The Pose Novel' (PMG, 21 May 1894, p 3) *is one of the more substantial light essays on literary subjects that Wells published in the* Pall Mall Gazette *in the months before he became that newspaper's drama critic. It introduces a concept—of authorial 'posing' or 'posturing'—that he later applied, usually for the purpose of derogation, as a literary critic for the* Saturday Review. *He thought enough of the essay to reprint it in his collection of 'mainly autobiographical' pieces,* Certain Personal Matters *(1898 [1897]; pp 98–103), from which the following text is taken.*[1]

I watched the little spurts of flame jet out from between the writhing pages of my manuscript, watched the sheets coil up in their fiery anguish and start one from another. I helped the fire to the very vitals of the mass by poking the brittle heap, and at last the sacrifice was over, the flames turned from pink to blue and died out, the red glow gave place to black, little luminous red streaks coiled across the charred sheets and vanished at the margins, and only the ashes of my inspiration remained. The ink was a lustrous black on the dull blackness of the burnt paper. I could still read this much of my indiscretion remaining, 'He smiled at them all and said nothing'.

'Fool!' I said, and stirred the crackling mass into a featureless heap of black scraps. Then with my chin on my fists and elbows on knees I stared at the end of my labours.

I suppose, after all, there has been some profit out of the thing. Satan finds some mischief still for idle hands to do, and one may well thank Heaven it was only a novel. Still, it means many days out of my life, and I would be glad to find some positive benefit accruing. Clearly, in the first place, I have eased my mind of some execrable English. I am cleaner now by some dozen faulty phrases that I committed and saw afterwards in all the nakedness of typewriting. (Thank Heaven for typewriting! Were it not for that, this thing had gone to the scoffing of some publisher's reader, and another had known my shame.) And I shall not write another pose novel.

H. G. Wells as a Drama Critic

I am inclined to think these pose novels the wild oats of authorship. We sit down in the heyday of our youth to write the masterpiece. Obviously, it must be a novel about a man and a woman, and something as splendid as we can conceive of in that way.[2] We look about us.[3] We do not go far for perfection. One of the brace holds the pen and the other is inside his or her head; and so Off![4] to the willing pen. Only a few years ago we went slashing among the poppies with a walking-stick, and were, we said boldly and openly, Harolds and Hectors slaying our thousands. Now of course we are grown up to self-respect, and must needs be a little disingenuous about it. But as the story unfolds there is no mistaking the likeness, in spite of the transfiguration.[5] This bold, decided man who performs such deeds of derring-do in the noisome slum, knocks down the burly wife-beater, rescues an unmistakable Miss Clapton from the knife of a Lascar, and is all the while cultivating a virtuous consumption that stretches him on an edifying, pathetic, and altogether beautiful death-bed in the last chapter—— My dear Authorling, cry my friends, we hear the squeak of that little voice of yours in every word he utters. Is *that* what you aspire to be, that twopence-coloured edition of yourself? Heaven defend you from your desires!

Yet there was a singular fascination in writing the book; to be in anticipation my own sympathetic historian, to joy with my joys yet to come, and sorrow with my sorrows, to bear disaster like a man, and at last to close my own dear eyes, and with a swelling heart write my own epitaph. The pleasure remained with me until I reached the end. How admirably I strutted in front of myself! And I and the better self of me that was flourishing about in the book—we pretended not to know each other for what we were. He was myself with a wig and a sham visiting card, and I owed it to myself to respect my disguise. I made him with very red hair—my hair is fairly dark—and shifted his university from London to Cambridge.[6] Clearly it could not be the same person, I argued. But I endowed him with all the treasures of myself; I made him say all the good things I might have said had I thought of them opportunely, and all the noble thoughts that occurred to me afterwards occurred

H. G. Wells's Literary Criticism

to him at the time. He was myself—myself at a premium, myself without any drawbacks, the quintessence and culmination of me. And yet somehow when he came back from the typewriter he seemed a bit of an ass.

Probably every tadpole author writes a pose novel—at least I hope so for the sake of my self-respect. Most, after my fashion, burn the thing, or benevolent publishers lose it.[7] It is an ill thing if by some accident the tadpole tale survives the tadpole stage. The authoress does the feminine equivalent,[8] but I should judge either that she did it more abundantly or else that she burned less. Has she never swept past you with a scornful look, disdained you in all the pride of her beauty, rippled laughter at you, or amazed you with her artless girlishness? And even after the early stages some of the trick may survive, unless I read books with malice instead of charity. I must confess, though, that I[9] have a weakness[10] for finding mine author among his puppets. I conceive him always taking the best parts, like an actor-manager or a little boy playing with his sisters. I do not read many novels with sincere belief, and I like to get such entertainment from them as I can. So that these artless little self-revelations are very sweet and precious to me among all the lay figures, tragedy and comedy. Since the deception is transparent I make the most of the transparency, and love to see the clumsy fingers on the strings of the marionettes. And this will be none the less pleasant now that I have so narrowly escaped giving this entertainment to others.

I suppose this stage is a necessary one. We begin with ignorance and the imagination, the material of the pose novel. Later come self-knowledge, disappointments and self-consciousness, and the prodigals of fiction stay themselves upon the husks of epigram and cynicism, and in the place of artless aspiration are indeed in plain black and white very desperate characters. It is after all only another pose—the pose of not posing. We, the common clay of the world of letters, must needs write in this way, because we cannot forget our foolish little selves in our work. But some few there are who sit as gods above their private universes, and write without passion or vanity. At least, so I have been told. These be the true artists of letters, the white windows upon

H. G. Wells as a Drama Critic

the truth of things. We by comparison are but stained glass in our own honour, and do but obstruct the view with our halos and attitudes. Yet even Shakespeare, the critics tell us—and they say they know—posed in the character of Hamlet.

After all, the pose novel method has at times attained to the level of literature. Charlotte Brontë might possibly have found no other topic had she disdained the plain little woman with a shrewish tongue; and where had Charles Kingsley been if the vision of a curate rampant had not rejoiced his heart?[11] Still, I am not sorry that this novel is burned. Even now it was ridiculous, and the time[12] might have come when this book, full of high, if foolish aims, and the vain vast promise of well-meaning youth, had been too keen a reproach to be endured. Three volumes of good intentions! It is too much. There was more than a novel burning just now. After this I shall be in a position to take a humorist's view of life.

NOTES

1 Textual variants, when not merely a matter of punctuation or orthography, have been noted.
2 Wells had written a sentimental novel 'about a man and a woman' (*Lady Frankland's Companion*) while convalescing at Uppark in 1888—and then burned it. Hence the 'I' of this essay is itself a 'pose'.
3 PMG: 'look round us'.
4 PMG: 'and so off'.
5 PMG: 'The glorious transfiguration'.
6 PMG: 'my hair is very black'; 'from Oxford to Cambridge'.
7 PMG: 'lose them'.
8 PMG: 'equivalent of this'.
9 PMG: 'though, I'.
10 PMG: 'have a fancy'.
11 Charles Kingsley (1819–75), a leader of the Christian Socialist movement, expressed his vision of a regenerate priesthood working for social justice and unity in such books as *Alton Locke* (1850).
12 PMG: 'and a time'.

H. G. Wells's Literary Criticism

'THE SAWDUST DOLL'

This pointed attack on the unreality of the typical heroine of Victorian fiction (PMG, 13 May 1895, p 3) appeared two months after Wells had mercilessly exposed Grant Allen's idealization of the 'New Woman' in The Woman Who Did. *Of that novel's principal character Wells had written: 'She seems to us to be a kind of plaster-cast of "Pure Womanhood" in a halo, with a soul of abstractions, a machine to carry out a purely sentimental principle to its logical conclusion' (see 'Mr Grant Allen's New Novel').*

Who was it said that the heroines of fiction must be stuffed with sawdust from the neck downwards? The reading public will not let us have a real woman. The masters have tried their hands upon her, but the results are merely inoffensive; they are not interesting to the generation. Mr Meredith may draw his female characters after the most exquisite models, and Mr Hardy may turn us out variants of petulance. These command the attention and interest of a handful of critics, but the public does not approve of them. They are not stuffed with sawdust. 'If life is ugly', says a writer who is distinguished by a popularity among hundreds of thousands, 'it is our duty to make it pleasant in fiction'.[1] That is a point of view, and apparently the general point of view. A heroine must be a lay figure upon which to fling the costume of the hour. There is an unceasing demand for her, and the fashions are always changing; so the task should be fairly easy.

The study of Victorian heroines, should prove amusing to our grandchildren, though they will strive in vain to reconstruct the nineteenth-century woman by her. They have suffered many changes in particulars, these characters, but in principle they remain unchallenged. Once upon a time they were very brief in stature. The hero was fond of lifting the heroine in his arms and carrying her over puddles. She was a light and dainty creature, and there was nothing of her to speak of, as it were. This fragile little thing might now and then be plump; indeed, she was often plump as not. The hero liked her plump, and the Guy Livingstones[2] of those fierce days took her and crumpled her in a wild embrace.

H. G. Wells as a Drama Critic

She might on occasion be even plain, and a trifle insignificant. It was *Jane Eyre* [1847] that brought about this tolerance, but the fashion did not long survive, and on the whole we may safely say that she was preferred pretty. A number of variations were permitted in her details. There was no fixed colour for her eyes; her hair might be what it would, though gold was favoured; her nose was as a rule purely Greek, sometimes 'tip-tilted', never snub. They dwelt a good deal upon noses in those days, and that is how we come to know so well. The lips were 'scarlet', to that there was hardly any exception; and in terror or in any great emotion they grew white. Can you conceive her, this short, slight, dumpy little featherhead, all engirdled in a four-foot crinoline? These were the misses who, we are to suppose, are now our mothers.

It is difficult to see how they can well have been the mothers of the present heroines. For we have long since stepped out of the 'short' period, and are now living in an age of strapping lasses. Who is there, save a few belated Americans, who would dare fub us off with a little heroine at this time of day? You would find it very hard work to crumple a modern heroine. But otherwise she is not much changed. She no longer does crochet or crewel work; she plays lawn-tennis and golf. She is fair and graceful, and her complexion is wonderful. They did not insist so much upon complexions twenty years ago. But a generation has not added much to her character. She is still kept decorously stuffed with sawdust. It would be as wrong for her to have an individuality as it would be for her not to paint. The elder heroine was generally taken up with housework and good deeds. But she was sentimental for all that. Her successor has an easier time, what with balls and theatres and tennis parties. But she, too, does something in the way of good works; she can slum, if required, and has been known to become a hospital nurse. She cherishes the curate as persistently as her predecessor. And she has gained a little reserve in her sentimentality. In what does duty for the passion of love with her, she is more reticent and dignified. She does not cling quite so much, but she is just as sweet. You see we have got beyond the echoes of the *Sturm und Drang*. She would, of course, rather die than show any passion, as becomes a thing half sawdust. It is possible that she has a somewhat less pious obedience to her parents. In the old days a daughter sacrificed herself willingly and instantly to the command of a father, yearning and burning as she was, poor plump little creature, to marry the hero. She does not do that now, except in Sunday-school stories, which are obliged to enforce the Fifth Commandment. She reasons with her parents; she meets her lover clandestinely; she sometimes takes the law into her own hands.

But you must not suppose for the world that there is any impropriety in all this. That is how she shows what she is made of; but character, you must remember, must be consistent with the conventional morality that is the great literary canon which the public has laid down. There is a fair proportion of heroines about who have been wronged. These, to speak candidly, are venturesome creations. Not but what they are still sawdust. Oh, don't fly off with any notions to the contrary! They are quite respectable and quite nice, and you might safely introduce your daughters to them once in a while. What has happened is this. The hero, or hero-villain—for nowadays there is a tendency to combine the parts—has got out of hand, and our poor sawdust doll comes to figure in a tragedy. She cannot help it, poor creature; and she would give a great deal to be out of it; so you must not be hard upon her. But sorrow will purge her of her innocent offences, and she will turn up at the close, bright and smiling out of her glass eyes.

This conventional figure of the 'sweet English girl' has walked the stage a thousand times. One appearance differs from another only in the circumstances. You distinguish her on the various occasions by her changing names and changing frocks. These pick her out; for they are almost all the character that is allowed her. There are millions of her. Unluckily a serious attempt has been made to put her nose out of joint by the New Woman.[3] There are some malcontents who still clamour for a woman who is not stuffed with sawdust. The enterprise has had a temporary success, but we are glad to see that sounder and more wholesome views are returning. There is no reason to discard such a well-

H. G. Wells as a Drama Critic

established favourite, and, after all, is it not better to have a doll that merely moves its eyes when you press than an elaborate clock-work thing that kicks out its legs indecorously and makes horrid noises? The one is as conventional as the other, and not so pleasant. By all means give us back our sweet English girl, with her smile and her dispassion. She has nothing to do with life or human nature, but what odds is that? In the words of the illustrious novelist already quoted, if life is ugly we must take pains to alter it in fiction.

NOTES

1 The writer in question is probably Hall Caine, of whom Wells said: 'He shoots straight. There is no mistaking his drawing for truth, or his sentiment for revelation' ('Of Readers in General', SR 79: 30 March 1895, p 410).
2 Guy Livingstone is the eponymous blustering hero of George A. Lawrence's novel (1857).
3 See the headnote to 'Mr Grant Allen's New Novel'.

3 Literary criticism for the Saturday Review

Wells's association with the *Saturday Review* began when Frank Harris took over its management in 1894. The two and a half years or so (from November 1894 to April 1897) during which he regularly submitted brief essays and book reviews to Harris were formative ones for Wells. In those years he was at work revising *The Time Machine*, seeing to the publication of *The Wonderful Visit* and *The Wheels of Chance*, drafting *The Island of Dr Moreau*, *The Invisible Man*, and *Love and Mr Lewisham*, and assembling two volumes of his short stories. As if those projects were not enough to occupy his attention, he somehow found time to write speculative essays and review books on scientific subjects, while concurrently acting as the *Saturday Review's* principal reviewer of fiction.

Wells earned his post as a critic of fiction with a stinging attack on Grant Allen's *The Woman Who Did* in March of 1895 (see the headnote to 'Mr Grant Allen's New Novel'). Over the next two years, he was called upon to review more than 285 works of fiction.[1] Only a handful of his notices, beginning with 'The Well at the World's End' in October 1896, appeared over his initials; the rest were anonymous. Their anonymity, however, was in no way a reflection of disesteem. On the contrary, the surviving letters to Wells from the *Saturday's* editorial staff evince a high regard for many of his efforts. Of 'The Outcast of the Islands', for example, Harris's assistant, H. Blanchamp, wrote to say that 'The Editor . . . asks me to tell you that he thinks it one of the best pieces of literary criticism in the English Language'.[2] Wells, for his part, did his best to extract the maximum financial return from his work for Harris. In November 1895, perhaps with the thought of strengthening his bargaining position, he explored the possibility of contributing a monthly 'book causerie' to Jerome K. Jerome's

48

magazine the *Idler*.[3] Six months later, his pay was raised to the 'special rate' of two guineas a column, hitherto reserved for Bernard Shaw.[4] His reasons for relinquishing this employment are not on record; but chief among them must have been a desire to devote more time to the writing of fiction—and especially to his first 'serious novel', *Love and Mr Lewisham*—now that he no longer needed to rely on an income from journalism for his subsistence.

In making his appearance as a critic, he no doubt subscribed to the opinion of his editor, that 'It is always well . . . for a writer to have a weekly review wherein to slay his enemies, if necessary' (Blanchamp to Wells, 20 November 1895). As an author of 'scientific romances' whose ambitions lay in what he regarded as the more demanding field of realistic fiction, Wells's chosen enemies were among the popular novelists of his day—above all, the practitioners of the adventure story and the historical romance—and also the commercially-minded critics who showered adulation upon them while remaining lukewarm, or worse, towards the efforts of such novelists as Hardy, Turgenev, and Meredith. His declaration that 'one chapter of *Jude the Obscure* or of *Esther Waters* is worth all that Mr [Anthony] Hope has written and much to boot' is typical of his anti-populist stance. 'Popular Writers and Press Critics', the essay in which this statement appears, is not so much a personal attack on Hope as a general dissection of the 'decay of criticism' in the face of millions of new readers 'ignorant of life' and 'contemptuous of its probabilities'. Unlike his contemporaries, Wells as a critic is never content to offer an inert 'appreciation' of a book under review, and is often outspoken in defence of intellectual and artistic standards.

Since his impact as a reviewer depended on his ability to amuse as well as instruct his readers, he found from the beginning that the best way of enforcing his judgements on popular novels was to subject them to ridicule. A sarcastic commentary, spiced with abundant and aptly-chosen quotations, is his most usual procedure. Thus, reviewing *Joan Haste*, a 'realistic' novel by Rider Haggard, he joyfully mocks at what happens when the bloodthirsty romancer of the Zulus turns his attention to the 'savages of East Anglia'.

Similar treatment is dispensed to Andrew Lang ('On Lang and Buchan'), 'Ian Maclaren' ('The Simple Art of Popular Pathos'), Mrs Hodgson Burnett ('A Servants' Hall Vision'), and Wilson Barrett ('An Adelphi Romance'). His antipathy to these writers derives partly from a contempt for artistic ineptitude, and partly from his sense of the intrinsic limitations of the romance form itself. Romance, as he views it, 'prohibits anything but the superficialities of self-expression; . . . sustained humour, subtle characterization are [alike] impossible [in it]' ('The Lost Stevenson'). Because its characters tend to be wooden and stereotypic and its situations repetitive and improbable, the romance militates against that expression of the author's 'individuality', or 'uniqueness', which Wells holds to be one of the primary values in literature (see above, pp 7–8). Only when he comes to *An Outcast of the Islands* does he set aside this formal objection. Conrad's 'real romance—the romance that is real!' opens up a 'new and wonderful field' for fiction, and leaves no doubt of its author's 'greatness'. Yet in welcoming exceptions of this kind, Wells seems at a loss for a language in which to describe the positive achievements of the romance, both in Conrad's work and in that of others, like Stevenson and Morris. His admiration for Conrad is more fully manifest in his lengthy and painstaking criticism of the stylistic excesses of *An Outcast of the Islands* than in his commendation of the book's 'living realities'. Stevenson, he suggests, is not a romancer but a novelist at heart—albeit a novelist 'entangled in the puerilities of romance' ('The Lost Stevenson'). (The account that he gives of Stevenson's career may reflect his own anxiety not to be type-cast as a writer of 'scientific romances'.) And his praise of the 'clean strong sentences' and 'stout oaken stuff' of *The Well at the World's End* seems to apply more to Morris's ethical calibre than to the quality of his literary workmanship.

As his stress on 'living realities' indicates, the qualities that Wells holds most dear are, first and foremost, those of the social-realist novel. In 'Flickers of Imagination and a Flare', he singles out the portrayal of the pure-hearted prostitute—a character who 'would not be out of place in a good sympathetic realistic novel'—as the one redeeming

Literary criticism for the Saturday Review

feature of Robert Hichens's sensation-filled and melodramatic fiction: 'indisputably, Mr Hichens has taken a real girl and studied her furniture, her costume, her hours of employment, her ways of speech and some of her ways of thought very carefully'. Wells implies that the element of integrity which this portrait introduces into a novel otherwise revelling in 'Sin' and sexual coyness is one of the few ingredients which might stand in the way of its 'inevitable popularity'. It would be wrong, however, to assume on the basis of this passage that he approved of the 'documentary' approach to realism practised by the naturalists. Wells was not an admirer of French naturalism or its English imitators. If his ideal of realism is defined in opposition to the unreality of the popular romance, it is also carefully distinguished from what he called the '"colourless" theory' or scientific impersonality in fiction (see 'The Paying Guest'). 'The theory of a scientific, an impersonal standpoint, is fallacious', he declares ('The Method of Mr George Meredith'). Nevertheless, his general endorsement of verisimilitude brings him closer in outlook to the social realists, such as Gissing, than it does to their romantic opponents.

Time and again Wells returns to the idea of a narrative steeped in the personality of its author. Stevenson, he argues, lacked 'that saving obstinacy, that inflexible self-conceit' which is the 'essence of originality' ('The Lost Stevenson'). A writer possessing these attributes, Wells believed, should display them in his work, rather than suppressing them, as the naturalists did. The novelist should not be afraid to 'laugh, talk and point with his finger . . . and generally assert his humanity' ('The Paying Guest'). The novelist's personality, however, should be conveyed by artistic means, and not in the form of direct preaching. Grant Allen's 'independence of spirit' does not make up for his manifest aesthetic deficiencies ('Mr Grant Allen's New Novel'). Richard Le Gallienne is likewise taken to task for his fondness for 'the Gospel touch' ('The Lost Quest'). In opposition to propagandist fiction such as that of Le Gallienne and Grant Allen, Wells affirms his admiration for the richly idiosyncratic style and narrative 'Method of Mr George Meredith'.

H. G. Wells's Literary Criticism

Even more than Meredith, Wells was a novelist with strong comic instincts, and the aspect of naturalistic fiction with which he least sympathized was its asceticism, its deliberate abandonment of the vigorous authorial presence associated with Dickens, Thackeray, and their predecessors in the English tradition. The disappearance of the omniscient narrator entailed the loss of much of the novel's potentiality for 'satire, irony, laughter, and tears' ('The New American Novelists'). On the other hand, Wells was not blind to the advances made by the new school of realism, and especially by the Russian novelists Turgenev and Tolstoi. In Turgenev, and also in the Hardy of *Jude the Obscure*, he recognized an authenticity of sociological vision and social statement which drew his highest praise as a critic. Here was a fiction based on strictly modern experience which avoided both the restricted social range of a novel like Morrison's *A Child of the Jago* and the lifeless abstractions of a Grant Allen. The achievement of Hardy, and still more of Turgenev, lay in developing a mode of characterization at once 'individual' and 'typical'. Turgenev's people are 'not avatars of theories nor tendencies', but 'individuals living under the stress of this great social force or that' ('The Novel of Types'). In his response to *Fathers and Children* and *Jude the Obscure*, Wells was able to celebrate the conjunction of the artistic excellence so lamentably lacking in popular fiction with a sort of realism which satisfied his unwavering, post-Arnoldian conviction that literature should aspire to a genuine and far-reaching 'criticism of life' (see note 5 below).

If Wells's emphasis on the role of authorial personality in fiction points towards his belief in the anarchic and experimental nature of artistic creation, his insistence that characters should be 'typical individuals' suggests that the novelist's task is that of a sociologist or social historian. The conflicting tendencies here are resolved in his social novels of the Edwardian decade, rather than in his criticism, which does not aspire to a formal or unified aesthetic. His protests against the suppression of the author's personality by the realists make him to some extent a forerunner of the 'self-conscious' fiction of recent years. At the same time, his rejection of the artistic self-discipline enjoined by the naturalists left him open to the charge of aesthetic conservatism. Wells's stance here should be contrasted with that of Arnold Bennett, as revealed in the critical articles collected in *Fame and Fiction* (1901). Bennett's attack on his friend's novelistic criteria, in a letter written in 1903—'You still cling to the Dickens-Thackeray standards, and judge by them' (Bennett to Wells, 24 August, in Wilson, p 95)—serves to reveal the traditionalist aspect of Wells's notion of the 'good sympathetic realistic novel'.

As is usually the case with a creative artist in his formative years, Wells's views on fiction must be understood in relation to his own artistic development. In his sequence of social comedies from *Love and Mr Lewisham* through *Kipps, Tono-Bungay*, and *The History of Mr Polly*, Wells comes nearest to realizing his ideal of a kind of fiction that would be at once socially representative in its range and highly personal in its idiom. The individual and the social are brought together in the character of George Ponderevo, the first-person narrator of *Tono-Bungay*, who introduces his story with the announcement that 'I want to tell—*myself*, and my impressions of the thing as a whole, to say things I have come to feel intensely of the laws, traditions, usages, and ideas we call society . . .'. In *Tono-Bungay*, the two main characters, George and Edward Ponderevo, are at once 'typical individuals' living in the shadow of great social forces, and the central figures of a narrative which is a uniquely Wellsian experiment.

Although his Edwardian social novels are the culmination of the creative effort presaged by his writings for the *Saturday Review*, he was soon dissatisfied with his achievement in them, feeling that the realistic novel no longer exerted the direct influence on ideas and social attitudes that he now wished to exercise. His outspoken championship of nineteenth-century realism in his early reviewing may help to explain the vehemence of his later disillusioned repudiations of the 'Novel'. There has been much comment on the irony of his abandoning, at the time of his confrontation with Henry James, the faith in the values of art that is such a marked feature of his early criticism. But it is equally relevant to remember that his championship of realism was itself first conceived in reaction against his success as a writer of 'scientific romances'. Indeed, the real irony behind Wells's remarkable performance as a critic upholding the standards of the 'great tradition' of Dickens, Thackeray, Meredith, Hardy, and Turgenev in the 1890s is that it was achieved at the expense of a full understanding of the possibilities of science fiction, romance, and fantasy. That Wells had an instinctive grasp of those possibilities he proves not only by his own work, but in his immediate response to the writings of Crane and Conrad. Yet his instinct never quite became a conscious conviction, in large measure because Wells saw little in the debased tradition of mindless romances to encourage him to believe that 'a genuine effort towards a criticism of life'[5] could be undertaken outside the confines of the realistic novel.

NOTES

1 See R. M. Philmus's bibliography, which provides abstracts of 92 reviews and review-articles that can now be identified with some certainty as being by Wells.
2 Letter from Blanchamp to Wells, 23 May 1896 (in the University of Illinois Wells Collection). For further quotations from this correspondence, see Gordon Ray's bibliography.
3 A manuscript 'dummy' for this prospective column, together with a draft of an undated letter to Jerome, survives in the Wells Collection at Urbana.
4 Ray, p 31.
5 Wells uses this phrase in his 'Fiction' column, SR 80: 9 November 1895, p 624.

Literary criticism for the Saturday Review
'JOAN HASTE'

Sir Henry Rider Haggard (1856–1925) *made his reputation with romances such as* King Solomon's Mines *(1885) and* She *(1887).* Joan Haste *was both a departure from his usual South African settings and the most substantial novel of his to appear during the 1890s. For Wells (in SR 80: 21 September 1895, p 386), it was a sitting target.*

Mr Haggard has made a new departure in his latest book; that generous thirst of his for blood is under wonderful restraint. From the Zulus he has transferred his attention to the savages of East Anglia, and apart from the killing of his heroine in a momentary lapse, a pheasant massacre, the smashing of a respectable innkeeper's face till it was like 'a squashed pumpkin with no eyes left for a sinner to swear by', the killing of the dog Towser, and a broken leg or so, there is really no violence worth speaking about in the volume before us. From his blood-and-thunder romances, the discovery of which was one of Mr Lang's many brilliant feats of criticism,[1] Mr Haggard has turned to the pure conventional; conventionality with dyspepsia, to be precise and brief. Just as the real hero of *Paradise Lost* is Satan, so the leading part in *Joan Haste* is that gloomy but magnificent villain, Samuel Rock. Even the name has a sinister note in it. 'Samuel Rock was a Dissenter', we are told at the very beginning; we hear of Joan's 'terror' of him, and he enters, 'smiling his most obsequious smile' [1:8]. What can one expect after that but villainies? 'Not uncomely in appearance', Mr Haggard tells us with a fine sense of impartiality, and adds, with an artistic air of inadvertency, that his eyes were 'shifty', and his long white hands (they had, for no particular reason, filbert nails that any lady might envy, albeit Samuel was a tiller of the soil) were 'never still'; there was 'something furtive and unpleasant about them, capable as they were of the strangest contortions' [2:9]. By this simple manipulation you have the man damned beyond sympathy and ready for all the native violence of the Haggard Fates. He makes love to Joan most unpleasantly in

55

intense whispers—Mr Haggard has evidently been studying love on the English stage—with obligato 'strangest contortions', and retires rejected, 'walking through the grass of the graves with a slow and somewhat feline step' [2:15]. A pretty phrase that—it is pleasant, for instance, to think of Samuel Rock shaking his foot at a puddle. Mark, too, the restrained beauty of that 'somewhat'. Heedless youth would have had that step all feline or not feline at all; but Mr Haggard, full of the wise caution of the mature artist, qualifies. A proper feline step is quadrupedal. No doubt, too, it was snaky in parts, and occasionally passed insensibly into the gross movements of the gorilla.

Joan, the heroine, it is needless to say, is the flower of her species. Her face was a 'flawless oval' (like a well-made dish), she had arched brows, and we are specifically told that her eyes shone 'beneath them'. Her arms, too, are 'set on to the shoulders with a peculiar grace', and not at any less suitable point of her anatomy. She was beautiful under any circumstances, and Mr Haggard never lets you forget it. She is the kind of heroine who would be beautiful if you tarred and feathered her. Even seen from behind, 'she looked like a person of some refinement', and Captain Henry Graves (R.N.), coming upon her birdnesting, stopped to 'study the appearance of the loveliest woman that he had ever beheld' [3:19]. Captain Graves—curious how needlessly sombre Mr Haggard is even in his names!—is the kind of young man you see on the illustrated price-lists of ready-made clothing people. Naturally they loved, with disastrous consequences to Joan, and she would not marry him for fear of spoiling his future. She was only a poor village girl at the time, having been, like the majority of her class, changed at birth, and his duty to society demanded a mercenary marriage. Consequently she followed the usual law of romance and married the nearest villain, which villain was Rock. The sole but sufficient reason adduced is that the thought of him made life seem hateful to her. After a hundred pages or so of tattered passions, Rock, whose fingers are probably getting tired, realizes that the book ought to be ended, goes mad, and starts out to shoot Sir Henry, formerly Captain, Graves. Joan hastily dresses herself in a hat and coat from nowhere in particular—'there upon the pegs hung a man's coat and hat not unlike those which Sir Henry was wearing that day' [40:411], and Heaven knows how they got there, for Rock never wore anything but a clerical overcoat, a soft felt hat, and top-boots—and hurries out to get shot in her lover's place. Which happens with dramatic precision, for Mr Haggard's providence, if a trifle misanthropic, is an admirable stage manager.

'"Dead!" shrieked the madman, wringing his hands', repeated 'Dead, dead!' and then, without further parley, 'he was gone' [40:420]; and for all that Mr Haggard tells us of his subsequent fate, he may be going still through the East of England, insulting every casual passenger with the furtive and unpleasant motions of his gesticulating digits. Sir Henry arrives in the nick of time for Joan to say, 'Kiss me—I am dying' (dies) [40:423]. The curtain comes down dismally on the news of the murder, while Ellen, Henry's sister, declaims a moral about sowing the seed and 'the decrees of Providence' [40:425], which in this world of Haggard are certainly terrible enough. It is indeed a melancholy book, full of forcible foolishness, a jerry-built story with a stucco style, and it fully justifies Mr Haggard's position beside Messrs Hall Caine and Crockett[2] as one of the most popular writers of our time. Mr [F. S.] Wilson's illustrations are a relief to the letterpress. His conception of Samuel Rock is quite sufficiently satanic, and should give considerable satisfaction to the churchmen among the obscure multitudes who read this writer; but his ideas of a horse's paces are apparently derived from instantaneous photographs, and are quite unlike any impression that has ever been received by the present reviewer.

NOTES

1 Andrew Lang and Rider Haggard were friends and sometime collaborators. Their acquaintance seems to date from 1885, when W. E. Henley asked Lang to report on the manuscript of *King Solomon's Mines* (see R. L. Green, *Andrew Lang* [Edmund Ward, Leicester, 1946], pp 120–38, 166, 176). Thereafter Lang became Haggard's principal champion: in the pages of the *Contemporary Review* for October 1888, for instance, he defended him from an anonymous attack, the previous month, in the *Fortnightly*.

2 Hall Caine (1853–1931) and S. R. Crockett (1860–1914) were two best-selling authors whom Wells considered to be virtually devoid of literary merit. On 22 January 1898, Wells wrote to Gissing: '. . . have you seen something like this about [here he has drawn a 'picshua']. If so—shoot it! It's not human. It's Hall Caine . . . His damned infernal . . . book [*The Christian*] has sold 100,000 (one hundred thousand) copies. One hundred thousand copies [another 'picshua']. . . . Otherwise he has no claim upon our attention' (see also 'The Sawdust Doll', note 2). As for Crockett, Wells had found his short stories 'positively painful' (SR 79: 20 April 1895, p 513) and had reviewed his novel *Cleg Kelly* under the rubric 'Beyond Criticism' (SR 82: 11 July 1896, pp 40–1).

Literary criticism for the Saturday Review
'MR GRANT ALLEN'S NEW NOVEL'

Grant Allen (1848–99) was a prolific writer of almost everything from short stories to Baedekers. His The Woman Who Did *(1895) was the first novel that Wells reviewed for Frank Harris (SR 79: 9 March 1895, pp 319–20; reprinted in part in ExA 8:2). Though he confessed privately his 'agreement with Allen's ideas' (ExA 8:2), in print he objected not only to the aesthetic failings of* The Woman Who Did *but also to its design of promoting the 'New Woman', 'emancipate[d] . . . from monogamy'. To Allen's next production,* The British Barbarians: A Hill-Top Novel, *he likewise reacts negatively—and does so despite some striking resemblances between its satiric fiction and that of his own recent fantasy,* The Wonderful Visit.[1] *However, in this case (SR 80: 14 December 1895, pp 785–6), he takes exception not so much to the content of Allen's 'sermon' as to his use of an art-form for conveying it.*

If the voice of the critic is the voice of the people, as the more optimistic of them fondly imagine, the great British public must be very angry with Mr Grant Allen. To judge from his preface, however, Mr Allen seems to have anticipated that his fellow-countrymen would scarcely hear themselves assailed as 'barbarians' and turn the other cheek. This last story has been written, so he tells us, to please himself: 'simply and solely for the sake of embodying and enforcing my own opinions'. He is weary of expressing other people's opinions and suppressing his own, of providing milk for babes when he 'wished to purvey strong meat for men'. Therefore he has called his story 'A Hill-Top Novel', and dedicated it 'to all who have heart enough, brain enough, and soul enough to understand it'. As for the general reader, he is counselled to leave it or take it at his will, which, seeing that *The Woman Who Did* is in its nineteenth edition, is a tolerably safe challenge.

Now, we have no fault whatever to find with Mr Grant Allen's attitude towards the public. It is in every respect the right attitude for the author—the only possible attitude for the artist. This independence of spirit may not of itself produce literary masterpieces, but assuredly no masterpiece was ever begotten of the subjection of writer to reader. The question is not one of fitness, but of idiosyncrasy. The reader's view of life may be the more just, the writer's intensely, pathetically distorted. What does it matter, so long as the author writes up to the fullness of his undivided conviction or indifference? Thus far we are in entire accord with Mr Grant Allen. But to start fair is not enough, after all, to win the race. To accomplish any supreme achievement in the writing of novels it is necessary that the author be an artist, and *The British Barbarians* is even farther from the sphere of art than *The Woman Who Did*, which is saying a very great deal.

At the threshold of the book Mr Grant Allen admits that he selects the form of fiction because through this medium he can more easily preach and teach his philosophy to women and to the young, who are the chief consumers of novels. The story is to him, therefore, a mere pretext for an attack upon all existing laws and customs which he considers noxious or useless. This particular story is, he further declares, 'a protest in favour of purity'; but Mr Grant Allen's idea of purity is not the average person's idea of purity. In this instance he makes its champion a mystic being from the twenty-fifth century, who miraculously visits this age and country in the guise of 'a perfect gentleman' clad in a grey tweed suit [1:7]. Mr Bertram Ingledew, who is descended both from a Duke and a cobbler, is re-incarnated in the highly respectable suburb of Brockenhurst and casts his 'clear blue eye, very deep and truthful' [1:5], upon Frida Monteith, the wife of a 'moneyed man of oil in the West African trade' [4:55], with a Scotch parentage and evangelical principles. Mr Ingledew burst like a bomb upon Brockenhurst society, whose conventions he freely described as savage taboos, and whose laws he derided and defied. At length his proposal to play tennis on Sunday and his original interpretation of the Seventh Commandment aroused the ire of Mr Monteith to the extent of forbidding his wife to receive him. But Frida, who had all the average woman's appreciation of sedition, especially when expressed with 'that ineffable air of distinction as of one royal born' [4:56],

Literary criticism for the Saturday Review

flies to the arms of the mysterious alien, whereupon her husband, being subject to ordinary human passions and prejudices, follows Frida and her lover intent on vengeance. Having shot Bertram Ingledew, he is disposed to forgive Frida, but she prefers to follow her lover to the twenty-fifth century through the trout-ponds at Broughton.[2]

To consider such a production as a work of art would be absurd. To do Mr Grant Allen justice, he does not even claim such consideration. Judged from this point of view, his book is redolent of bad taste and bad English, destitute alike of dramatic incident and character analysis. Bertram Ingledew is a mere lay figure who serves as a mouthpiece for Mr Grant Allen's diatribes against the existing laws relating to morality and property. True, Mr Allen takes occasion to say a good many things that require saying, and suggests a good many reforms that would, if adopted, bring our present legal code more into harmony with modern humanity and the exigencies of its development. But the sooner Mr Allen realizes that he cannot adopt an art-form and make it subservient to the purposes of the pamphleteer, the better for humanity and for his own reputation as a thinker and a man of letters. Far be it from us to curb Mr Allen's desire to reform his generation. Let him preach to it from his hill-top till he mends it or it ends him, but let him call his sermon a sermon and be content. But the philosopher who masquerades as a novelist, violating the conditions of art that his gospel may win notoriety, discredits both himself and his message, and the result is neither philosophy nor fiction.

Thus it is not the prejudices of the reader but the limitations of his chosen medium which must bind the artist. From the first bond the novelist must emancipate himself if he would see literary salvation; from the latter he breaks away at his peril. Mr Grant Allen has so broken away, and the result is *The British Barbarians*, futile alike as an ethical treatise and as a work of fiction. But with *The Wom[a]n Who Did* in its nineteenth edition, Mr Allen no doubt deems himself justified of his temerity.

NOTES

1 See David Y. Hughes, 'H. G. Wells and the Charge of Plagiarism', *Nineteenth-Century Fiction* 21, 1966, pp 85–90.
2 At the end of Allen's novel, Frida Monteith, now a Liberated Woman, hoping that suicide will enable her to join her lover in the twenty-fifth century, 'walked on by herself . . . across the open moor and purple heath, towards black despair and the trout-ponds at Broughton'.

Literary criticism for the Saturday Review
'THE METHOD OF MR GEORGE MEREDITH'

Meredith (1828–1909), who had succeeded Tennyson to the Presidency of the Society of Authors in 1892, was at the height of his critical reputation when he wrote The Amazing Marriage. *Wells, while acknowledging the difficulties that Meredith's subtle narrative technique presents for the average reader of novels, nevertheless argues (SR 80: 21 December 1895, pp 842—3) that it is preferable to the impersonality of the naturalistic school.*

Lord Ormont and his Aminta [1894] had, to the sense of some of us, a touch of autumn. There were whispers that Mr George Meredith was growing old. But here is the dispelling of such doubts, a book fit to stand beside anything that he has ever written. Of his previous work it is most like the *Egoist* [1879]. Lord Fleetwood, the central figure, is a wealthy young nobleman, a monster of aristocratic self-respect, 'the slave of his word',[1] surrounded by a group of toadies, yet anxious to do his duty by the country so far as a busy and somewhat preoccupied country will permit, encourager of field sports, and especially of the noble art. But he has far finer possibilities in him than the Egoist, and carries us at last altogether out of comedy. He begins magnificently with a fine ambition to be the idol of his countrymen and countrywomen and perishes at last 'of his austerities' [47:281], Brother Russett in a mountain monastery. The other party to the marriage is another of Mr Meredith's triumphant androgynes, a wonderful girl with a man's heart, born and bred in the remoteness of the Carinthian mountains, flung suddenly thence to be nursed, married, hated, discarded, insulted, and finally (too late) loved by the imperial Fleetwood. And set about these two are the *eyes*, the wonderful chorus of characters which Mr Meredith uses so persistently and with such amazing effect. The difficulty and peculiar individuality of his style lie not so much in his phrasing, distinctive though it is, as in his method of telling his story indirectly, through the means of puppet proxies. It is in her failure to understand this, in her endeavour to suggest Meredith by mere verbal inversions and obscurities that 'John Oliver Hobbes'[2] shows the insufficiency of her study of her master. Take, for instance, the fight upon the Haslemere Punch Bowl in the vivid short story of three chapters [1–3] which forms the introduction to the main narrative. 'Dame Gossip' asks: 'Who then was the gentleman who stopped the chariot with his three mounted attendants, on the road to the sea, on the heath by the Great Punch Bowl?' 'Countess Fanny must have known him, and not once did she open her mouth to breathe his name. Yet she had no objection to talk of the adventure, and tell how. . . .' [2:19] And so on for a vivid paragraph. Then, 'Simon Fettle was a plain, kindly creature, without a thought of malice, who kept his master's accounts. He fired the first shot at the foremost man, he relates, . . .'[3] and so we go on for a space, hearing more of the business from Simon Fettle. Then comes a wonderful miniature of Charles Dumps, the postillion, who made a little fortune talking about the business, but contradicted himself sadly. 'Yet we have the doctor of the village of Ipley, Dr Cawthorne, a noted botanist, assuring us . . .' [2:25].

It is this perpetual shifting of the standpoint that limits Mr Meredith's public. As a method of narrating pure incident, as in this case, it is certainly not a little tiresome to many a well-meaning reader. But where it comes in with superlative success is in such an employment as the analysis of the effect of Carinthia, who is by common standards a plain girl, upon Fleetwood. We have among the chorus one Woodseer, a character remarkably suggestive of the Stevenson of the Overland Voyage,[4] a phrase-maker with a note-book. It is he calls her, 'A beautiful Gorgon—a haggard Venus' [8:84]. He writes again, 'a panting look, a look of beaten flame; a look of one who has run, and at last beholds' [8:85]. Woodseer himself, we see—to the black finger nails—through the unfriendly comments of Sir Meeson Corby. He follows us through the book, to marry at last the girl Madge, who is there as exponent of all the feminine sympathy, the activity and usefulness of Carinthia. Besides Woodseer's memoranda we have fluttering on the edge of the tale, the pages of the book Carinthia's father wrote long ago (only a few copies extant) of 'Maxims of Men'. Out of it all, out of her effect on Dame Gossip, on Woodseer, on Madge, on

Literary criticism for the Saturday Review

Fleetwood, and on Lady Arpington, one conceives the woman, and how living she is! So blurred at the outline she has atmosphere, perspective—you turn to some explicit impersonal writer, and behold sheet-tin as men walking! Plausible and well coloured perhaps from the one right point of view, but even from that, harsh of contour, and from elsewhere, *showing the edge*.

There is no one right method of telling a story—only the preposterous unknown of *How to Write Fiction*[5] believes that. But for the presentation of a human being, at least, this artifice of seeing through the eyes of characters is supremely effective. Otherwise you can have only the author's view. The theory of a scientific, an impersonal standpoint, is fallacious. The really logical scientific method would be to deal with Carinthia as so many pounds of bone, muscle, blood, and flesh, and state velocity, orientation, latitude and longitude, from moment to moment. But a soul is determined by its surfaces of contact with other souls. It may be Mr Meredith sometimes carries his indirect method to excess, and puzzles a decent public, nourished on good healthy, straightforward marionettes. But we can find it in us to return thanks even for his excesses. And assuredly this book is as fine, and vigorous, and subtle as anything he has ever written.

NOTES

1 The editors have not found this phrase in *The Amazing Marriage*. In the title of chapter 11, however, Meredith refers to Fleetwood as 'the prisoner of his word'.
2 The pseudonym of Mrs Pearl Teresa Craigie (1867–1906), whose *The Gods, Some Mortals and Lord Wickenham* (1895) Wells had found amiable largely, if not solely, because of its 'Meredithisms' (SR 79: 11 May 1895, pp 624–5).
3 Meredith's text at this point reads: '. . . the foremost man, as he related in after days' (2:20). The word 'tell', in Wells's previous quotation, does not appear in the novel.
4 Probably an allusion to, if not a misprint for, *An Inland Voyage* (1878).

5 Wells had written about this anonymous manual in 'The Secrets of the Short Story' (SR 80: 23 November 1895, p 693). There he had ridiculed its assumption that Literature can be produced through the mechanical application of invariable Rules.

Literary criticism for the Saturday Review
'THE NOVEL OF TYPES'

As the opening paragraph of this review (SR 81: 4 January 1896, pp 23–4) indicates, the impact of the Russian novel came relatively late in England. However, one of the two novels by Turgenev (1818–83) noticed here was soon to achieve 'classic' status: Fathers and Children, *in Constance Garnett's translation. Wells argues (with some daring) that Turgenev's characters in* Fathers and Children *and* Spring Floods *are 'typical individuals', and that this makes him a more genuinely 'contemporary' writer than any English novelist of 1896. He was later to revise this opinion in favour of Gissing, whose 'contemporaneity' and historical sense he affirmed in his 1897 essay on that novelist (see 'The Novels of Mr George Gissing').*

It is a remarkable thing how few of the educated public read Turgenev. For one reader of Turgenev one can find a dozen of the incoherent, and sometimes almost amorphous, Tolstoi. Your cultivated young man responds 'Certainly' to *The Woman Who Did*,[1] he is familiar with George Egerton[2] and *Anna Karenina* [1873–77], he is reading *Trilby*[3] now, and Turgenev—he knows by name. The comparative neglect of these wise and wonderfully constructed novels, especially in England, is to us unaccountable. Perhaps it is the fault of the newspaper critic. What can one expect when the worthy *Times*, in its weekly *réchauffé*, welcomes *A Sportsman's Sketches* [1847–51] among its 'Recent Novels', gives it just one-third of the space devoted to the praises of the very newest version of the Scotch 'jocks', and, by way of criticism, tells us that 'these tales are a pleasing corrective of much affected and unwholesome modern nonsense'. 'The *format*', it adds, 'paper and print are all commendable'.[4] Turgenev, so treated, becomes a mere page in attendance upon an obscure and unreadable imitator of Mr Maclaren's imitations of Mr Barrie.[5] He stands a Lilliputian beneath the towering columns that commemorate the latest triumph of Mrs Humphry Ward.[6] Surely abuse had been more honourable.

The peculiar characteristic of Turgenev's genius is the

extraordinary way in which he can make his characters typical, while at the same time retaining their individuality. It is the easiest thing in fiction to invent a character that is merely typical; to drive a bundle of views or habits or traditions, void of all idiosyncrasy, through a series of incidents. In a recent novel,[7] for instance, was a Cynic, Cynicism heaped up and brimming over, Cynicism neat, as free of any personality as oil of water, and Mr Grant Allen's 'Herminia' was a Theory against Marriage, insufficiently personified.[8] But Turgenev people are not avatars of theories nor tendencies. They are living, breathing individuals, but individuals living under the full stress of this great social force or that. The force is not the individual, any more than the voice of the preacher is the sounding board. But every note in the tumult of living opinion finds here and there through a country its own proper resonator, and Turgenev's seems to throw together in the most natural way a group of these resonators. In *Spring Floods* the theme is the sudden awakening of erotic emotions in a man, and the destructive effect of the sexual energy disengaged by that awakening. Young Sanin returning to Russia is delayed at Frankfort, and falls in love with a girl, Gemma, in a confectioner's shop. He fights a duel for her, supplants her accepted suitor, and, under a promise to marry her, goes on to Russia to settle his affairs. There he meets Marie Nikolaieva, the adventurous wife of a complaisant husband, confides his love for Gemma to her—and never returns to Gemma. But at the very end of this story, the individuality of the actors falls away, the symbolism shows through. He goes, the serf of sensuality, with Maria and her husband to Paris, and as they pass through Frankfort all the chief actors in the Gemma idyl, save only Gemma herself, stand and stare contempt at him from the street corner. The book resembles a little in its leading idea Mr Hardy's *Jude the Obscure*,[9] and undoubtedly Mr Hardy is inclining, from his old elaboration of local colour, to experiments in the typical; but, while much of *Jude the Obscure* is still local and personal, *Spring Floods* is catholic, without superfluity or redundance, a thing simple, complete, and beautiful.

In *Fathers and Children* we have the characters carried, not

Literary criticism for the Saturday Review

upon the tides of a man's development, but upon the secular advance in opinion which maintains a perpetual conflict between young and old. 'Bazarov', written five-and-twenty years ago, is still typically modern—earnest to get behind sentimentality, idealism, to go hand in hand with truth. He is, says Mr Edward Garnett, in italics, *'the bare mind of Science first applied to Politics'*;[10] and that is admirably the essence of the matter. And yet he is human, perfectly human; and therein is the wonder of Turgenev's art. One must compare the book with Mr Bernard Shaw's somewhat similar *Unsocial Socialist* [1887] to appreciate the artistic feat Turgenev has performed. Give the *Unsocial Socialist* to any decent body ignorant of Mr Bernard Shaw's particular line of thought, and the book is simply unsympathetic and unconvincing. But *Fathers and Children* has been tried by the present reviewer upon such a simple soul, and the verdict upon Bazarov is that he is a rude, conceited, and singularly unfeeling young man—just the impression the living man makes upon that refined old gentleman Pavel Petrovitch. Mr Bernard Shaw sympathizes, and expects us to sympathize, only with his hero. Turgenev links us not only with Bazarov, but, if you be so disposed, you may take the timid philanthropist and hero-worshipper Arkady to your heart; or Arkady's father, a man of forty-four, fond of tender poetry, and playing abundantly and badly on the violoncello; or those dear old parents of Bazarov, who apologize to him so touchingly for inviting the village priest to meet him. The old mother—but a quotation is better. The only son, after years from home, has revisited them.

> She was sitting, as before, near her son (she did not play cards); her cheek, as before, propped on her little fist: she only got up to order some new dainty to be served. She was afraid to caress Bazarov, and he gave her no encouragement; he did not invite her caresses, and, besides, Vassily Ivanovitch had advised her not to "worry" him too much. "Young men are not fond of that sort of thing," he declared to her....
>
> "No!" he said to Arkady, the next day, "I'm off from here to-morrow. I'm bored; I want to work, but I can't work here. I will come to your place again; I've left all my apparatus there too. In your house one can at any rate shut oneself up. While here my father repeats to me, "My study is at your disposal—nobody shall interfere with you," and all the time, he himself is never a yard away. And I'm ashamed somehow to shut myself

away from him. It's the same thing, too, with my mother. I hear her sighing on the other side of the wall, and if one goes in to her, one's nothing to say to her." [21:234-6]

In *Fathers and Children*, as in *Rudin* [1856] and *On the Eve* [1860], Turgenev uses a structural form of which he is very fond. The type, the back-bone figure of the story, is precipitated into new surroundings, into a quiet country houseful of educated people in each of the three cases. So we see the stanger in his most vigorous reactions, explaining himself, striking out sympathy in this personage and antagonism in that. We know him solid by the shadows he casts. In the *Universal Socialist*[12] you may find by comparison the advantage of this method. There, as an imperfect artist naturally would do, the story opens upon the type. In this matter of method Mr Meredith and Turgenev meet. Mr Meredith's theme is ever a personality, Turgenev's ever a principle; but in the use of subsidiary comment their workmanship, externally so dissimilar, is in the essentials the same.

It is curious that in casting about for a comparison to Turgenev one should alight on a book now, I believe, out of print, by a man who is scarcely known to the general public as a novelist. But an equivalent to Turgenev does not exist among contemporary writers; modern types, modern influences play an astonishingly small part in modern fiction. We may count Mrs Humphry Ward, perhaps, and George Egerton, and Mrs [sic] Tirebuck,[13] and one or two others; but their books are statements, not studies of opinion. The highest form of literary art, the Turgenev novel, the novel of types, does not live at present in this country.[14]

NOTES

1 See the headnote to 'Mr Grant Allen's New Novel'.
2 The pseudonym of Mrs Mary Chavelita Dunne (1860-1945), two of whose books Wells had reviewed earlier in SR 79: 30 March 1895, pp 416-17.
3 George DuMaurier's best-selling triple-decker, published in 1894, sold 80,000 copies in the first three months following its appearance.

Literary criticism for the Saturday Review

4 'The very newest version of the "Scotch Jocks"' refers to George MacDonald's *Lilith*, the novel which was given pride of place in the *Times* review of 'Recent Novels' (5 November 1895, p 11) from which Wells quotes phrases about *A Sportsman's Sketches*. The same review contains a hostile and patronizing discussion of *The Wonderful Visit* by 'H. S. Wells' (*sic*). The reviewer may have been Andrew Lang (for this conjecture, see Gordon N, Ray's article in the *Library*, p 31).

5 'Ian Maclaren' was the pen name of John Watson (see 'The Simple Art of Popular Pathos'), who, Wells hints, borrowed his sentimentalism from Sir James Barrie (1860–1937).

6 Wells had no great liking for Mrs Ward's productions. Though her treatment of her subject often has 'the indisputable stamp of truth', he wrote of *Sir George Tressady*, it has 'neither very much humour nor very much wit' (SR 82: 10 October 1896, p 397).

7 Michael Dure's *An Impression . . ., Called 'The Imagination of Their Hearts'*, reviewed by Wells in SR 82: 25 July 1896, p 96.

8 The heroine of Grant Allen's *The Woman Who Did*.

9 Compare 'Jude the Obscure'.

10 Edward Garnett (1868–1937), the son of Richard and father of David Garnett (see the 'Preface to *The Scientific Romances*'), introduces his wife Constance's translation of *Fathers and Children*. He later (1917) wrote a book on Turgenev.

11 Wells had reviewed *On the Eve* in SR 79: 25 May 1895, pp 675–76, but at the time had preferred Jonas Lie's *One of Life's Slaves* over it.

12 Probably a misprint of the Shaw title mentioned above.

13 Wells had found William E. Tirebuck's study of a collier family, *Grace of All Souls* (1895), 'rich with irrelevant detail': 'it is not so much a novel written as a mass of writing with the stuff of a novel therein' (SR 81: 25 January 1896, pp 107–8).

14 Compare Wells's remarks on Turgenev in 'The Novels of Mr George Gissing'.

H. G. Wells's Literary Criticism
THE THREE IMPOSTORS

Arthur Machen (1863–1947) is known chiefly as the author of occult or supernatural tales of horror. The Three Impostors *was his second work of fiction in that genre. Wells's discussion of the merits and (mainly) the faults of Machen's rather loosely connected series of 'Adventures' follows, but remains separate from, his consideration of George Gissing's* Sleeping Fires *('Fiction', SR 81: 11 January 1896, p 49).*

Mr Machen is an unfortunate man. He has determined to be weird, horrible, and as outspoken as his courage permits in an age which is noisily resolved to be 'healthy' to the pitch of blatancy. His particular obsession is a kind of infernal matrimonial agency, and the begetting of human-diabolical mules.[1] He has already skirted the matter in his previous book, the *Great God Pan* [1894], and here we find it well to the fore again. This time, however, it simply supplies one of a group of incoherent stories held together in a frame of wooden narrative about a young man with spectacles. This young man falls into a circle of Black Magicians, who are practising indecorums and crimes at which Mr Machen dare only hint in horror-struck whispers. Aghast—all Mr Machen's characters are aghast sooner or later—the young man takes to flight, and, instead of informing the police, runs to and fro about London, trying to hide. The chase assumes this form: Again and again a Mr Dyson sees the young man, and again and again this Mr Dyson is accosted by people who tell him stories, remotely apropos of the unhappy fugitive. They are members of the secret society, and bent apparently upon inciting Mr Dyson to murder him. Mr Dyson proving sluggish, the young man in spectacles is caught by other hands, tied down to the floor of a deserted house in the west of London, and live coals are, very properly, piled upon his chest. He smells of cooking, and perishes, and the ubiquitous Mr Dyson comes in and sees his remains. Tableau. 'They [. . .] clung hard to one another, shuddering at the sight they saw', did Mr Dyson and Mr Phillips, his friend ['The Adventure of the Deserted Residence', p 214]. That is

Literary criticism for the Saturday Review

the climax of Mr Machen's invention; he ends there. Other effects are the murder of a respectable citizen, whose remains are, for no earthly reason, outraged by being incontinently mummified; a man who, also for no earthly reason, vanishes; a witches' meeting in California; the inventor of an instrument of torture caught in his own trap, and the mongrel creature already alluded to. Mr Machen has one simple expedient whereby he seeks to develop his effects. He piles them up very high, and makes his characters horror-struck at them. This kind of thing:

> He seemed to pour forth an infamous jargon, with words, or what seemed words, that might have belonged to a tongue dead since untold ages, and buried deep beneath Nilotic mud or in the inmost recesses of the Mexican forest. For a moment the thought passed through my mind, as my ears were still revolted by that infernal clamour, "Surely, this is the very speech of hell"; and then I cried out again and again, and ran away shuddering to my inmost soul. ['The Adventure of the Missing Brother,' pp 90–91]

But it fails altogether to affect the reader as it is meant to do. It fails mainly because Mr Machen has not mastered the necessary trick of commonplace detail which renders horrors convincing, and because he lacks even the rudimentary conception of how to individualize characters. The framework of the book is evidently imitated from Mr Stevenson's *New Arabian Nights* [1882], a humorous form quite unsuited, of course, to realistic horrors. Mr Machen writes with care and a certain whimsical choice of words, so that his style is at least distinctive.

NOTES

1 Page 115 of *The Three Impostors* contains a somewhat obscure account of the rape of a peasant woman by a mysterious and diabolical serpentine creature.

H. G. Wells's Literary Criticism
'POPULAR WRITERS AND PRESS CRITICS'

Ironically subtitled 'An Informal Appreciation', this brief essay (SR 81: 8 February 1896, pp 145–6) reveals Wells as being far from appreciative of the romances and novels of Sir Anthony Hope Hawkins (1863–1933). In fact, 'Anthony Hope' figures in Wells's analysis as an instance of those writers whose popularity he can account for only in terms of sociological factors affecting the readership of fiction.

To account for the vogue of certain books, the popularity of certain writers, has always been difficult, and in our time the task appears to have become impossible. It is comparatively easy to see why our grandfathers and grandmothers went into ecstasies over *Jane Eyre* [1847], and our fathers and mothers had still more reason to extol *Never Too Late to Mend* and *The Woman in White*.[1] But between those times and ours there is an impassable gulf. The passing of the Education Act in 1870[2] and the coming to reading age in 1886–1888 of multitudes of boys and girls, have changed the conditions of journalism and literature in much the same way as the French Revolution changed the conditions of political thought and action. The popularity of *Tit-Bits, Pearson's Weekly, Answers, Ally Sloper*, and a multitude of other periodicals,[3] is only to be accounted for by the advent of the Board-school scholar. And while the male of this species has chiefly exerted his influence in the degradation of journalism, the debasing influence of the female, reinforced by the free libraries, has been felt chiefly in the character of the fiction. 'Arry reads *Ally Sloper* and *Tit-Bits*, 'Arriet *Trilby* and *The Sorrows of Satan*.[4] We only use these extreme examples to account for what would otherwise be unaccountable—the comparative popularity to-day of scores of books whose relation to life is of the slightest, and whose connexion with Art is purely accidental. It is scarcely too much to say that every writer of our time who can be called popular owes three-quarters of his or her fame to the girls who have been taught in Board schools. This is the true explanation, we believe, of the vogue of

Literary criticism for the Saturday Review

The Heavenly Twins, A Superfluous Woman, and other similar productions.[5]

The evil goes deeper. The influx of these millions of readers, who are so ignorant of life that they are contemptuous of its probabilities, and who display the same impartial indifference to the laws of language as to those of Art, has degraded not only creative writing, but also criticism. Let us suppose, for example, that a critic condemns the construction of *The Heavenly Twins*, shows that the story from which the book takes its name is merely an episode intercalated in a hysterical diatribe against the tyranny exercised by man over woman. The episode itself, he points out, is based upon an absolutely impossible assumption, and has no connexion whatever with the main current of the narrative. Such a critic is forthwith met by the fact that fifty thousand copies of the book have been sold, and he may congratulate himself if his dictum is not pilloried in publishers' advertisements side by side with the announcement of the book's success. Popularity that has no relation to merit constitutes, perhaps, the chief reason why criticism to-day has been almost entirely displaced in the columns of the Press by mere adulation.

There are, however, subsidiary reasons for this decay of criticism which in their turn deserve to be noted. Not a few publishers have found it to their profit to employ a critic as a member of their staff, and to turn this guide of public opinion into the herald of their wares. Thus A.B., the critic of *The Daily Snuffler*, receives a salary as the reader of the great publishing house of X. A.B., in the discharge of his duties as publisher's reader, recommends Messrs X. to publish certain books, and when these books are published the same gentleman, as critic of *The Daily Snuffler*, uses the columns of that paper to puff these very books into popularity. Occasionally, too, this same gentleman writes a leader deploring the venality of French newspapers, and holding the *Figaro* up to public contempt because a book may be puffed in its columns by paying so much for a notice. In these days when readers are distinguished by an indiscriminating voracity, it is only natural that the panegyrist should be better paid than the critic, and so criticism declines and puffery increases, till Walter Besant is regarded seriously as a man of letters,[6] and a rag-bag journalist is spoken of as 'a master-mind' in the columns of a great daily paper.

We have written all this as a mere excuse for our inability to criticize seriously the works of two men which have been much applauded in the Press. For years past our curiosity has been excited about the novels of Mr Anthony Hope by 'notices' in this paper and in that. When the *Chronicles of Count Antonio* [1895] appeared, a few weeks ago, accompanied by puffs that ran from half a column to nearly two, we sat down to read it. We found it dull beyond belief. A series of episodes in the main impossible take place in a country as least as vague as Cloud Cuckoo Land.[7] Not wishing to rest under such an impression of so belauded an author, we procured the rest of Mr Hope's books, and began with the *Prisoner of Zenda* [1894]. It was not as dull as the *Chronicles of Count Antonio*, but all its interest came from a quick succession of extraordinary incidents, all founded upon the family likeness between the brother of an English Earl and a German Grand Duke. The scene of the story is laid in Germany, if indeed that can be called a scene which has neither local nor national colour and no relations either to place or time, and if that can be called a story which whirls giddily from improbability to improbability, where names stand for characters, and illusion does not seem even to be desired. Nevertheless we went on with our task. We felt sure that Mr Anthony Hope must have done something better than the *Chronicles of Count Antonio*, or the *Prisoner of Zenda*. We fell upon *The Indiscretion of the Duchess* [1894] as the smallest of his books, and regretted the choice. It can only be compared with its own brethren, and we are fain to acknowledge that it is a little better than the *Chronicles*, though a little worse than the *Prisoner of Zenda*. And then we forswore Mr Hope's novels of adventure.

On the advice of a friend we turned to Mr Hope's more realistic performances, and we shall run over them briefly. *A Man of Mark* [1890] is the worst of them. It stands in our memory as one of the very worst attempts at novel-writing that we have ever come across. *A Change of Air* [1893] is not much better; but by comparison *Mr Witt's Widow* [1892],

Literary criticism for the Saturday Review
Father Stafford [1891], *Half a Hero* [1892], and *The God in the Car* [1891] are good. *Father Stafford* and *The God in the Car* are examples of spurious realism attained by taking some well-known public character as the hero. Let us examine *The God in the Car*, which has run through six editions, and which is declared by the *Standard* to be 'a brilliant book . . . one of the most remarkable works in a year that has given us the handiwork of nearly all our best living novelists'. This is comparing Mr Anthony Hope's story with the *Esther Waters* [1894] of Mr George Moore, with the second *Jungle Book* [1895] of Mr Kipling, and with *Jude the Obscure* of Mr Thomas Hardy.[8] To challenge such a comparison is to disgrace English journalism. One chapter of *Jude the Obscure* or of *Esther Waters* is worth all that Mr Hope has ever written and much to boot. The dialogue is the best thing in the book. It is smart with the little epigrams of the society talker, but there is no real characterization and no construction. In essentials the writer has no grip. The whole book is flaccid and limp. As in *Father Stafford* and *Half a Hero*, so in *The God in the Car*, the author is at pains to work up to a situation which he proves unable to handle worthily. *Father Stafford* and *The God in the Car* fizzle out in the weakest way imaginable, while *Half a Hero* wins to a dramatic ending by outraging probability—the hero of the book, who is supposed to be the Premier in one of our colonies, meets his death in a labour-riot.

NOTES

1 Charles Reade's *It is Never too Late to Mend* (1856); Wilkie Collins's *Woman in White* (1860).
2 This Act provided, among other things, for increasing the number of places for pupils in the day school system. In the first ten years the Act was in force, the elementary school population more than doubled.
3 Popular weeklies whose circulation, at the time Wells was writing, averaged half a million each. All were founded between 1880 and 1890. '[George] Newnes [of *Tit-Bits*], [Alfred] Harmsworth [of *Answers*], and [Cyril] Pearson [of *Pearson's Weekly*] . . . revolutionized the lowest level of cheap journalism', says Richard Altick. 'Apart from circulation-boosting stunts like prize contests and insurance schemes, their policy was to fill their papers with anecdotes, jokes, excerpts, riddles—nothing

which required sustained attention on the part of their readers, let alone concentration' (*The English Common Reader* [University of Chicago Press, 1957], pp 363–4; see also p 396).

4 On *Trilby*, see 'The Novel of Types', n 3; *The Sorrows of Satan* (1895) was one of Marie Corelli's best-sellers (to which Wells alludes later, in 'Flickers of Imagination . . .').

5 Two triple-decker romances, the first (1893) written by Frances Elizabeth MacFall (1862–1943) under the pseudonym Sarah Grand; the other (1894) by Emma Francis Brooke (d. 1926).

6 Wells himself did not take Besant (1836–1901) seriously. He declared *Beyond the Dreams of Avarice* (1895), for example, to be notable chiefly for its soporific power (SR 79: 30 March 1895, pp 420–1). See also 'Jude the Obscure', n 6, and 'Flickers of Imagination . . .,' n 2.

7 The imaginary utopia in Aristophanes' satiric comedy *The Birds*.

8 See 'Jude the Obscure'.

Literary criticism for the Saturday Review
'JUDE THE OBSCURE'

The clamour of indignation with which Jude the Obscure *was received no doubt helped persuade Thomas Hardy to stop writing novels. Wells found himself virtually alone among contemporary reviewers in his unstinting praise of the book. Even now, some readers may think that he is too uncritical in his admiration, that his empathy for the title character has blinded him to Hardy's weaknesses as a novelist. Yet Wells does put Hardy's achievement in perspective elsewhere (see 'The Novel of Types'). Here, instead, he makes a case for* Jude *as introducing 'the voice of the educated proletarian, speaking more distinctly than it has ever spoken before in English literature' (SR 81: 8 February 1896, pp 153–4). If he overstates the novel's merits, he perhaps does so with the design of counterbalancing the cries of strident condemnation.*

It is doubtful, considering not only the greatness of the work but also the greatness of the author's reputation, whether for many years any book has received quite so foolish a reception as has been accorded the last and most splendid of all the books that Mr Hardy has given the world. By an unfortunate coincidence it appears just at the culmination of a new fashion in Cant, the Cant of 'Healthiness'. It is now the better part of a year ago since the collapse of the 'New Woman' fiction began. The success of *The Woman Who Did* was perhaps the last of a series of successes attained,[1] in spite of glaring artistic defects, and an utter want of humour or beauty, by works dealing intimately and unrestrainedly with sexual affairs. It marked a crisis. A respectable public had for a year or more read such books eagerly, and discussed hitherto unheard of topics with burning ears and an air of liberality. The reviewers had reviewed in the spirit of public servants. But such strange delights lead speedily to remorse and reaction. The pendulum bob of the public conscience swung back swiftly and forcibly. From reading books wholly and solely dependent upon sexuality for their interest, the respectable public has got now to rejecting books wholly and solely for their recognition of sexuality, however incidental that recognition may be. And the reviewers, mindful of the fact that the duty of a reviewer is to provide acceptable reading for his editor's public, have changed with the greatest dexterity from a chorus praising 'outspoken purity' to a band of public informers against indecorum. It is as if the spirit of McDougallism has fled the London County Council to take refuge in the circles called 'literary'.[2] So active, so malignant have these sanitary inspectors of fiction become, that a period of terror, analogous to that of the New England Witch Mania, is upon us. No novelist, however respectable, can deem himself altogether safe to-day from a charge of morbidity and unhealthiness. They spare neither age nor sex; the beginner of yesterday and the maker of a dozen respectable novels suffer alike. They outdo one another in their alertness for anything they can by any possible measure of language contrive to call *decadent*. One scarcely dares leave a man and woman together within the same corners for fear of their scandal; one dares scarcely whisper of reality. And at the very climax of this silliness, Mr Hardy, with an admirable calm, has put forth a book in which a secondary, but very important, interest is a frank treatment of the destructive influence of a vein of sensuality upon an ambitious working-man. There probably never was a novel dealing with the closer relations of men and women that was quite so free from lasciviousness as this. But at one point a symbolical piece of offal is flung into Jude's face. Incontinently a number of popular reviewers, almost tumbling over one another in the haste to be first, have rushed into print under such headings as 'Jude the Obscene', and denounced the book, with simply libellous violence, as a mass of filth from beginning to end.

If the reader has trusted the reviewers for his estimate of this great novel, he may even be surprised to learn that its main theme is not sexual at all; that the dominant motive of Jude's life is the fascination Christminster (Oxford) exercises upon his rustic imagination, and that the climax of its development is the pitiless irony of Jude's death-scene, within sound of the University he loved—which he loved, but which could offer no place in all its colleges for such a man as he. Only as a modifying cause does the man's sexuality come in, just as much as, and no more than, it

Literary criticism for the Saturday Review

comes into the life of any serious but healthy man. For the first time in English literature the almost intolerable difficulties that beset an ambitious man of the working class—the snares, the obstacles, the countless rejections and humiliations by which our society eludes the services of these volunteers—receive adequate treatment. And since the peculiar matrimonial difficulties of Jude's cousin Sue have been treated *ad nauseam* in the interests of purity in our contemporaries, we may perhaps give her but an incidental mention in this review, and devote ourselves to the neglected major theme of the novel. . . .[3]

It is at Christminster that he, being already married to the runaway Arabella, meets and falls in love with his cousin Sue. And this development of the sexual side of the man is a necessary part of his complete presentation. He is energetic, he is deeply emotional, and the complication was inevitable. The man of the lower class who aspires to knowledge can only escape frustration by ruthlessly suppressing affections and passions; it is a choice of one tragedy or another. To have veiled the matter, to have ignored sex altogether in deference to the current fashion, would have gone far to make Jude the Obscure into a John Halifax, Gentleman.[4] Sue, however, is no mere figure of sexual affection, as Arabella is of passion; she is the feminine counterpart of Jude's intellectual side, clearer minded, unimpassioned, an exceptional but a possible woman. She points the moral of the Churchminster defeat with her acute modern-spirited comments, and participates so far in the main theme of the story, in addition to her rôle as a detracting feminine influence. But her coldbloodedness seems, for some incomprehensible reason, to have roused the common reviewer to a pitch of malignant hatred.

It is impossible by scrappy quotations to do justice to Mr Hardy's tremendous indictment of the system which closes our three English teaching Universities to what is, and what has always been, the noblest material in the intellectual life of this country—the untaught. Sufficient has been quoted to show how entirely false is the impression that this book relies mainly upon its treatment of sex trouble—that it is to be regarded as a mere artistic and elaborate essay upon the great 'Woman Who' theme. That is really as much criticism as is needed here just now. The present reviewer will not even pretend to taste and dubitate, to advise and reprimand, in the case of a book that alone will make 1895 a memorable year in the history of literature. Let it suffice further to quote the last scene of all, the death of Jude, one of the most grimly magnificent passages in English fiction. . . .[5]

That is the voice of the educated proletarian, speaking more distinctly than it has ever spoken before in English literature. The man is, indeed, at once an individual and a type. There is no other novelist alive with the breadth of sympathy, the knowledge, or the power for the creation of Jude. Had Mr Hardy never written another book, this would still place him at the head of English novelists. To turn from him or from Mr Meredith to our Wardour Street romancers and whimpering Scotch humourists[6] is like walking from a library into a schoolroom.

NOTES

1 Grant Allen's novel spawned a number of imitations. Wells briefly noticed two of them—*The Woman Who Wouldn't* and *The Woman Who Didn't*—and found them to be 'without the faintest appeal to any human being . . . except to those who are still in the "curious" stage of sexual development' (SR 80: 21 September 1896, 387; see also the headnote to 'Mr Grant Allen's New Novel').
2 Sir John McDougall (1844–1917) was Chairman of the London County Council, in which capacity he led a campaign to clean up London's music-halls.
3 Wells's plot summary of *Jude's* opening chapters has been omitted here because it consists for the most part of long quotations (from i:3 and ii:6).
4 The eponymous hero of Mrs Craik's (Dinah Maria Mulock's) sentimental novel about a poor boy who greatly improves his social position through honesty, education, and hard work.
5 At this point Wells quotes at length from Hardy's account of Jude's death (vi:11:509–10).
6 Sardonic epithets for authors of pseudo-archaic historical romances (eg, Walter Besant) and cloyingly sentimental novels (eg, S.R. Crockett and 'Ian Maclaren').

Literary criticism for the Saturday Review
ON LANG AND BUCHAN

Andrew Lang (1844–1912) the literary critic was someone whom Wells regarded as a pernicious influence on the republic of letters.[1] *He therefore seized upon* A Monk of Fife *as offering an opportunity to ridicule the chief proponent of the Scott tradition. In his review (SR 81: 22 February 1896, pp 208–9), he exposes Lang's shabby performance both for what it is and for being the consequence of Lang's threadbare critical precepts. To complete the job of demolition, Wells ends by comparing Lang's 'wooden' romance unfavourably to* Sir Quixote of the Moors, *the first book-length work of fiction by John Buchan (who is perhaps best-known as the author of* The Thirty-Nine Steps [1915]*).*

We have all heard of Mr Henley's incurable boyishness.[2] Of Mr Lang also boyishness is an attribute—a boyishness of a sort not quite so much a matter of the emotions and rather more of the intelligence than Mr Henley's. Mr Henley's boyishness declines to grow old, Mr Lang's declines to grow up. With the former it is an emotional persistence, with the latter it is an arrested development. Most people, at some time or other, have come upon the clever little boy of the preparatory school. Learning has already marked him for her own. For him are no rambles in the summer's lanes, no daylong truancies, no 'mugging' fads; 'stinks' or pets; stamps or furtive tobacco. He cares for none of these things. At the utmost he will entertain a 'favourite subject'. On the other hand, there are no wearisome imprisonments, no perennial impositions in his life. He takes his exercise regularly, decent cricket or decent football, attentively developed, and in the fullness of time passes on, to all appearances, sane and healthy, by way of scholarship and fellowship towards the minuter, more specialized learning of the University. Of such a type is the boyishness of Mr Andrew Lang, a decorous bookish puerility—regularly taking the air in the playing-fields, and bearing itself according to prescription in all the relations of life. It is not so much boyishness proper as prize-boyishness: a fine sense of the humour of defective scholarship; a fine contempt for experience, a memory and a trick of imitation admirably trained, a crippled imagination, and an unqualified preference for parody over original work. He is naturally at his best in those chuckling literary leaders of his in the *Daily News*, bristling with allusions, apt misquotations, and clever mimicry. As a critic he is amusing when he is not irritating, and if he could only keep his hands from romance he would cut a very respectable figure among contemporary writers. But clearly he does not understand the limitations his curiously dwarfed imagination imposes, and at intervals he continues to fail conspicuously in this branch of literary endeavour.

The new effort is mainly an offering to the memory of Stevenson. What there is human of Norman Leslie is extract of David Balfour: Catriona[3] appears in the story under the name of Elliot, but, eluding Mr Lang's pursuit, she is, like Daphne, incontinently changed to wood. The crown of Mr Lang's imagination is Noiroufle, an inferior Mr Maskelyne,[4] only too conspicuously disguised in a vast Hebraic nose and a long black beard. He cannot read (for the purposes of this story), but he can do all the current tricks of a European juggler, and his wonderful device of imitating men's voices is Mr Lang's culminating inspiration. For it was not Flavy who betrayed Joan of Arc, but the wonderful Noiroufle, who boldly transcended the possibility of ventriloquism, imitated Flavy's voice, and so got the drawbridge raised and cut off her retreat. A whacking fight was going on beyond the drawbridge, about Flavy was a tumultuous uproar, and yet the men whose duty was at the cranks and pulleys trusted to their ears rather than their eyes [ch. 26]. So Joan was taken, and Elliot would not marry David—Norman, that is—out of sorrow for her. 'If she [herself] bids me do as you desire', said Elliot, 'then I would not be disobedient to that Daughter of God' [30:262]. Nothing remained for a romance hero but the quest of this permission. Going to Joan in her dungeon was exceedingly simple. You disguised yourself in English costume and went to the nearest seaport; there you found a fisherman and an east wind, and went to one of the Cinque Ports; there were always bands going to France, and you joined one. 'As fortune would have it, the wind went about, and we on board, and with no long delay

Literary criticism for the Saturday Review

we were in Rouen town' [30:370]. Then you made three things your 'chief care'. You got a lodging near the castle, you purveyed your three horses of the fleetest, and won the favour of Sir Thomas Grey, who forthwith took you as his galloper, and gave you his signet to 'open the town gates' [31:370–71]. 'Moreover the man who has the chief charge and custody of the Maid was the brother's son of Sir Thomas'. What could be simpler? This miscreant you often met at his uncle's table, and you laughed at his jests and did him what service you might. Finally, when 'he had well drunk', you lost that one of your three horses to him 'which most he coveted' [31:373]. 'I will do thee a good turn', said he. 'You crave to see this Puzel. . . .' 'At his wording I set down an order to the Castle porter. . . . This pass he signed with his name [,] and sealed with his seal [*ring*] bearing his arms' [31:375], and the thing was done! The planning of this elaborate scheme and its successful execution reflect almost equal credit on the intelligence and invention of Norman Leslie and his creator. A day's delay would have been fatal—she was to be burnt on the morrow. Happily things went without a hitch, and she signed an order on Elliot for marriage to Norman Leslie.

The book professes to be a translation from the French into English; but the dialogue is largely annotated Scotch, after the Crockett fashion,[5] and the rest of the text is set with 'belike', 'perchance', 'gentle damsel', and so forth, on the good old model of such romances as Mr Martin Tupper's *Steph[a]n Langton* [1858]. With a certain elderly childishness, an erudite sham appendix is affixed, and the book is printed in a heavy dark type with elaborate initials, and illustrated to suggest the illuminations of a manuscript. As Mr Lang's pretence is that he has translated this book from the old French, the seasoning of archaic English and modern Scotch dialect is simply absurd. In one place comes a quaintly characteristic touch. The text refers to 'that great Danish knight who was with us under Orleans, Sir Andrew Haggard', and an obsequious footnote adds 'Substituting "or" for "argent", his bearings were those of the distinguished modern novelist of the same name.—A.L.' [31:374]. He gets through a game of golf this time, however, without any playful reference to Mr Horace Hutchinson.[6]

To turn from Mr Lang to Mr Buchan is to realize how natural

and inevitable a thing story-telling is. You have it or you have it not. Here, on the one hand, is a man who has been carrying on a desultory attack upon fiction for years, and on the other a new writer, presumably young, and with his trade still to learn. But the books are out of comparison. *Sir Quixote of the Moors* is stirring, living in every character, and with a fine emotional quality. It is evidently an imitation of the work of Mr Stanley Weyman,[7] but then everybody begins with imitation. It is certainly neither senile nor very inferior. It is Mr Stanley Weyman with a Scotch accent. Mr Buchan has the essentials of a fine novelist—a picturesque imagination, a sense of close sequence, and some insight. Let him bear in mind that the proper thing for a young writer to do is not to feast on the broken meats of the popular favourites of to-day, and he may do well. A story of his about a Salvation Army captain, that the present reviewer has read elsewhere,[8] was altogether fresher and finer than this book.

NOTES

1 Lang was no doubt *a* (and probably *the*) principal target of Wells's later attack on the 'Academic School' of reviewers, whom he accused of perpetuating the deleterious influence of 'classical' authors like Sir Walter Scott ('Certain Critical Opinions', SR 82: 11 July, 1896, pp 32–3.) See also 'Joan Haste', n 1 and 'The New American Novelists', n 2.
2 Wells perhaps has in mind Shaw's comment in a review of the (revised) printed version of *Macaire*, a play written by William Ernest Henley in collaboration with R. L. Stevenson.

> The charm of the pair [writes Shaw] was their combination of artistic faculty with a pleasant boyishness of imagination. . . . That amusing mixture of pedantry and hero-worship survives unabated and unenlightened in Mr Henley's cult of literature. . . . [A]t every turn of his pen he shows that cardinal quality of youth, its incapacity of apprehending life at first hand . . . (SR 79: 8 June 1895, p 757).

Wells was, of course indebted to Henley, who had promoted the young author by publishing both serial versions of *The Time Machine* (1895).
3 The hero and heroine of Stevenson's *Kidnapped* (1886).
4 Probably John Nevil Maskelyne (1839–1917), the conjuror, who wrote books on spiritualism and the supernatural.
5 See 'Joan Haste', n 2.

Literary criticism for the Saturday Review

6 Horatio Gordon Hutchinson (1859–1932), golfer and writer of books and newspaper columns on the art of golfing.
7 Wells frequently invokes Stanley Weyman (1855–1928) as one of the inventors of contemporary English adventure fiction. Weyman 'quite fairly borrowed' the episodic procedure of Dumas *fils*, Wells writes in one review, but 'instead of human beings, he introduced marionettes, which were more easily managed' (SR 82: 4 July 1896, p 21).
8 'A Captain of Salvation', *The Yellow Book*, 8 (January 1896), pp 143–58. (Wells's 'A Slip under the Microscope' appeared in the same number).

H. G. Wells's Literary Criticism
'AN OUTCAST OF THE ISLANDS'

This review of An Outcast of the Islands *(SR 81: 16 May 1896, pp 509–10) resulted in a correspondence between Wells and Joseph Conrad (1857–1924) that led in turn to their becoming close friends. Though their relations were undoubtedly strained early on, when Wells refused to give his blessing to the proposal that Conrad collaborate with Ford Madox Hueffer (later Ford), Conrad's letters stand as testimony to an admiration that Wells reciprocated. Conrad saluted the young 'scientific romancer' as the 'Realist of the Fantastic'; and it seems likely that he remembered* The Invisible Man, *which had 'powerfully impressed' him in 1898, when he came to write* Heart of Darkness *(1900).[1] He also kept in mind Wells's particular objections here to his verbosity (see n 3 below).*

Last year there was published an East Indian romance, *Almayer's Folly*, which was praised, it is to be feared, rather more than it was read.[2] Reviewer after reviewer hailed the new writer more or less pithily, promised him a brilliant future, and thought no more of the matter. 'Mr Conrad', said the *Daily Chronicle*, thumbs up, so to speak. 'Mr Conrad may go on'. 'We have been struck by the book'. 'He will find his public, and he deserves his place'. And Mr Conrad has availed himself of this generous permission, and has gone on—to a remarkably fine romance indeed. One fault it has, and a glaring fault; and that one may deal with first, and put aside to proceed to the more grateful enterprise of praise. Mr Conrad is wordy; his story is not so much told as seen intermittently through a haze of sentences. His style is like river-mist; for a space things are seen clearly, and then comes a great grey bank of printed matter, page on page, creeping round the reader, swallowing him up. You stumble, you protest, you blunder on, for the drama you saw so cursorily has hold of you; you cannot escape until you have seen it out. You read fast, you run and jump, only to bring yourself to the knees in such mud as will presently be quoted. Then suddenly things loom up again, and in a moment become real, intense, swift.

Here, to get this painful part over, is Mr Conrad at his

Literary criticism for the Saturday Review

worst. In Chapter iii of Part V, he wishes to show us the intolerable boredom of Willems, the outcast, left alone, satiated, in Lakamba's deserted settlement, with the woman he loved so passionately. He has to give us a glimpse of the savage woman's aching perplexity at this changed demeanour, and of her gleam of happiness when for a moment he tried to relieve his tedium by blowing at the whitened ashes of his passion. Indisputably, Mr Conrad has imagined it all; for if you feel about in this chapter, however hastily and eager, grasping the tangible facts, and letting the haze drive by you, you will, after an interval, see quite distinctly the pathetic beauty of the episode he has conceived. And this is how he begins: 'On Lingard's departure solitude and silence closed round Willems'. This apparently misses the effect sought, because of the turn of the phrase—'closed' cripples the idea of being derelict almost as much as if one spoke of a man being thickly swathed in isolation. Silence and solitude do not close round any one; they sit down afar off and watch. So much Mr Conrad seems to have felt, and to modify it he adds, 'The cruel silence [*solitude*] of one abandoned by men', and still dissatisfied proceeds, 'the reproachful silence which surrounds an outcast rejected by his kind'. But there is something unsatisfactory about that silence, and the only remedy within Mr Conrad's reach seems to be more words; so 'the silence unbroken by the slightest whisper of hope', and then, getting angry, 'an immense, an [*and*] impenetrable silence, that swallows up without echo the murmur of regret and the cry of revolt' [p 348]. And having given the battered silence its unsatisfactory quietus with this, Mr Conrad leaves it. The curious thing is that this trampling army corps of dependent clauses, this silence correcting silence, leaves no impression of silence at all. For ten pages altogether does Mr Conrad toil away, multiplying words. Here is a sample chosen haphazard, which, indeed, might almost serve as a criticism of him in itself: 'His wandering feet stumbled against the blackened brands of extinct fires, kicking up a light black dust of cold ashes that flew in drifting clouds and settled to leeward' (naturally enough) 'on the fresh grass sprouting from the hard ground, between the shade trees. He moved on, and on; ceaseless, unresting, in widening circles, in zig-zagging paths that led to no issue; and the marks of his footsteps, pressed deep into the soft mud of the bank, were filled slowly behind him' (not in front, mind you) 'by the percolating water of the rising river, caught the light, and shone in a chain of small reflected suns along the broad expanse of black slime, of the dull and quivering mire where he struggled on, objectless, unappeased; struggled on wearily with a set, distressed face behind which, in his tired brain, seethed his thoughts: restless, sombre, tangled, chilling, horrible and venomous, like a nestful of snakes' [v:3:349].[3]

Notice here how the one finely expressive symbol of the shining footsteps is lost in this dust-heap of irrelevant words, and in particular how the last eleven words, with that needless inappropriate image of snakes, rob the whole of its last vestige of effect. It never seems to occur to Mr Conrad to put forth his effect and leave it there stark and beautiful; he must needs set it and explain it, and refer to it, and thumb and maul it to extinction; and it never seems to dawn upon him that, if a sentence fails to carry the full weight and implication it was meant to do, the remedy is not to add a qualifying clause, but to reject it and try another. His sentences are not unities, they are multitudinous tandems, and he has still to learn the great half of his art, the art of leaving things unwritten.

Now all this is set down without any desire of detraction. It is the least any one must say who is setting out to give Mr Conrad his meed of praise as a romancer. After all this has been said, one can still apply superlatives to the work with a conscience void of offence. Subject to the qualifications thus disposed of, *An Outcast of the Islands* is, perhaps, the finest piece of fiction that has been published this year, as *Almayer's Folly* was one of the finest that was published in 1895. It is hard to understand how the respectable young gentlemen from the Universities who are engaged in cutting out cheaper imitations of the work of Mr Stanley Weyman and Mr Anthony Hope[4] can read a book like this and continue in that industry. Think of the respectable young gentleman from the University, arrayed in his sister's hat, fichu, rationals, and cycling gauntlets, flourishing her

Literary criticism for the Saturday Review

hat-pin, and pretending, in deference to the supposed requirements of Mr Mudie's public,[5] to be the deuce and all of a taverning mediaeval blade, and compare him with Willems the Outcast, late confidential clerk to Hudig & Co. Here you have (a little pruned of words[6]) the picture of Willems in his glory:

In the afternoon he expanded [*expounded*] his theory of success over the little tables, dipping now and then his moutaches [*moustache*] in the crushed ice of the cocktails; in the evening he would [often] hold forth, cue in hand, to a younger [*young*] listener, across the billiard-table. *The billiard balls stood still as if listening also,* under the vivid brilliance of the shaded [oil] lamps. . . . Through the big windows [and the open doors] the salt dampness of the sea, the vague smell of mould and flowers [from the garden of the hotel] drifted in and mingled with the odour of lamp-oil. . . . Willems would win the game[.With a remark that it was getting late, and that he was a married man], he would say a patronizing "Good night," and step out into the long empty street.[. . .] He would walk in the middle, his shadow gliding obsequiously before him. He looked down on it complacently. The shadow of a successful man! He would be dizzy with [the] cocktails and [with the intoxication of] his own glory. . . . As he often told people, he came East fourteen years ago, a cabin-boy. A small boy. His shadow must have been very small at that time. . . . And now he was looking at the shadow of the confidential clerk of Hudig & Co. going home. . . . He had not done himself justice out [*over*] there [in the hotel]; he had not talked enough [about himself], [he had] not impressed his hearers enough. Never mind. Some other time. Now he would go home and make his wife get up and listen to him. . . . A man of his stamp could carry off anything, do anything, aspire to anything. In another five years those white people who attended the Sunday card-parties of the Governor would accept him—half-caste wife and all! Hooray! He saw his shadow dart forward and wave a hat, as big as a rum barrel, at the end of an arm several yards long. . . . Who shouted hooray? . . . He smiled shamefacedly to himself, and, pushing his hands deep into his pockets, walked faster with a suddenly grave face.

How that reeling swaggerer lives! And the strange thing is that Willems lives through 383 pages, and dies living, shot by his savage mistress in a flash of jealousy:

Something stopped him short, and he stood aspiring [in his nostrils] the acrid smell of the blue smoke that wheeled about him [*that drifted from before his eyes like an immense cloud*]. . . . Missed, by Heaven! Thought so! [. . .] And he saw her very far off[, throwing her arms up]; while the revolver, very small, lay on the ground between them! . . . Missed! . . . He would go and pick it up now. Never before did he understand[,] as in that second[,] the triumphant delight of sunshine and of life. His mouth was full of something salt and warm. He tried to cough; spat out. . . . Who shrieks? [. . .] He dies! [—] Who dies? [—] Must pick up. . . . Night! [—] What? . . . Night already. [v:4:383–84][7]

Then compare Mr Conrad's wonderful Aïssa with the various combinations of Mr Hope's *Duchess* and Mr Weyman's fitful lady that do duty in contemporary romance. How she lives and breathes through all this jungle of tawdry pretentious verbiage! . . .[8]

Surely this is the real romance—the romance that is real! Space forbids anything but the merest recapitulation of the other living realities of Mr Conrad's invention—of Lingard, of the inimitable Almayer, the one-eyed Babalatchi, the Naturalist, of the pious Abdulla—all novel, all authentic. Enough has been written to show Mr Conrad's quality. He imagines his scenes and their sequence like a master, he knows his individualities to their hearts, he has a new and wonderful field in this East Indian novel of his—and he writes despicably. He writes so as to mask and dishonour the greatness that is in him. Greatness is deliberately written; the present writer has read and reread his two books, and, after putting this review aside for some days to consider the discretion of it, the work still stands. Only greatness could make books of which the detailed workmanship was so copiously bad, so well worth reading, so convincing, and so stimulating.

NOTES

1 See Conrad's letter to Wells of 4 December 1898, as quoted by G. Jean-Aubry in *Joseph Conrad: Life and Letters*, 2 vols. (Doubleday, New York, 1927), I, pp 249–50.
2 Wells had hailed Conrad's first novel as 'a very powerful story indeed . . . exceedingly well imagined and well written' (SR 79: 15 June 1895, p 797).
3 Conrad eventually cut 56 words from this passage ('and the marks . . . unappeased'): they appear in the second edition (1914) of *Outcast*, but not in the 1923 Uniform Edition.
4 See 'Popular Writers . . .', and 'On Lang and Buchan', n 7.
5 Charles Edward Mudie (1818–90) founded a circulating library system which from the middle of the nineteenth century on exerted a powerful

Literary criticism for the Saturday Review

Grundyish influence on the English publishing trade. Altick (*op. cit.*, p 214) speaks of 'his police power over newly-published novels'.

6 This is something of an understatement: the passage that Wells prunes 'slightly' is more than three times as long in the original. The last two sets of ellipsis points are Conrad's: the others, including those that the editors have added in brackets, indicate Wells's omissions.
7 Only the ellipsis points in brackets represent omissions.
8 A quotation from i:6:72–74 has been cut from this review.

H. G. Wells's Literary Criticism
'THE SIMPLE ART OF POPULAR PATHOS'

'Ian Maclaren' was the pseudonym of John Watson (1850–1907), a Presbyterian minister whose tales of Scottish life achieved enormous popularity from 1894 onwards. As Wells predicted in this review of A Doctor of the Old School *(SR 81: 30 May 1896, pp 557–8), the author's lecture-tours of America (in 1896, 1899, and 1907) were extremely successful. He died at Mount Pleasant, Iowa, on his third tour.*

It is a curious thing to pass immediately, in the promiscuous course of one's reviewing, from such a masterpiece as Mr Conrad's *Outcast of the Islands*,[1] true, powerful, and abundantly humorous, to such another masterpiece as *A Doctor of the Old School*. For indisputably the latter book is a masterpiece, though of a different art than the literary. It is a masterpiece of those seemingly simple yet really subtle and difficult expedients by which the favour of the great public is attained and secured; it appeals not to the intelligence and to the aesthetic sense, but against them—to something wider and deeper and greater, to something which we may very properly and beautifully speak of as the Great Heart of the People. Its methods are entirely different from those of the literary, and it would be surely unfair to Mr Ian Maclaren to subject him to the test of artistic standards. It would be as reasonable to do as much with the discourse of an electioneerer, or the prospectus of a patent pill. It would be as reasonable to condemn the crowbar of a navvy because it was not as beautifully chased and wrought as a Japanese sword. It is a lever to move gross, heavy objects, and if it is efficient, then it is as good a thing as the sword, in its own way. Because Mr Maclaren fails altogether to give us anything like human beings in his book, and because he keeps his work clear of either imagination or humour, that is no reason why he should bear himself abjectly before an artist like Mr Conrad in the improbable accident of a meeting. He has his uses, he touches the Great Heart, and the crowbar must ever precede the fine arts in the history of cities.

Literary criticism for the Saturday Review

And how vigorously and directly one must strike to touch that Great Heart! Here, for instance, is the kind of thing they like in America, a little paragraph from the preface: 'May I take this first opportunity', he writes, 'to declare how deeply my heart has been touched by the favour shown to a simple book by the American people, and to express my hope that one day it may be given me to see you face to face?' [0:9].

If you would touch, be touched, is indeed the first rule to be observed by the would-be popular writer. This simple, almost inadvertent, indication of the brilliant Transatlantic success of the story is preceded by another casual indication: 'From all parts of the English-speaking world', Mr Maclaren tells us, 'letters have come in commendation of Weelum MacLure, and many were from doctors who had received new courage. It is surely more honour than a new writer could ever have deserved to receive the approbation of a profession whose charity puts us all to shame' [0:8–9].

It becomes an interesting thing to study this little volume and see how it is done. It throws quite a vivid light on the Great Heart. An ambiguous style strikes one at the outset. Here is the opening sentence of the masterpiece:

Druntochty was accustomed to break every law of health, except wholesome food and fresh air, and yet had reduced the Psalmist's farthest limit to an average life-rate [1:13].

Of course Mr Maclaren does not really mean that Druntochty never broke food or really had reduced the Psalmist's limit; he means that the people really broke a great deal of food and had extended the limit, but that is his muffled way of writing it. Then, again, characterization is superfluous. A distinctive name, and in the case of the principal character plaid trousers with a patch behind, seems to be sufficient for the Great Heart. This is admirably shown—the want of characterization that is—in Mr [Frederick C.] Gordon's admirable drawing of the Doctor's funeral [p 197]. A long procession of Druntochty men winds adown the glen, all stern, all noble, all black-coated, all dour and canny, and all those other Scotch things; they recede into a remote perspective; you cannot tell one character of the story in the picture from another. There isn't one who wouldn't serve passably for Drumsheugh. You could not tell them in the book if the names were erased. Wives then would not tell their husbands there, or husbands their wives—for the women are all promiscuously 'snod' lassies. The only character you can distinguish through the illustrations is the Doctor, and him you tell by a huge beard and those breeches. No doubt they served as a kind of red lamp when he was mixed up with other people at kirk or elsewhere.

The book, says Mr Maclaren, in his preface to his friend the reader, 'has been illustrated by Mr Gordon after an admirable and understanding fashion' [0:7], and, although we do not admire his choice of adjectives, we entirely agree with his judgement.

The book, too, is never witty—that indeed perplexes and annoys the Great Heart very much—and it is never intentionally funny. From first to last it deals with dangerous illnesses, suppressed emotions, deaths and buryings. The Great Heart loves a burying. But above everything else it loves to read of great strong bearded manly fellows, talking huskily and with manifest difficulty the simple innocent sentimentalities of the boarding-school and the work-room. This kind of thing, when Drumsheugh pays a hundred pounds to bring down a doctor to save Annie.

> "She had given her heart tae anither, or a've thocht a' might hae won her, though nae man be worthy o' sic a gift. Ma hert turned tae bitterness, but that passed awa beside the brier bush whar George Hoo lay yon sad simmer time. Some day a'll tell ye ma story, Weelum, for you an' me are auld freends, and will be till we dee."
>
> MacLure felt beneath the table for Drumsheugh's hand, but neither man looked at the other.
>
> "Weel, a' we can dae noo, Weelum, gin we haena mickle brichtness in oor ain hames, is tae keep the licht frae gaein' oot in anither hoose. Write the telegram, man, and Sandy 'ill send it aff frae Kildrummie this verra night, and ye 'ill hae yir man the morn."
>
> "Yir the man a'coonted ye, Drumsheugh; but ye'ill grant me ae favor. Ye'ill lat me pay the half, bit by bit—a' ken yir wullin' tae dae't a'—but a' haena mony pleasures, an' a' wud like tae hae ma ain share in savin' Annie's life." [2:70–73]

How strangely unlike the farming folk and general practitioners the Great Heart meets in life, is it not? That bit of cheap emotion, wrung, as it were reluctantly, out of a strong

Literary criticism for the Saturday Review

man, never fails to touch the Great Heart. Nose-blowing and spectacle-wiping in particular it never tires of. . . .[2]

It may seem exceedingly simple to do this sort of thing, the babbling of green fields and 'mithers' on deathbeds, the impossible self-sacrifices, the nose-blowings and spectacle-wipings, the faithful beast business, and the sentimental addresses to the unknown reader, but the point is that everybody does not do it, and Mr Maclaren does. Since it pays remarkably well, and since people do not seem to object to doing a great many other tawdry things that pay well, it follows that everybody cannot do this kind of thing. It follows, further, that Mr Maclaren deserves the success he has won both in kind and quantity. It does not follow, because he is contemptible as a literary artist, and because he cannot write English, that he is to be despised. It is a good thing to touch the Great Heart; perhaps even in the eternal balances it is a better thing than to have testified to the truth in the details of character. At any rate, we wish him well. The American trip his preface foreshadows will inevitably succeed, and the stimulus sales will receive by that face-to-face encounter, should carry him past Messrs Caine and Crockett[3] to the very summit of successful fiction writers. It is not only a showy but an influential position.

NOTES

1 See Wells's review of Conrad.
2 A series of quotations and extracts (from 3:122–5; 4:144, 165–6; and 5:176–85, 201), interspersed with brief passages of comment and summary, has been omitted.
3 See 'Joan Haste', n 2.

H. G. Wells's Literary Criticism
MORE HAGGARD

This brief notice appeared on May 30, 1896 (SR 81:562–3). A month earlier, Wells had condemned Raymond Raife's The Sheik's White Slave *on the grounds that it was a poor imitation of Haggard and lacked that master's 'dyspeptic pessimism' (SR 81: 25 April 1896, p 436). But here he discovers that Haggard's latest romance,* Heart of the World, *is an even worse imitation of Haggard.*

Mr Rider Haggard, discouraged no doubt by his essay in novel-writing, has returned again to his own familiar romance. It is just the old story over again: writing on a stone, hidden city; big, fat, beautiful, irresistible Englishman of the public-schoolboy type; amorous native princess, love, marriage all right and proper, sunbeam shining into temple, jealous native, copper daggers, intrigue, tragedy, catastrophe, city destroyed, princess destroyed, fat Englishman and admiring Indian friend walk out by another door and come home through a series of secret passages, much impressed by all they have seen. The Englishman never gets hurt, never gets humiliated, the beautiful woman of the story inevitably falls in love with him, and so forth. It's tiresome reading for a reviewer, but there's not the shadow of a doubt that very little boys like to identify themselves with a successful 'bounder' of the type of the Rider Haggard hero. Whether it is good for them is another matter. It must take up a lot of their time reading the replicas of the romance over and over again, and it must fill their heads with very silly ideas about the invulnerability and other privileges of the Englishman abroad. And, apart from this pandering to the gross egotism and egotistical patriotism of the British small boy, the book is not nearly so effective in its own particular line as Mr Raife's *Sheik's White Slave*. At the game of impossible romance Mr Haggard's imitators are beating their master. He must try again.

Literary criticism for the Saturday Review
'THE LOST STEVENSON'

Posthumous publication of Weir of Hermiston *gave Wells the chance to survey the career of its author. Although there is something movingly elegiac about the resultant little essay (SR 81: 13 June 1896, pp 603–4), it is less a eulogy of Stevenson for his solid achievements in fiction than a lament for his considerable talents dissipated 'in the Scott line of business'.*

Perhaps none of all the generation that is now in its prime suffered more through the peculiar qualities of contemporary criticism—maudlin appreciation for the most part, tempered by defects of temper and a care for the public morals—than Stevenson. That the man who could write such a novel as *Prince Otto* [1885], such a fantasia as the 'Isle of Voices' [1893] and such a masterpiece of the trickery of effect as the *Strange Case* [of *Dr Jekyll and Mr Hyde*: 1896], should settle down at last into the hard ruts of purely conventional romance is, indeed, a pitiful instance of the way in which wrong-headed flattery, a feminine book-market, and a man's own talent may triumph over his genius. In *Weir of Hermiston* we have, in the essentials, a superbly clever book—in the Scott line of business—built about a central conception that would appeal to Mr Hall Caine[1]—romantic, effective, insincere, written down, if ever a book was written down, to a public upon which Stevenson fancied his hold was slipping. That the inherent power of the man shines through the artificialities of his method is undeniable. For an unknown writer it would win a great reputation, and coming from such a source we could award it nothing but praise; but as the work of Stevenson's maturity, we must needs deal with it in a different fashion. To praise copiously and indiscriminatingly because the man is untimely dead would be to dishonour criticism; to call this fragment the 'highest' of his writings, as Mr Sidney Colvin[2] does in his editorial note, is to dishonour Stevenson's memory. It would, indeed, have been a masterpiece of a sort had it been completed, a masterpiece largely in his own despite. One can see how straight it was flying to its mark, albeit it lies now not halfway there. It would have made—it has made—such organs of cheap criticism as the *Daily Chronicle* cry aloud by the familiarity of its effects and the powerful conventionality of its treatment.[3] By that praise the quality of its design is marked. That it would have crowned the permanent work of this master—that, when the hot fit was over and the book bound and printed, he would still have regarded it with unmixed satisfaction, it is altogether impossible to believe. . . .[4]

The strength of the book lies, of course, in the great Lord Justice Clerk, and that he is strongly done is undeniable. He is done, indeed, with astounding strenuousness; black! he is not so much painted black as tarred and feathered. He is so violently vivid that he is already pulling the story crooked in this fragment; the Black Brothers, albeit four in number, succumb to him, and decline upon humour. Assuredly there is no man living who could complete the tremendous figure Stevenson has indicated—foul-minded, grimly honest and laborious, brutally intellectual. The tremulous, gentle Mrs Weir, and his sardonic dismissal of her impotent dinners, is faultlessly conceived. 'Puir bitch!' he says at her death-bed, with a tender touch [1:33]. And in the third chapter, 'In the Matter of the Hanging of Duncan Jopp', in which the Lord Justice delivers sentence, the fragment culminates. The first few paragraphs of that chapter may serve to give an idea of its quality:[5]

> Presently, after she was tremblingly embarked on her story, "And what made ye do this, ye auld runt?" the Court interposed. "Do ye mean to tell me ye was the panel's mistress?"
> "If you please, ma loard," whined the female.
> "Godsake! ye made a bonny couple," observed his lordship; and there was something so formidable and ferocious in his scorn that not even the galleries thought to laugh. . . . In the course of sentencing, my lord had this *obiter dictum*: "I have been the means, under God, of haanging [*sic*] a great number, but never just such a disjaskit rascal as yourself." [pp 49–50]

That rings true; that is the Stevenson whose death is a loss. It is magnificent. That 'under God'! But, on the other hand, he becomes a man and a brother again, just a Scotch romancer like his imitators with the Four Black Brothers and their melodramatic hunting of their father's murderers; to rise

Literary criticism for the Saturday Review

again sharply to the humorous description of their middle-age years. . . .[6]

But after reading that, call to mind that these good souls, and the decent body their aunt, the housekeeper at Hermiston, are to break prison and rescue Archie! This humour, good as it is, is a blunder, in view of the story's necessities. It deadens at once the shouting vehemence of their title of the Black Brothers—the scowling and clattering which the deafening quality of Hermiston absolutely necessitates. It is a lapse from the devices of romantic storytelling to the humanities of the novel. One may doubt if it would have appeared in the finished work.

It is an ungrateful but a necessary task thus to examine this unrevised fragment. It has been made necessary by the fulsome praise poured out upon it. The two women are finely done, but indeed they are no revelation. Put young Kirstie and old Kirstie beside Stevenson's other women, beside Seraphina and his Countess von Rosen, and you see them at once for the mere brilliant workmanship they are. And Weir, tremendous as he is, becomes merely a violent, forcible old man retouched to tragic unreality if you contrast him with such creations as Pinkerton, Gondremark, and the incomparable Gotthold.[7] Archie, too, is a shadow to Prince Otto, and even to David Balfour. Sufficient is done for us to take the measure of the whole. The work would have been another of Stevenson's Scotch romances, doubtfully the strongest, and that is all one can say for it; another brilliant testimony to the ultimate mastery of Scott, with gleams here and there of humour, of subtlety, of a whimsical stoicism curiously delightful, of all that Stevenson might have been had not the Scott tradition laid hold of him.

Another of Stevenson's Scotch romances! It is the tragedy of Stevenson's career, that the friendly critic, his own emotional patriotism, and the book-buying public, conspired to drive him along the pathway of traditional romance. He became the fellow of Mr Rider Haggard in popular esteem.[8] No doubt in *Treasure Island* [1883] and the *Master of Ballantrae* [1891] he did it, saving a heroine, almost as well as it could be done; but to work that set formula there were and are so many passably clever men. The romance form prohibits anything but the superficialities of self-expression; and sustained humour, subtle characterization, are impossible. And no one who has read *Prince Otto* but must recognize that in that, his first and last novel, for novel it was in spite of its romantic scenery, there was a promise of work that along its peculiar line might have placed Stevenson with Mr Hardy and Mr Meredith.[9] But relative to *Treasure Island, Prince Otto* failed, and it was Stevenson's weakness to let the acceptance of his books weigh on his self-judgement. The huge reputation, the glamour of Scott and Dumas,[10] confused him, and he shared the common delusion of Scotchmen that the proper study of mankind is the historical nobility of the Scotch character. And so even in the wonderful Pacific he gave himself to reminiscent fiction. Yet not only in *Prince Otto*, but even in this romance, one may see that Stevenson was not so much a romancer as a novelist entangled in the puerilities of romance. Those four brothers at home and the splendidly ruthless trial scene we have quoted are passages of the finest novel-writing, and so too is the third strongest thing in this fragment, the afternoon meditation in the chapter entitled 'Christina's Psalm Book'. The middle-aged housekeeper and Mrs Weir stand for whole pages together credible human beings. Then come the dabs of violent colour; the housekeeper's hair is suddenly an unfaded golden, and she glows romantically beautiful; the four brothers fly to cloak, boot, and rapier, and are fiercely chasing men over cardboard rocks by the light of a stage moon. Christina starts off up the hill-side, and in a trice is at the Weaver's Stone, half buried in lush melodrama; the Vast Weir at a touch is changed to a portentous stone hanging precipitously and ready to smash itself upon Archie in defiance of every law save that law of anachronism which governs romance. And it was all to end well and cheat the reader!

Bold and vigorous as the work is, we cannot join in the chorus of praise. The first quality of great art is sincerity. Stevenson had imagination; he had insight, a fine ear, a sense of and an ambition for style, and a persistent industry; but assuredly he lacked that saving obstinacy, that inflexible self-conceit, that is, perhaps, the essence of originality. His

Literary criticism for the Saturday Review

thought of things appears only by chance, as it were, in his Essays, in his travel books, in such verse as his 'Woodman'. The toy theatre laid hold of his imagination in his boyhood, and he never slipped its grip. He helped to hypnotize himself by his own ingenious criticisms. And his place has been at the figure-head of an artificial school, the excuse—the last unworthy of an innumerable host of industrious, scholarly writers who live by the fashion he revived in Scotch romance. No wonder that they who have nothing worth presenting in themselves sing the praises of this book; no wonder they annoy us by praising a work and those portions of it in which his personality is least apparent.

NOTES

1 See 'The Sawdust Doll', n 1, and 'Joan Haste', n 2.
2 Stevenson's friend, who edited his works and letters and wrote a rather 'sanitized' life of their author after Stevenson's death.
3 An unsigned but favourable review of *Weir* came out in the *Daily Chronicle* of 20 May 1896 (p 3).
4 Omitted at this point is a long quotation from chapter one (pp 24–6).
5 Wells, who after all was being paid on the basis of the number of columns that he filled, does indeed quote the opening paragraph of chapter three. His editors, however, have cut it and three other paragraphs that preceded the citation here.
6 Wells's quotation from chapter five (pp 139–40) has been left out.
7 Seraphina, the Countess von Rosen, Gondremark, and Gotthold are all characters in *Prince Otto*. Pinkerton figures in *The Wrecker* (1892).
8 Lang, for example, wrote to Haggard: 'I almost prefer it [*King Solomon's Mines*] to *Treasure Island*' (quoted in Green, *op. cit.*, p 120).
9 See Wells's reviews of *Jude The Obscure* and *The Amazing Marriage*.
10 Wells regarded Scott and Dumas as the forebears of the modern romance of adventure; see 'On Lang and Buchan', n 7.

H. G. Wells's Literary Criticism
'A SERVANTS' HALL VISION'

Frances Hodgson Burnett (1849–1924), author of Little Lord Fauntleroy *(1886), moved with her family to the United States when she was in her teens, and later returned to England as a best-selling novelist. The following review of her* A Lady of Quality *(SR 81: 20 June 1896, pp 627–8) is one of Wells's most gleeful onslaughts against the contemporary best-seller.*

Some twenty years ago a novel called *That Lass o' Lowrie's* [1877] attracted critical attention to a new writer. It was by no means a great book; but it showed freshness of observation, and a pleasant, if youthful, vivacity of style. In those days *The Ticket-of-Leave Man*[1] was being performed by half the dramatic amateurs of the land, and had given the Lancashire dialect a popular vogue, just as the Crocketts and MacLarens of to-day—or was it, haply, yesterday?—have dinned the accents of the kail-yard into the public ear.[2] *That Lass o' Lowrie's* might have been written by 'Bob Brierley' himself.[3] It was lucky, too, in its choice of scene and incident; for the coal-mine and its inevitable explosion had not then been worn to tatters in fiction and the 'penny reciters'.[4] But it was an interesting tale on its own account, well conceived and brightly told, and those whose business or delight it is to think of such things made a note of the author's name.

Other works followed which were not so good. *Haworth's* [1879] was an attempt to turn the English millhand to artistic use, as had been done with the collier; but it failed altogether. *Through One Administration* [1883] was constructed upon a much more ambitious scale, and it, moreover, essayed to depict, not the North-country life which the author had been born into and knew, but the essentially superficial notions of existence at Washington which a foreigner domiciled there could at best obtain. This book has been widely read both here and in America—principally, we believe, on account of its miraculously detailed and sympathetic analyses of the various clothes which the women in it from time to time wear. As a narrative of

Literary criticism for the Saturday Review

human emotion and action it is uninteresting to the last degree, and as an illuminating study of people and manners at the capital of the Republic it cannot be considered seriously at all. But, with all these faults, there was a certain suggestion of latent ability, a formless hint of the capacity to do so much better under more favourable conditions, which availed to save the book from utter condemnation. Then, in time, came *Little Lord Fauntleroy* [1886], and what the critics thought and said about that was of no importance to themselves or anybody else. The book swept like a wave over the entire English-speaking race, darkening the lives of scores of thousands of small boys who loathed the curls and velveteens and clean hands imposed upon them by its power; otherwise it afforded so much harmless amusement to the vast reading and play-going public of our time that it would be churlish to find fault with it. Two subsequent books concerned with children won less notice, perhaps because they were rather better written. Mrs Hodgson Burnett returned to her native land crowned with the laurels of an undoubted popular triumph. American newspapers confided to their readers the fact that she never wrote now for less than £30 per thousand words, the highest price ever heard of. There followed in due course little paragraphs in the journals—the mystery of how these things get about fascinates one more and more—hinting that at last *the* great work was coming. On the heels of these hints crowded announcements that it had been finished, and that it was very great indeed. Unhappily, most of the reviews seem to have been based upon these announcements rather than on the book itself.

Frankly, *A Lady of Quality* is the poorest and least worthy piece of work that has been offered to the public by an author of any reputation for many years. We may go further, and express the conviction that, if the manuscript had been sent round on its own merits, unaccompanied by the author's name, there would not have been a publisher in London of the first class who would have taken it at his own risk.

The self-respecting gorge rises at the very title-page. We are told there that it is 'a most curious, hitherto unknown history, as related by Mr Isaac Bickerstaff but not presented to the World of Fashion through the pages of *The Tatler'*, and now for the first time written down. This calm assumption of Richard Steele's most important pseudonym challenges comparisons from which the cleverest and wittiest of our writers might well shrink.[5] The author of *Lord Fauntleroy* is not afraid, but the fearlessness is of the kind which suggests that she has little or no notion of what she is doing. The introductory chapter is, indeed, laboriously Tatlerized, as the job might be done by an amateur with a deficient ear and an untrained hand, and throughout the book one encounters numerous sporadic attempts to bring the writing into harmony with what the writer conceives to be Steele's style. But the most successful of these performances only suggest Richardson[6] at his dullest and most slipshod moments, and the great bulk of the book is written in a jargon which has not been English at any period, but has been *Family Herald*[7] for all time. An ambitious nurserymaid, prematurely snatched from the village Board school to go into service, would think of noble lords and ladies of a bygone age in exactly the spirit which informs this book. If she went to the length of putting her thoughts into words, and especially if she invented conversations between these gilded puppets of her fancy, the result would bear a recognizable resemblance to *A Lady of Quality*. It is a dream of the servants' hall.

Sir Jeoffrey Wildairs is a bad rural Baronet, drunken, malicious, poverty-stricken, ignorant, brutal. His ill-used wife dies after having given birth to a daughter, whom she tries to smother in her dying moments. The child grows to the age of six, living under her father's roof, but the country-houses of poor baronets were so spacious in those days, that she never happened to see or hear of him till then. When they do meet, they are not at first drawn to each other. He offers her physical violence, coupled with rude remarks. She assails him with his own hunting-crop, 'beating his big legs with all the strength of her passion, and pouring forth oaths such as would have have done credit to Doll Lightfoot herself. "Damn *thee*! damn *thee*!" she roared and screamed, flogging him. "I'll tear thy eyes out! I'll cut

Literary criticism for the Saturday Review

thy liver from thee! Damn thy soul to hell!"' [2:25]. The Baronet's heart is touched by this, and he at once loves and admires his little daughter. He dresses her in boy's clothes forthwith, and she spends nine happy years riding astride the wildest and most incredible horses that an impoverished Baronet's stables ever afforded, or bandying lewd jests with grooms, kennel-boys, and the obscure alcoholized shadows who are spoken of always as her father's 'booncompanions'. She reads no books, meets no civilized companion; but on her fifteenth birthday she suddenly decides to be a lady—and presto! she is one. The metamorphosis is magnificent in its abruptness. Her father gives a dinner-party on the occasion, and when the cloth is removed she stands on her chair, breeched and smiling.

'"Look your last on my fine shape", she proclaimed in her high, rich voice. "You will see but little of the lower part of it when it is hidden [*hid*] in farthingales and petticoats. Look your last before I go to don my fine lady's furbelows"' [4:54]. She returns on the stroke of midnight, clad in sumptuous feminine apparel; what is more, 'the majesty of her eye and lip and brow made up a mien so dazzling that every man sprang to his feet beholding her' [4:56].

More than three hundred pages remain of the book after this, and about one-half of them are devoted to rhapsodies about this Clorinda's beauty, wisdom, strength, daring, culture, wit, and general miraculousness. It is true that what she is represented as saying is invariably stupid, and that she never helps out by any action of her own the portrait which the author imagines is being drawn. But then it is not a portrait, but a shapeless mass of adjectives heaped against the skeleton conception of a heroine as stucco is plastered on a wall. The most sympathetic imagination could not fancy that there is such as person as Clorinda. The other marionettes make even less pretence of being alive. There is another wicked Baronet, a young man, Sir John Oxon by name, and he is very bad indeed. 'Few men there lived who were as vile as he, his power of villany lying in that he knew not the meaning of man's shame or honour' [16:241]. This gentleman seems to have seduced Clorinda at some period of her infancy to win a wager, although this episode is wrapped in the profoundest mystery by the author. At any rate, he is on terms of intimacy sufficient to enable him to cut from her head without her knowing it a lock of hair five feet long, and get away with it unobserved. He intends to use this trophy with diabolical effect later on, but unhappily mislays it, and cannot remember where it is. This renders him temporarily powerless, and he is forced to stand by and see Clorinda marry another, and become the greatest lady in England, if not Christendom. Her aged husband thoughtfully dies in a fit, after there has appeared upon the scene a third person, who is usually referred to in awed fashion as his Grace of Osmonde, whose palace was at Camylotte. This hybrid of the *Idylls of the King* and Ouida's *Othmar*[8] surpasses both parents. '"Twas said that he was the most magnificent gentleman in Europe; that there was none to compare with him in the combination of gifts given by both Nature and Fortune. His beauty both of feature and carriage was of the greatest, his mind was of the highest . . . he had no equal in polished knowledge and charm of bearing' [10:141]. He had remained unmarried through a delicate feeling that no woman was up to his mark; but to see Clorinda was to abandon that notion. 'He was too high and fine in all his thoughts to say to himself that in her he saw for the first time the woman who was his peer, but this was very truth' [10:144].

But at this point the depraved Sir John suddenly recalls where he put that lock of hair, and after several chapters of ostentatious lurking about the premises, muttering and shaking his fist, he says so, and the lady faints. The only clue to her excessive perturbation seems to lie in the fact that, whereas on page 108, when Clorinda finds that her tresses have been rifled, the lock of hair is described as five feet long, on page 229 we find Sir John declaring, after a lapse of years, that it is now 'like a raven's wing, and six feet long'. This uncanny circumstance might readily unnerve any lady of quality, all the more as Sir John looked at her 'with this secret exultant glow in his bad, beauteous eyes' [15:228]. She recovers herself, however, and asks Sir John to call with his keepsake, and prepares herself by reading 'a book of sermons, such as 'twas her simple habit to pore over with

Literary criticism for the Saturday Review

entire respect and child-like faith' [15:230–31]. When he comes she brains him with his own loaded whip, and hides the corpse under the sofa until the evening, when she carries it to the cellar and buries it. She marries the Duke—'she was so goddess-like and beautiful a being, her life one strangely dominant and brilliant series of triumphs, and yet she came to him with such softness and humility of passion, that scarcely could he think himself a waking man' [20:309]—and she wisely says nothing about the cellar. She lives happily, 'adored and obeyed with reverence by every man and [or] woman who served her and her lord [21:316]. . . . Royalty honoured them . . . and Mr Addison and Mr Steele, Dr Swift and Mr Pope, were made welcome in the stately rooms' [21:316]. She bears a son, 'even at his first hour, of limbs and countenance so noble that nurses and physicians regarded him amazed' [21:369]. Her glorified existence is ended only by 'the ripeness of years' [24:368]; and her epitaph leaves it in doubt whether Immortality is not her debtor rather than her creditor. No poor 'slavey', musing in her half-lighted basement upon the clouds up above the area railings, ever dreamed a more gorgeous or satisfactory vision.

The book has not a gleam of conscious humour from cover to cover. There is not a person in it who lives, or could ever have lived. It contains no incidents of any relevancy save those which are enumerated in the not ungenerous sketch we have given above. There is not a thought in it to remember, or a phrase to repeat, except by way of a joke. It has not even the merit of giving a sustained and craftsmanlike imitation of the work to which it has the assurance to liken itself. Yet we gather that it is one of the so-called 'Books of the Year'.

NOTES

1 A melodrama (1863) by Tom Taylor (1817–1880).
2 S. R. Crockett and 'Ian Maclaren' were the best-known practitioners of the Kailyard School. See also 'Joan Haste', n 2, and 'The Simple Art of Popular Pathos'.
3 Bob Brierly is the naive and blustering hero of Taylor's play.
4 'Penny reciters' or 'penny readings' were parochial entertainments

consisting of music, readings, and so forth, for which the admission charge was one penny.
5 Richard Steele was the founder and co-editor (along with Joseph Addison) of *The Tatler* (1709–11), to which he contributed essays under the pseudonym of Isaac Bickerstaff (originally one of Jonathan Swift's pen names).
6 That is, Samuel (1689–1761), author of *Pamela, Clarissa,* and *Sir Charles Grandison*.
7 A popular weekly (1842–1940), at the time something of a Victorian equivalent of the *Saturday Evening Post*.
8 Tennyson's poem appeared in 1859; *Othmar* (1885) is a romance by the prolific Louise de la Ramée ('Ouida'), of whom Wells wrote: 'Modern life has shown her its face and taught her its jargon, but its soul is hid from her eyes' (SR 80: 16 November 1895, p 661).

Literary criticism for the Saturday Review
'THE WELL AT THE WORLD'S END'

William Morris (1834–96) had died on October 3rd. In this signed review (SR 82: 17 October 1896, pp 413–5), Wells recalls the impression that the artist, poet, and socialist orator had made on him as a science student in the 1880s. Even then, Wells was a conscious opponent of 'aesthetic' socialism; and his opinion of the Morrisian romance—and specifically of The Well at the World's End—*is distinctly lukewarm here. Nevertheless, his own later work often brings to mind Morris's utopian vision; see, for example,* In the Days of the Comet *(1907) and* Men like Gods *(1923).*

The present reviewer last saw William Morris nearly ten years ago. He drifted, as most students in London in those days drifted sooner or later, to that little conventicle in the outhouse beside Kelmscott House,[1] at Hammersmith, and enlisted with something of the emotion of a volunteer. In those days economic reform was in the air, and Socialism was a possible force in politics. And this present reviewer, impecunious and adolescent, imagined that here he was to meet the resolute nucleus, the little leaven of clear-headed men, that was presently to dominate the country—such as himself shouting and shoving in the yeasty tumult. And assuredly had the huge mass of feeling that social stresses had then evolved, and Henry George and Bellamy[2] contributed to shape, found for itself a directing mind, a great Socialist party might to-day have sat in Westminster with Radicalism under its wing. But happily for the permanence of the existing social order, it found no directing mind. Intelligent and emotional adolescence sitting shy but earnest in the back seats slowly forgot its ideas of a council of war, and by the end of the meeting was being vastly entertained by a comedy of picturesque personalities. The more prominent seats were full indeed of personalities, signifying the same to the most casual eye, even in their dress. And the discussion was earnest and quaint and original, and for the most part, as it seemed, irrelevant. Art was for ever straying into the talk and denunciations of the *bourgeois*. The Chicago

Anarchists,³ too, were inextricably interwoven with the business. There was also a disposition to restore the Thirteenth Century⁴ well in evidence. But as to a sane enterprise towards expropriating landlords . . .! And earnest adolescence being above all things impatient, presently gave up attending these meetings.

Most of the personalities of these gatherings have somehow got more or less entirely effaced from the present reviewer's memory. He recalls fragments: a blue serge jacket, for instance, a flannel collar, an inordinate orange tie, and a lank neck with a vast Adam's apple passing upward into mist. The head, the voice of that personality have left no trace whatever. And another faceless figure of black and gold, like a banker. And a wonderful girl, designed, it seems, by Mr Walter Crane.⁵ And a miscellany of hair ends, and ties, and voices. There was ever a cheerful cackle among these intimates before the meeting began. But above the confusion of these memories two figures remain distinct. Mr Bernard Shaw, physically individualized with extraordinary decision, a frequent speaker, and always explicit and careful to make himself misunderstood; and the grand head, the rough voice, the sturdy figure, sedulously plain speech, and lovable bearing of William Morris.

This present volume comes to remind one of those absurd younger days, when one seriously imagined we were to be led anywhere but backward by this fine old scholar. As soon might one have taken a Herrick as a leader! His dreamland was no futurity, but an illuminated past. For him the appointed task was to restore the fragments that Rabelais and Cervantes scattered long ago, and show how beautiful that old romantic land had been. And never did he do it so sweetly and well as in this present story. *Ci-devant* adolescence, robbed of many of its downy illusions and most of its impatience, may now follow him cheerfully enough with something of the relief of bathing after a hot and dusty road, into that land of the ancient glamour.

It is Malory, enriched and chastened by the thought and learning of six centuries, this story of Ralph and his Quest of the Well at the World's End. It is Malory, with the glow of the dawn of the Twentieth Century warming his tapestries

Literary criticism for the Saturday Review

and beaten metal. It is Malory, but instead of the mystic Grail, the search for long life and the beauty of strength. And women as well as men go a questing. Tennyson, too, gave us Malory,[6] but with the Grail—as remote and attenuated indeed as the creed of a Broad Churchman, but the Grail still, and for the simple souls of the future and the past, all the involved gentilities of the middle Victorian years. Morris is altogether more ancient and more modern.

Save that its spirit is living, the story does not seem to be coherently symbolical. Such analysis as a transient reviewer may give discovers no clue to a coherent construction. Life is too short for many admirable things—for chess, and the unravelling of the *Faerie Queen* and for such riddles as this. Ever and again the tale is certainly shot and enriched with allegory. But as we try to follow these glittering strands, they spread, twist, vanish, one after the other, in the texture of some purely decorative incident. . . .[7]

The book is to be read, not simply for pleasure. To those who write its pages will be a purification, it is full of clean strong sentences and sweet old words. 'Quean' and 'carle', 'eme', 'good sooth', 'yeasay' and 'naysay', we may never return to, nor ever again 'seek *to*' a man, but 'fain' and 'lief' and 'loth' and 'sunder' and the like good honest words, will come all the readier after this reading.

And all the workmanship of the book is stout oaken stuff that must needs endure and preserve the memory of one of the stoutest, cleanest lives that has been lived in these latter days.

NOTES

1 Morris's London home, which he used for socialist meetings in the 1880s. 'Outhouse' presumably means 'out-building'.
2 The Americans Henry George, author of *Progress and Poverty* (1880), and Edward Bellamy, author of *Looking Backward* (1888), both exercised a powerful impact on early British socialism. Wells himself records Henry George's influence on him, in *ExA* 4:4.
3 August Spies, Samuel Field, Albert Parsons, and five other men were tried and executed in 1887 for allegedly instigating the Chicago

H. G. Wells's Literary Criticism

Haymarket Riot (4 May 1886). For years afterwards, their case was the same kind of *cause célèbre* that Sacco and Vanzetti's would later be.
4 A reference to the 'medievalist' leanings which Morris shared with his fellow Pre-Raphaelites.
5 The Pre-Raphaelite painter (1845–1915).
6 Tennyson's *Idylls of the King* is based on Sir Thomas Malory's prose romance, the *Morte d'Arthur* (1485).
7 The column and a half omitted here consists almost exclusively of two long quotations from *The Well at the World's End* (ii:3:169–74 and iii:17:79–80).

Literary criticism for the Saturday Review
'A SLUM NOVEL'

With A Child of the Jago, *Arthur Morrison (1863–1945) established himself as the leader of the so-called 'Cockney school' of novelists, including Edwin Pugh, Richard Whiteing, and William Pett Ridge, who wrote of working-class life in London's East End. Wells (in SR 82: 28 November 1896, p 573) praises Morrison's book for its authenticity; but questions its didactic purpose, which even its far-too-narrow sociological perspective cannot validate. The review is evidence of his rejection of the 'slice-of-life' objectivity of contemporary naturalistic fiction.*

The son of the alcoholic proletarian, the apparently exhausted topic of Dr Barnardo,[1] has suddenly replaced the woman with the past in the current novel. We have had him clothed in Cant as with a garment in the popular success of *Cleg Kelly*,[2] and we have had him presented, out Mr-Henry-James-ing Mr Henry James in pursuit of the *mot juste*, in the amiable *Sentimental Tommy*.[3] And two men of knowledge as well as ability have been dealing with him in the new spirit of sincerity.[4] No doubt this is, as yet, but a beginning. Next year the artful publisher will be asking his young authors for books about poor boys born in sin and vermin and displaying with infinite pathos the stunted rudiments of a soul, and the still more artful bookseller will be passionately overstocking himself with innumerable imitations. It is indisputable that the rediscovery of Oliver Twist is upon us. The imitator, that pest of reviewers, that curse of literature, will catch him and keep him. After the fashion of these latter days, we shall all be heartily sick of him long before we are allowed to hear the last of him. So far, however, he has been a fairly interesting person.

A Child of the Jago is indeed indisputably one of the most interesting novels this year has produced. We have admired Mr Morrison already for his 'Lizer'unt';[5] we have disliked him for his despicable detective stories;[6] and we will frankly confess we did not think him capable of anything nearly so good as this admirably conceived and excellently written story. It deals with a well-known corner of the East End, not only with extraordinary faithfulness, which indeed is attainable to any one reasonably clear of cant and indolence, but also with a really artistic sense of effect. It is beyond doubt that Mr Morrison must be full of East End material, and never once through this book does he drop into the pitfall of reporting. *A Child of the Jago* is one of those rare and satisfactory novels in which almost every sentence has its share in the entire design.

The design, it must be confessed, is a little narrow. It is as if Mr Morrison had determined to write of the Jago and nothing but the Jago. It is the Jago without relativity. The reader will remember the spacious effect at the end of Mr Conrad's *Outcast of the Islands*, when Almayer shook his fist at the night and silence outside his sorrows.[7] Mr Morrison never gets that spacious effect, although he carries his reader through scenes that would light into grandeur at a glance, at the mere turn of a phrase. The trial scene of Josh Perrott for the murder of Weech, and the execution scene that follows, show this peculiar want of breadth in its most typical manner. Mr Morrison sticks to Josh Perrott, hints vaguely at the judge, jerks with his thumb at the Royal Arms, moves his head indicative of policemen, as though he was uneasy in such company. The execution is got off in three pages with a flavour of having been written in a hurry, is, indeed, a mere sketch of one of the characters for the fuller picture there should have been. It seems all the slighter, because it comes immediately after an elaborately written murder, action as finely executed as one could well imagine, and just before the equally stirring concluding chapter, the killing of Dick Perrott in a street faction fight. Moreover, by this brevity the latter chapter is brought too close to the murder chapter. Instead of crest and trough, a rise and cadence of emotion, we end in a confusion, like water breaking on a rocky beach. Had the father and son been presented in antagonism with some clearly indicated creative and destroying force, with Destiny, with Society or with human Stupidity, the book might have concluded with that perfect unity of effect it needs and does not possess.

But this want is not a failure with Mr Morrison so much as the expression of his peculiar mental quality. He sees the

Literary criticism for the Saturday Review

Jago, is profoundly impressed by the appearance of the Jago, renders its appearance with extraordinary skill. But the origin of the Jago, the place of the Jago in the general scheme of things, the trend of change in it, its probable destiny—such matters are not in his mind. Here, perhaps, is his most fundamental utterance, *à propos* of a birth:

> Father Sturt met the surgeon as he came away in the later evening, and asked if all were well. The surgeon shrugged his shoulders. "People would call it so," he said. "The boy's alive, and so is the mother. But you and I may say the truth. You know the Jago far better than I. Is there a child in all this place that wouldn't be better dead—still better unborn? But does a day pass without bringing you just such a parishioner? Here lies the Jago, a nest of rats, breeding, breeding, as only rats can; and we say it is well. On high moral grounds we uphold the right of rats to multiply their thousands. Sometimes we catch a rat. And we keep it a little while, nourish it carefully, and put it back into the nest to propagate its kind."
>
> Father Sturt walked a little way in silence. Then he said: "You are right, of course. But who'll listen, if you shout it from the house-tops? I might try to proclaim it myself, if I had time and energy to waste. But I have none—I must work, and so must you. The burden grows day by day, as you say. The thing's hopeless, perhaps, but that is not for me to discuss. I have my duty."
>
> The surgeon was a young man, but Shoreditch had helped him over most of his enthusiasms. "That's right," he said, "quite right. People are so very genteel, aren't they?" He laughed, as at a droll remembrance. "But, hang it all, men like ourselves needn't talk as though the world was built of hardbake. It's a mighty relief to speak truth with a man who knows—a man not rotted through with sentiment. Think how few men we trust with the power to give a fellow-creature a year in gaol, and how carefully we pick them! Even damnation is out of fashion, I believe, among theologians. But any noxious wretch may damn human souls to the Jago, one after another, year in and year out, and we respect his right—his sacred right." [28:273–74]

There speaks Mr Morrison. It is practical on the face of it, and quite what would occur to a man looking so nearly at Whitechapel that the wider world where the races fight together was hidden. But the fact is that neither ignorance, wrong moral suggestions, nor parasites are inherited; the baby that survives in the Jago must needs have a good physique, the Jago people are radically indistinguishable from the people who send their children to Oxford, and the rate of increase of the Jago population is entirely irrelevant to the problem. The Jago is not a 'black inheritance' [28:273], it is a black contagion—which alters the whole problem. And Mr Morrison knocks his surgeon's case entirely to pieces by his own story; for he shows, firstly, in Mrs Perrott that to come into the Jago is to assimilate oneself to the Jago; and secondly, in Kiddo Cook, that a vigorous, useful citizen may come out of it.

NOTES

1. Dr Thomas John Barnardo (1845–1905), the philanthropist, wrote a number of books about alcoholism and the miseries of lower class life in East End London.
2. A novel (1896) by S. R. Crockett (see 'Joan Haste', n 2).
3. Wells deemed this book (1896) to be 'a step nearer the coherent and starkly sincere novel we may reasonably expect and reasonably require from Mr [James] Barrie before his writing days are done' (SR 82: 14 November 1896, p 527).
4. Morrison and Stephen Crane (see below, p. 137).
5. Of the short stories comprising *Tales of Mean Streets* (1894), 'Lizerunt' got the most attention, thanks to the scenes of violence that it depicts.
6. Wells had been somewhat more charitable towards *Martin Hewitt, Investigator* (1894) in his review of that book (SR 79: 30 March 1895, p 421).
7. At the close of Conrad's novel, Almayer shouts 'impudently into the night'.

Literary criticism for the Saturday Review
'AN ADELPHI ROMANCE'[1]

Wilson Barrett (1846–1904) was a prominent actor-manager and dramatist. His play The Sign of the Cross *opened at the Lyric Theatre in London on 4 January, 1896, and ran for a year. The novel of the same name, reviewed here (SR 82: 12 December 1896, pp 629–30), was an adaptation from the stage play, lacking none of the latter's melodramatic absurdities.*

There must be searchings of heart in the deanery of Canterbury to-day. The author of *Darkness and Dawn* is outdone, and the kindred arts of gushing and gloating have found a still bolder practitioner than Dr Farrar.[2] We have long feared that someone might arise who would oust the Dean from his proud pre-eminence in classical romance. Fitted, like another Shadwell, to reign where Shadwell reigned,[3] he has always presented one weak point to the enemy. Dean Farrar could never quite throw off the results of a sound Greek and Latin education. With all the later pre-occupations of his style and mind, there was a terrible danger lurking for him in the fact that he was once really a very fair scholar. But when the master-creator of Neronian society arrives, fresh from the green-room, with all his paint and all his wig upon him, wrapped in a Liberty toga and with a chaplet of tinfoil laurel on his brows, the Dean withdraws. Not even the magic pen which gave us the scenes in *Eric; or, Little by Little*, can claim attention now. When Mr Wilson Barrett treads the boards none are seen but he.

The process on which the new romance-writer has worked appears to be this. You take down one or two common handbooks of Latin history, and you copy out what is said there about, let us say, Nero. You then consult an authority on Roman upholstery and dress, and take notes of some agreeable articles and garments. Then, being thus amply supplied with local colour and a few Latin words, you let the Genius of Christianity have her fling, tincturing the whole with the kind of broad, tepid sentiment which experience has taught you is most welcome on Saturday nights at the back of the pit. Before you know it, and to your equal pleasure and surprise, your romance is written; it is 'a story of Christian Martyrdom under Nero', and you call upon the clergy to shudder and approve. To represent the dangers of this facile plan would be useless. If a man is capable of writing in this way, he is incapable of perceiving that any other way has advantages. To those who have some idea of the varieties of classical treatment, as it is called, we may give a notion of Mr Wilson Barrett's book by saying that it reminds one of what an amateur would produce who tried to imitate a picture by the late Edwin Long.[4]

If Mr Barrett possessed any power of telling a narrative or of creating a character, his extraordinary ignorance of all the features of antique society might be forgiven him. We know that a predecessor of his on the boards possessed 'little Latin and less Greek', and yet contrived to write a *Julius Caesar* that was a masterpiece. But a mind less creative, less observant than Mr Barrett's we have rarely met with. Propriety of action, the art of making his personages do and say what people in their position would be likely to say and do, is absent in him to a degree really phenomenal. On the second page of his tale, a little girl between four and five years of age—as the author is precise in telling us—replies in these beautiful words to a little boy who has asked her to be his wife:

"Make me thy wife?" lisped the little maid demurely. "Nay, that thou shalt *never* do. I am very, very grieved, dear Melos, to deny thee *aught*, but *that* I *cannot* promise. Do not let it vex thee, for, though I cannot let thee make me thy wife, I will be thy dearest friend, dear, dearest Melos."

"But, Mercia," began the lad.

"No, Melos, no, I cannot," firmly replied the child. "Pray thee do not ask such things." [1:2]

It might be thought almost impossible that the book should be sustained at the level of psychology, style and verisimilitude reached by this brilliant passage. But it is so sustained; we cannot conscientiously say that it ever flags. We have often wondered whether the complex and sinister figure of Nero, so mysterious and pathetic, so gorgeous and incomprehensible, seen vaguely by us through a mist of terror and detraction, with its genius and its folly, its penetrating intelligence, and its frenzied neuresthesia, would ever find a

Literary criticism for the Saturday Review

creative biographer who would illuminate its darkness. We have not waited in vain. This is how Mr Wilson Barrett records the conversation of 'the implacable, beautiful tyrant, having Death in his hands':

> "Come, come, Marcus, taste thou hast—of a kind. Indeed, that last banquet of thine was a marvel—but cold, my Marcus, cold! The women were beautiful—that is, what one could see of them, but somewhat frigid, eh? Reserved, eh? Not like these, eh? Look at that. There's life, eh? And fire, eh?" and the bloated sensualist pointed to a group in one of the open tents. [3:14]

It is like a pork-butcher at a cattle-show!

Turn we, as the author would say, to the home-life of antiquity. Some people have thought that Mr Alma Tadema's conception of it is fairly exact;[5] others, more youthful spirits, incline to the *moeurs* of M Loüys' wonderful (but-not-intended-for-the-clergy) *Aphrodite*.[6] A perusal of *The Sign of the Cross* sets all these doubts at rest. It was not the least like either—it was like Brompton, Passionate Brompton.[7] Here is the heroine's 'reception'-room:

> It was plainly, though not poorly furnished, and was brightened by flowers, palms and evergreens. Mercia's lute and tambour-frame were on the stone bench resting on a cushion covered with embroidery wrought by her own hands. Mercia was busily spinning, humming the while softly to herself the refrain of a Christian hymn that she was committing to memory, the metre and time of which would not harmonize with the tap-tap of a sculptor's hammer chiselling out the base of yet another statue to Nero across the road. [4:20]

Of the refinement and classic grace of Mr Wilson Barrett's style we almost despair of giving an idea. As he would eloquently say, it must be seen to be appreciated. It is of the florid order, and when it shrinks from so curt a word as 'men' it simply says, 'again the male sex may be particularly implied'. When it wishes, with dainty irony, to refer to the fact that a man is drunk, it says, 'Hast thou not worshipped the ruby wine-god enough already, good Glabrio?' [7:45]. When it represents Roman nobles in conversation, it coruscates in this way:

> "Will there be no ladies present?"
> "I think I may truly say there will be no ladies present" [8:65],

meaning, in its delicate waggishness, that those present will

H. G. Wells's Literary Criticism

be 'no ladies'. It leads the characters to address one another, on all occasions, as 'my Marcus', 'my Tigellinus', 'my Poppaea'. But quotation alone can do justice to the higher ethical flights of this histrionic chronicler of Neronian Rome:

> Again they rushed at the good old man as though he were some wild and dangerous beast.
> Now down the street sped a girl so lightly and swiftly that she appeared to skim rather than tread the ground. Clad in pure white, she seemed to the brutal mob a daughter of the gods rather than of earth, and for the moment they shrink [slunk] back, awed and ashamed. It was Mercia. On her way to the house of her friend, Favius, she had seen a crowd of people attacking an apparently helpless man, and, not pausing to count the probable cost of her action, had run boldly forward to assist, and, if possible, save the victim of their fury. With a force and energy amazing in one so seemingly slight and frail, she pushed the men away, and stood protecting the fallen Favius, braving the mob. How divinely beautiful she looked! Her arms were outstretched as if to shield the old man from further peril, her eyes shining with the fire of righteous wrath, and her lovely face alight with inspiration. [7:48]

The bosom which is not stirred to its depths by this beautiful passage must be impervious to the still, small voice of chromolithography. . . .[8]

NOTES

1 See 'An Ideal Husband', n 1.
2 Frederic William Farrar was author of both of the books Wells mentions in this paragraph: *Darkness and Dawn; or, Scenes in the Days of Nero* (1891) and *Eric, or Little by Little* (1858). By 1890, the latter had run through 24 editions.
3   . . . from Ireland let him reign
      To far Barbadoes on the western main
                              John Dryden, *MacFlecknoe*, 11.139–40
By this allusion, Wells intimates that Dr Farrar's fiction is superlatively dull.
4 Long (1829–91) was a painter of biblical subjects and oriental scenes that appealed to the religious sentiment of the viewer.
5 Lawrence Alma-Tadema (1836–1912) was highly popular for his idealized depictions of Greek and Roman life.
6 Subtitled *Moeurs antiques*, this somewhat salacious novel (1896) was the work of Pierre Loüys (1870–1925).

Literary criticism for the Saturday Review

7 Wells is perhaps referring to Brompton Oratory, a nineteenth-century neo-baroque Roman Catholic church designed by Herbert Gribble which has about it 'an atmosphere of Italian devotion and Italian fervour' (Nikolaus Pevsner, *The Buildings of England: London except the cities of London and Westminster* [Penguin Books, Harmondsworth, 1952], p 245).
8 Wells concludes by criticizing the Bishop of Truro for his commendatory preface to Barrett's book.

H. G. Wells's Literary Criticism
'THE LOST QUEST'

Wells was not an admirer of Richard Le Gallienne (1866–1947). He had already found the aestheticism and passionlessness of that author's Prose Fancies *objectionable (SR 82: 1 August 1896, pp 113–4). None the less, he is willing to concede that* The Quest of the Golden Girl *(reviewed in SR 83: 6 March 1897, pp 249–50) is harmlessly pleasant to read . . . until it turns serious.*

The divided mind has been at work again. We picture Mr Le Gallienne—he pictures himself—setting out to be gay, freakish, fantastic, impossible, a thing of Charm, a whimsical picturesque Personality, starting in the quest of Girls and fluttering merriment. Sterne is dead, Heine is dead[1]—one must take what one can get. It will not be profoundly original we know, but Mr Le Gallienne's reminiscences are sometimes very pleasantly done. And it begins fairly well, the modern pilgrim dining copiously through some chapters, and dreaming afterwards of the arms of the Golden Girl. The phrase for the old Surrey town, 'a cluster of ripe [old] inns' [i:6:26], is indisputably pretty. But clusters run overmuch in Mr Le Gallienne's mind, and the heavenly housemaid whose bosom was like a 'happy handful of wonderful white cherries' is altogether too suggestive of the accredited description of Diana of Ephesus for a vulgar Christian taste.[2] However, a slip in the spirit of the book is endurable, and one goes on to a harmoniously interwoven imitation of Mr Hardy—the great lady and the village schoolmaster[3]—and a passable snivel in the manner of Mackenzie.[4] I loathe Mackenzie, wet or dry; but it is not my business now to criticize Mackenzie. Then on to The Mysterious Petticoat [i:14–16:66–68]—picturesque suggestiveness, evidently but quite creditably after the master. So far the book is very pleasant irresponsible reading, and it goes half-way to its end at that level. The trout story and Nicolete [ii:3–11:112–69] are amiably contrived, and the suggestions of the quality of the contrast between love at seventeen and love at thirty are cleverly made. And

Literary criticism for the Saturday Review

then!. . . . Something comes into the book—how can one express it? Imagine a picnic, dining informally but agreeably, amidst sylvan surroundings, and there arrive in succession a brass band of three Golden-Haired performers, with an air of having been expected, and then a man with a gospel. The picnic proceeds to these accompaniments.

It will probably be the enduring misfortune of Mr Le Gallienne's life that he wrote a book—not a bad or criminal book, be it understood, but just a well-meaning, youthful, cloudy sort of book: a book, in fact, that any one might have written—called the *Religion of a Literary Man* [1893]. The vaguely serious young man, the vaguely serious young woman, and, what was far worse, the Dissenting minister, judging by the title and a certain air of toleration for God, took it seriously. The book was consequently a success. These people will take anything seriously that is respectfully free with sacred names and sacred ideas; and 'the gospel of simplicity' and 'a book that makes for righteousness' are specimen extracts from appreciative reviews. The support of the Dissenting pulpit and the liberal serious was certainly a very considerable factor in the making of Mr Le Gallienne's earlier career, and this section of the public continued for some time to listen to his lecturing and to read his books with an air of profound understanding. We must not be too hard upon a young writer, writing to live, if he reacts to this influence—its pressure is upon most of us. Casting about for the Gospel touch, and knowing the intellectual quality of these people, Mr Le Gallienne, with 'rare spiritual insight', as the Detroit reviewer (a victim) puts it, has selected the gospel of picturesque promiscuity for both sexes as the required moral intention. As this is realized the spirit of one's reading alters. A frieze of a satyr and nymphs may be delightful as decoration, but if it is proffered as 'Teaching' the sooner the thing is broken up the better. Mr Le Gallienne's good offices are not required. Our Mother Nature has provided quite sufficiently for that sort of thing.

One may doubt if the moral idea became operative until the book was half written. Then it cropped up as an outcome of the Nicolete episode. 'She had never suffered' [ii:12:174]. '"Grant me," I asked, "but this—*A Woman who has suffered*"' [ii:12:175]. And suddenly out of the tangle of trivial prettiness, the quest sets off to a sort of restaurant by the sea, Yellowsands on the Sly, to find a tainted woman. The first encounter is with a red-haired woman asleep by a bicycle. That instrument accentuates the change. We are topical—we have come out of the atmosphere of Sterne, Mackenzie and Stevenson, and we are alone with Le Gallienne and the modern spirit. After the bicycle [iii:1–4:176–203], the Twelve Golden-Haired Barmaids. 'It was, he explained, the name given to a favourite buffet at the Hotel Aphrodite, which was served by twelve wonderful girls, not one under six feet in height, and all with the most glorious golden hair. It was a whim of the management, he said' [iii:7:225]. And that is the vein of the second part, a sort of copper-gilt magnificence, like the Holborn Restaurant. After a nonsensical episode neither real nor pretty, the quest ends in this glittering place with Sylvia Joy, the actress, the woman who 'has suffered' [see iii:10:255], duly foreshadowed in the petticoat episode of the first part. The last touch of prettiness is the picture of Sylvia dancing in the moonlight [iii:11:264–66], and then the story collapses. But it does not end. Mr Le Gallienne's gaiety has long since fled: he has something in his mind—that unfortunate resolution to find an unfortunate woman! Sylvia really has not suffered, except technically, and her morals are not half bad enough for the new gospel. At the eleventh hour the heroine's situation becomes vacant.[5] But there is always the 'Venusberg of Piccadilly'. We come to it after a hesitation of some chapters, and there at last is the real Golden Girl, a 'tall noble figure', a 'haughty head', at the street corner [iv:2:296]. Her soul is still pure. So he marries her, and they have a little child—which is nice for the child—and the mother subsequently dies, and the last chapter, I learn from the American notices, is extremely pathetic. The 'little feet' patter about the house—a 'fairy patter sweet and terrible to the heart' [ii:3:308]. As I read the passage, grotesque as it may seem, it is the case of the father, and not of the child, that is presented as pathetic.

On the whole, I suppose Mr Le Gallienne would have his book taken seriously. But seriously there is very little to say.

Literary criticism for the Saturday Review

Throughout his book he ignores the manifest fact that sexual affairs primarily concern children, that sex represents the species in the individual. He attacks the matter from the standpoint of individual happiness, and that is not the way to get even at the happiness of the individual. He would seem to argue, after the manner of G.B.S. or Nietzsche, that a man is a unique individual pitted against the universe. From that point of view the more varied the past, the more assertive, copious and unhampered the activities of a man or woman, the finer the human being is. But the truth is the individuality of a man is not his complete expression. A man is a specimen of a species of social animal—plus a specimen of some sort of culture, plus a slight personal difference. If his culture has been sane, his desires, his emotions, his abiding happiness, lie in the good of the species—in the good of the generations to come. Morality is only a selfishness enlightened, and all sane morality is for the welfare of the children. This is not a cant or a Teaching; granted the accepted body of biological science, it is one of the things that must be.[6] To isolate one's interest from the species is finally to make life mean and death horrible. The end of the magnificent individual is commonly grotesque; corpulence, baldness, paralysis, a bitter solitude, for the woman sooner than the man. To regard sexual matters as a means of irrelevant amusement, as Mr Le Gallienne apparently would have us do, and in the case of a woman as a convenient financial resort, is therefore simply to confess a spacious ignorance of fundamental things. That is taking the book seriously. But that such a book should admit to being taken seriously is simply to say that its art fails.

Mr Le Gallienne has spoilt a pretty piece of work. But his Teaching leaves a good half of the book and many subsequent passages very pleasant reading. It is certainly his most sustained and most finished performance so far. But it is a pity that he will not abandon the attempt to combine deleterious instruction with his entertainment.

NOTES

1 Wells is alluding to Laurence Sterne's *A Sentimental Journey* (1768) and Heinrich Heine's *Die Harzreise* (1826–31).
2 The many-breasted Diana of Ephesus, that is (see 'On George Macdonald'). The phrase that Wells misquotes is actually more 'suggestive' as Le Gallienne wrote it: 'two happy handfuls of wonderful white cherries' (i:9:35).
3 Perhaps Wells has in mind Eustacia Vye and Clym Yeobright in *The Return of the Native* (1878).
4 Henry Mackenzie (1745–1831), author of *A Man of Feeling* (1771).
5 That is, the post of Golden Girl seems to be in want of further applicants.
6 Wells's argument for a moral stance grounded on biological realities is one that he had developed at length elsewhere, notably in his speculative essays on 'The Duration of Life' and 'Death' (see EW, pp 132–9). Here he contrasts that position of his with Le Gallienne's 'individualistic' view that 'Love for ever completes the world, for it has no future of higher achievement, no expectation of greater joy. . . . Love can dream of no greater blessedness than itself, of no heaven but its own' (*Quest*, iv:3:305).

Literary criticism for the Saturday Review
'FLICKERS OF IMAGINATION AND A FLARE'

Robert Hichens (1864–1950) had his first popular success with The Green Carnation *(1894), a satire on the aesthetic movement. In the following appraisal (SR 83: 3 April 1897, pp 355–6), Wells contrasts the vulgar sensationalism of Hichens's* Flames *with the genuine effects achieved by the prolific Hungarian novelist Mór (Maurus) Jokái (1825–1904) in his romance* The Green Book, or Freedom under the Snow. *This was Wells's final appearance as a reviewer of fiction for the* Saturday Review.

Mr Hichens having served the public with a witty portrait and with an artistically finished story, has turned, in an experimental spirit, I presume, to the production of rubbish. For 'copious rubbish' describes the greater part of *Flames*. He must be gratified at his success. The *Daily Chronicle* lit up at the book in a sort of holy ecstasy,[1] and Mr Hichens is a-booming. His book has all the essentials of a popular success, and I find it hard to believe the wit of *The Green Carnation* [1894] can be unaware of the quality of its attributes. In the first place, it is inordinately long—414 closely printed pages. Such a length, as Sir Walter Besant has recently pointed out,[2] is in itself one of the chief factors in popular appreciation. Sir Walter, and the public generally, hold that it is a sort of cheating to tell a story in less than 80,000 words—the reader 'gets through it' so soon. The public does not want ideas, it does not want memories, it does not want an elaborated, meditated, and sedulously pruned story; it wants 'a good long read', and Mr Hichens has set himself at last to meet that demand. The public may eat over the book, talk over it, lose its 'place' here and begin again there, mark its 'place' with bits of paper, sleep over it, and get up next day to it, with lots of 'reading' still left—it may be made to last from Saturday to Monday without an effort. A self-respecting novelist with any sense of form could have got every effect in the book in one quarter the length, but that sort of thing does not lie within the purview of the booming reviewer.

The story is judiciously stale, and exquisitely adapted to a popular form of silliness. It is about hypnotism and diabolical possession. It is surely one of the duties of the popular novelist—only the popular novelist invariably shirks his duty—to do his best to laugh that sickly and mischievous nonsense out of the public mind. But Mr Hichens and the *Daily Chronicle* are on the other side. A young gentleman of ladylike manners, 'the Saint of Victoria Street', the 'wonderful purity' of whose face suggested 'the ivory peak of an Alp, the luminous pallor of a pearl' [i:1:14], lived in a chastely furnished flat in company with a Steinway grand piano, a picture of 'The Merciful Knight', architectural photographs, books, and an arrangement of violets. Considering that this is a hot and dusty world with a great many things urgently needed to be done in it, I would submit that a highly educated young male who lives like that deserves to be roughly handled. But Mr Hichens evidently thinks that this costly and inane loafing is a life without Sin. Sin! In company with a young man named Julian this person with the piano, having nothing better to do with his time, begins a series of séances; and about seventy pages further on the reader discovers is possessed of a devil. As a consequence of this possession he papers his room with a sort of red that on minute examination was only too evidently wrought of 'tiny flames' [iv:2:258], he replaces his pictures with nastily suggestive furniture (which Mr Hichens describes), and, instead of those violets, portrays his soul in orchids—which is hard on Mr Chamberlain.[3] 'It was easy to imagine them'—the orchids—'whispering to each other soft histories of unknown sins', and so forth [iv:2:254]. For the uncleanness of Mr Huysmanns[4] is the uncleanness of Mr Hichens. Music, flowers, furniture—the nastiness of sexual suggestiveness is over it all. And among other symptoms of possession little dogs are scared to death at Valentine and big dogs try to bite him. And Dr Lev[i]llier felt 'a sick repulsion' [i:7:49]—the description of which is a lapse into Mr Hichens's more artistic self.

The devil in possession—it becomes evident in a few score pages—is a remarkably silly sort of devil indeed, and instead of the spacious and humorous enterprises any intelligent devil would have undertaken, simply resorts to what Mr Le Gallienne calls the 'Venusberg of Piccadilly',[5] and attempts by

Literary criticism for the Saturday Review

various idiotic proceedings to lead the ridiculous Julian into Sin. To Mr Hichens 'Sin' means only one thing, and on the whole I prefer Miss Marie Corelli's Satanism.[6] This devil takes Julian to an exciting music hall with a young person of 'pure heart' and tarnished morals, sends them home in a cab together, and thereby Julian's first step in Sin is taken. After that this devil—even a devil must amuse himself—plays the piano and sings. The music brought one

> 'to the verge of some sphere in which the sordidness attained by our race would be sneered at as delicacy, in which our lowest grovellings of the pigstye would be as lofty flights through the skies . . . hideous eccentricity . . . wanton desolation. . . . The voice was not Valentine at all, but the voice of a stranger, powerful, harsh and malignant. . . . A thick hoarseness dressed it as in disease, and at moments broke it and crushed it down . . . deadly song . . . not the faintest touch of humanity. . . .
> "Stop him," Julian murmured.
> "You!" answered Lev[i]llier [iii:2:180–81].

Why they did not hit him remains unexplained. These devilries proceed. He kills a little dog with fright, and he introduces Julian to one, Molly. But the 'pure heart' of the young woman of the initial Sin comes to the rescue. There is an inexplicable struggle between her and the possessed Valentine. She works to prevent Julian committing Sin again, and Valentine to induce him to do so. The struggle is complicated, and I find it difficult to follow. Dr Lev[i]llier fusses about in a number of chapters. We seem to be out on the tiles—to employ a convenient idiom—for three books, and the business is over. Excellent reading, all of it, for the thoughtful household. Julian dies, the spirit departs out of Valentine, and his body, having really been dead a year, collapses very effectively in the way *She* rendered popular.[7] Whether the young woman dies or lives is not particularly clear to me, and I doubt if it was perfectly clear to Mr Hichens. But so loose is the symbolism of the story that it really does not matter.

The description of this young woman of 'pure heart' and indifferent morals is the worst and best of the book; it is quite out of place, but good descriptive work. The substance of her is a portrait. Indisputably, Mr Hichens has taken a real girl and studied her furniture, her costume, her hours of employment, her ways of speech and some of her ways of thought very carefully. She is really a commonplace, good-hearted 'unfortunate', and would not be out of place in a good sympathetic realistic novel. But with a curious lack of imaginative adaptation he has thrust her into this silly story, and endowed her, not with the sane dislike of nastiness such a girl would periodically experience, but with a consistent continuous objection, an insane and physiologically impossible opposition to Sin, as he conceives it. Heaven forbid that I should minimize the conflict every man of energy must wage for the sake of his worldly efficiency against the more seductive pleasures! But this sort of unreality only serves to make the whole business sentimental and ridiculous. Mr Hichens—the Mr Hichens of *Flames*—has, like Miss Marie Corelli, a good strong undisciplined imagination; his literary workmanship is infinitely better in its detail; his 'form' is as lax and copious, and his want of insight, his want of that sanity, that abiding sense of proportion and distance which is the essence of humour, is just as marked. In addition, his sexual prepossession is a powerful one. I think I may safely congratulate him on an inevitable popularity.

There is an objectionable quality in all serious fiction, fiction professing to be applicable to life, that is not saturated in humour, that is not true in its atmosphere, distance and proportion. Dead flat seriousness in a novel always affects me like high art out of drawing. It does not injure book sales of course; but if a man has no humour and wishes to do artistic work, his only hope of salvation lies in romance. One finds no humour, for instance, in the *Green Book*, but it is very delightful reading. The magnificent opening chapter presents you a dying man carried on a gun-carriage (for no earthly reason) across vast snowy wastes, his head waggling most effectively behind, and drops of blood falling on the snow. Behind this arrangement (also for no earthly reason) follows a horseman hung with icicles and riding slowly. 'As often as he sees a red rose on the snow he dismounts, kneels, and with a golden spoon'—no less—'takes up the crystallized token, and places it in an enamelled reliquary' [1:8]—also for no earthly reason. This first chapter has little or no bearing on the subsequent chapters, but for all that it is

Literary criticism for the Saturday Review

beautifully effective. And then the stag hunt through the fair, and the wonderful *'diva'* who kept the still more wonderful Green Book. 'In the very midst of the torch-lit crowd came a golden sledge, shaped like a swan. . . In it sat the prima donna, wrapped in her costly sables and literally covered with bouquets . . . drawn by a team of eight—such a team as the Czar himself had never been drawn by, since it was composed of eight young noblemen, the cream of Russia's *jeunesse dorée*' [7:55]. Chapter viii is entitled 'An Orgie over a Volcano'. So we proceed to astonishing conspiracies (for no earthly purpose) and astonishing betrayals. It is imagination blazing. It is magnificent—it is impossible, but it is not more impossible than the stuff of Mr Hichens, and it is far more brilliantly imagined, and in places picturesquely beautiful. There are dream-like memories to be found in the book that will linger long in the mind. But it will not be so popular as *Flames*. The sham 'Lesson' is absent,[8] and the serious young man may hunt through it in vain for details of 'temptations', for hints of 'unknown sins'.

NOTES

1 The editors have not been able to locate this reference.
2 A brief paragraph expounding Besant's views about the proper length for a story appeared two days earlier, in Besant's 'Notes and News' column in *The Author* (8 [1 April 1897], p 286).
3 Joseph Chamberlain (1836–1914), the British statesman, was famous for wearing a rare orchid bloom in his button-hole.
4 In his comments on J.-K. Huysmans's *En Route*, Wells had described that novel as being (unintentionally) 'a study of the mental disease resulting from want of employment and sensual excess, in which religion is a synonym for morbid abstinence, and even the Deity becomes at last merely an infinite, all-powerful sex maniac' (SR 82: 8 August 1896, p 139).
5 See 'The Lost Quest'.
6 As in *The Sorrows of Satan* (see 'Popular Writers . . .,' n 4).
7 On Rider Haggard's romance, see the headnote to 'Joan Haste'.
8 Compare Wells's objections to Le Gallienne in 'The Lost Quest'.

4 Gissing, Crane, and Joyce

Wells's essays on George Gissing, Stephen Crane, and James Joyce show his enthusiastic recognition of the work of three of his most talented contemporaries. While offering pioneering analyses of the individuality of each writer's achievement, these essays mark significant stages in Wells's own aesthetic development, showing him moving first towards and then away from a sense of common purpose with other major novelists of his time.

1

Although we do not know when Wells first read a Gissing novel, it is probable that he had been familiar with the older novelist's work for several years before their first meeting on 20 November 1896. His reviews of *Eve's Ransom* (SR 79: 27 April 1895, p 531) and *The Paying Guest* (SR 81: 18 April 1896, p 405) are tributes of admiration tempered by a degree of impatience with the grey pessimism of Gissing's vision of life (the same impatience is more sharply expressed in his review of *Delia Harding*). When the two men did meet, however, they took an instant liking to one another.[1] Gissing, whose second marriage was nearing collapse in 1896, found the Wellses' hospitality a welcome escape from his domestic trials, and in March–April 1898 he acted as their guide on their first visit to Italy. Despite Wells's antipathy to Gabrielle Fleury, Gissing's new companion, the two men remained on close terms, and in December 1903 Wells received a dramatic summons to his friend's deathbed at St Jean-Pied-de-Port in the French Pyrenees. This final visit is the source of Edward Ponderevo's death-scene in *Tono-Bungay* (1909).

Wells was second to none in his conviction of Gissing's stature as a novelist in the 1890s; yet at no time did he write of his *oeuvre* with unqualified approval. Reviewing *Eve's Ransom*, he judged that its author had fallen short of 'the true

Realism', which 'interweaves some flash of joy or humour into its gloomiest tragedy'. In regard to *The Paying Guest* he expresses his dislike of the style of authorial impersonality pioneered by the French naturalists. In its place, he advocates a return to the flamboyantly personal narrative methods of Thackeray and Sterne. Both this review and his longer essay, 'The Novels of Mr George Gissing', suggest Wells's buoyant faith in Gissing's powers of creative growth and regeneration—a faith for which Gissing, exhausted by nearly twenty years of public neglect, was undoubtedly grateful, although he himself could not share it. In 'The Novels of Mr George Gissing', Wells's misinterpretation of the ending of *The Whirlpool* (1897) results from his inability or refusal to admit the extent to which Gissing, like his character Harvey Rolfe, had come to rest in an attitude of resignation and withdrawal. Despite its warm appreciation of Gissing's work, the essay is not so much a retrospective appraisal as an attempt to discern the future direction of a novelist whose career was, tragically, almost at an end.

'The Novels of Mr George Gissing' is at once the earliest substantial critical discussion of its subject, and an important expression of Wells's developing aesthetic of fiction. The essay situates Gissing in relation to the earlier Victorian fictional tradition, and singles out for special consideration novels such as *New Grub Street* and *The Nether World*, which are still counted among their author's best. In addition, Wells elaborates the idea of the 'novel of types' incorporating a 'comprehensive structural design', which he had first advocated in his review of Turgenev (see 'The Novel of Types'). Gissing, he claims, is the one English novelist 'whose interest has been strictly contemporary'. His contemporaneity is not only a question of discovering new subject-matter (such as the many aspects of London's suburban life portrayed in Gissing's novels of the '90s), but of deploying that subject-matter in such a way as to reveal its broad social significance. In Gissing, Wells writes, the ramshackle plots of the early Victorians are being succeeded by the novel of contemporary history which displays 'a group of typical individuals at the point of action of some great social force'. This notion, which reflects the impact of

H. G. Wells's Literary Criticism

Tolstoi and Zola on English writers, and anticipates one of the major preoccupations of twentieth-century Marxist criticism, was certainly not a commonplace one when Wells was writing. (Modern readings of the later Dickens have frequently stressed the 'comprehensive structural design' of his novels, but neither Gissing nor any other late-Victorian critic of Dickens saw his work in that way.) Wells's own most successful embodiment of this 'new structural conception' was to be in *Tono-Bungay,* his 'social panorama in the vein of Balzac' (*ExA* 7:5). The conclusion of 'The Novels of Mr George Gissing', with its rejection of the 'conception of spacious culture' in favour of a Darwinian conception of 'struggle and survival', is also related to the direction that Wells's own writing was taking, especially in *Love and Mr Lewisham* (1900). The 'contemporary' quality of Gissing's novels that Wells celebrated in this essay was, more than anything else, what he desired at this time for his own work.

Wells returned to the subject of Gissing on several subsequent occasions. His draft of a preface to the historical novel *Veranilda* (1904) was rejected by the author's family, who objected to the veiled references to Gissing's private life, and felt that it portrayed him as a classicizing man of letters rather than a successful novelist. Wells presents the unfinished *Veranilda* as both a crowning expression of Gissing's personality, and as further proof of his powers of 'comprehensive design'.[2] Reviewing Frank Swinnerton's study of Gissing and Morley Roberts's *The Private Life of Henry Maitland* in 1912, Wells conceded that *Veranilda* was not a 'novel' or even a particularly good story, but declared it 'the only historical novel I have ever read that did not suggest to me stage scenery and contemporaries engaged in private theatricals'.[3] Wells's appraisal of Gissing in *Experiment in Autobiography,* like his review of Roberts and Swinnerton, has an air of barbed detachment at times, expecially when he is discussing his old friend's personal temperament. In the early writings reprinted here, however, the tone is utterly different. Wells is not merely summing up Gissing's strengths and weaknesses, but acknowledging the impact of a body of work which he knew intimately and which had become a sounding-board for his own novelistic ambitions.

2

Wells came to prominence in 1895 as author of *The Time Machine*. In the same year, Stephen Crane published *The Red Badge of Courage*. The success of this novel in England was followed by the appearance of two further works of Crane's, *Maggie* and *George's Mother*, both of which Wells discussed at length in the *Saturday Review* late in 1896. 'The New American Novelists' shows Wells responding to the Americanness of Crane's fiction, while extending the analysis of naturalism put forward in 'The Novel of Types' and 'The Paying Guest'. To the 'purely descriptive or scientific school' of Turgenev and his English followers, Gissing and George Moore, he now adds the 'Tolstoyan' school of Crane and Sherwin Cody, distinguished by an emphatic use of the interior monologue. As might be expected, he dissents from both forms, in favour of the 'novel tinged with essay', which he associates with Dickens and Meredith. Wells's sense of Crane's individuality is further developed in his signed review of *Maggie* (SR 82: 19 December 1896, p 655), in which he suggests that Crane's 'slum novel' is marred by a trivializing aestheticism: 'just as the mud of the Port of London has proved amenable to Mr Whistler, so the mud of the New York estuary has furnished material for artistic treatment to Mr Crane'. The result, though 'a work of art', is found to be distinctly lightweight beside the work of Arthur Morrison.

From this review it might appear that Wells was largely out of sympathy with Crane's concerns. Nevertheless, the two men had many things in common—their early success with a 'new' form of fiction, their journalistic involvements, their invalidism, and their irreverence towards cultural tradition—and they became close friends after Crane and his wife Cora arrived in England in 1898. Crane, who was dying of tuberculosis, took a lease on Brede Place, an Elizabethan mansion a few miles from Wells's home at Sandgate. Wells wrote 'Stephen Crane. From an English Standpoint' within a few weeks of his friend's death on 5 June 1900. This brief but masterly essay is much more than a formal tribute to its subject. While it delicately intimates the Whistlerian quality of Crane's work, even at its finest, it is a salute to a fellow-novelist whom Wells had come to regard as an accomplice, as someone who shared his own defiance of tradition and his advocacy of a new art worthy of the twentieth century. Crane, Wells writes, is 'the first expression of the opening mind of a new period, or, at least, the early emphatic phase of a new initiative—beginning, as a growing mind must needs begin, with the record of impressions, a record of a vigor and intensity beyond all precedent'. This open-minded encomium for a writer whose work he saw as born of an amalgam of Whistler and Tolstoi has proved to be the foundation of Crane's modern reputation.

3

Born in 1882, Joyce belongs to the modernist literary generation whose emergence after 1910 was largely responsible for the eclipse of the Edwardian sociological novel of Wells, Bennett, and Galsworthy. Since Joyce, like James, has become one of the high priests of modern aestheticism, the part that Wells played in the growth of his reputation is of peculiar interest. He first took notice of Joyce in 1915, when Ezra Pound wrote to him to see if he could help the Irish writer to find some financial support. A year later, Pound, who had decided to publish *A Portrait of the Artist as a Young Man* under the specially-created imprint of the Egoist Press, again applied to Wells as part of his search for suitably influential reviewers of the book. Wells's notice of the *Portrait* shows remarkable discernment of its author's literary qualities, and is, besides, a historic document in several respects.

Wells picks out two of what have since become the 'classic' episodes of the *Portrait*, comparing the Christmas dinner scene to Sterne and the hell-fire sermon to Conrad. He notices the novel's formal innovations, such as the final change from third- to first-person narration and Joyce's avoidance of inverted commas. The main theme of his review, however, is the realism of the *Portrait* and the unique insight that it gives into Irish education, religion, and politics. True to his Edwardian loyalties, Wells views the *Portrait* as a *Bildungsroman* in which the hero is a 'typical individual' (like his own Kipps and George Ponderevo) formed by contemporary social pressures. The result, he declares, is 'by far the most living and convincing picture that exists of an Irish Catholic upbringing'.[4] Wells's essay remains a superb statement of the reasons for the *Portrait*'s abiding popularity.

Besides Sterne and Conrad, Wells compares the *Portrait* to the work of Jonathan Swift—a double-edged compliment, since his reference to Joyce's 'cloacal obsession' was to haunt its object for many years. Pound's immediate response was to write to Joyce on 1 March 1917 that '[Wells] IS a bloody damn fool, but a full page from him ought to do a good deal of good to your sales'. When Joyce sent him the Nausicaa episode of *Ulysses* two years later, however, Pound felt obliged to point out that '*obsessions* arseore-ial, cloacal, deist . . . shd. be very carefully considered before being turned loose'.[5] The subsequent history of responses to Joyce's 'cloacal obsession' would make a scholarly article, if not a book in itself.

With the publication and banning of *Ulysses* (1922), Joyce became a byword for literary modernism; yet the linguistic experimentation of *Work in Progress* (later *Finnegans Wake*) led to his desertion by Pound and some of his other early admirers. In the late 1920s, Joyce met Wells for the first time, and asked him for a public expression of support for the aims of his new book. Wells's refusal is an exceptionally lucid statement of the differences of upbringing and outlook that separated him from Joyce, and of his sense of the inferior claims of experimental art to those of experimental science—here represent by Pavlov's work on conditioned reflexes. There is no doubt of his continuing respect for Joyce's work, and the signs are that the two men remained on cordial terms. Wells summed up his sense of the contrast between them—all too sweepingly, it must now be said—in his preface to Geoffrey West's *H. G. Wells: A Sketch for a*

H. G. Wells's Literary Criticism

Portrait (p 13): 'I am outside the hierarchy of conscious and deliberate writers altogether. I am the absolute antithesis of Mr James Joyce'. But if Wells had really been the absolute antithesis of artists such as Gissing, Crane, and Joyce, he could never have written the essays and reviews which follow.

NOTES

1 The hundred or so letters that they exchanged between 1896 and 1903 (see Gettmann) indicate the closeness of their friendship.
2 The essay is reprinted in Gettmann, pp 260–77.
3 See the Literary Supplement to *Rhythm*, December 1912, pp iii–iv.
4 One of the factors influencing this review was Wells's lifelong detestation of the Catholic church—which eventually found expression in the vitriolic *Crux Ansata* (1942).
5 See *Pound/Joyce*, ed. Forrest Reid (Faber, London, 1967), pp 94, 158.

Gissing, Crane and Joyce
'THE PAYING GUEST'

Under the heading 'The Depressed School', Wells had protested against the 'greyness' of the life that Gissing had depicted in Eve's Ransom (see 'Delia Harding', n 1). His comments about The Paying Guest *(SR 81: 18 April 1896, pp 405–6) show him to be still divided—almost one year later—between his high admiration for the realism of Gissing's shorter novels of the mid 1890s, and his dislike for the severity of the 'naturalistic' narrative method that Gissing employs in them.*

Here is Mr Gissing at his best, dealing with the middle-class material he knows so intimately, and in a form neither too brief for the development of character nor too lengthy for the subtle expression of his subtle insight to grow tedious. The paying guest is a young person, 'not quite the lady', who has quarrelled with her stepfather and half-sister at home; and the genteel entertainers are the Mumfords of Sutton. They are thoroughly nice people are the Mumfords, and they know the Kirby Simpsons of West Kensington and Mrs Hollings of Highgate; and, indeed, quite a lot of good people. Then there are the Gentimans—'nice people; a trifle sober, perhaps, and not in conspicuously flourishing circumstances; but perfectly presentable' [1:7]. The Mumfords live at Sutton, 'the remoteness of their friends favoured economy; they could easily decline invitations, and need not often issue them. They had a valid excuse for avoiding public entertainments—an expense so often imposed by mere fashion' [1:6]. What a delightful analysis of the entire genteel spirit that last phrase implies! And they kept three servants to minister to their dignity, although entertainments were beyond their means. In the remote future, when Mr Gissing's apotheosis is accomplished, learned commentators will shake their heads over the text, well nigh incapable, in those more rational times, of understanding how these two people with their one child could be so extravagantly impecunious. Yet we, in this less happy age know how true it is. In and about London there must be tens of thousands of Mumfords, living their stiff, little, isolated, pretentious, and exceeding costly lives, without any more social relations with the people about them than if they were cave-dwellers, jealous, secluded, incapable of understanding the slightest departure from their own ritual, in all essentials savages still—save for a certain freedom from material brutality. Mrs Mumford's great dread was that this paying guest of hers would presently drop an aspirate; but that horror at least was spared her. But the story of the addition of the human Miss Derrick to the establishment, her reception, her troubles, and her ignominious departure, must be read to be believed. The grotesque incapacity of every one concerned to realize for a moment her mental and moral superiority to the Mumfords is, perhaps, the finest thing in an exceedingly entertaining little volume. Why, one may ask, is it so much more entertaining than the larger novels of Mr Gissing? Mr Gissing has hitherto been the ablest, as Mr George Moore is perhaps the most prominent, exponent of what we may perhaps term the 'colourless' theory of fiction. Let your characters tell their own story, make no comment, write a novel as you would write a play. So we are robbed of the personality of the author, in order that we may get an enhanced impression of reality, and a novel merely extends the purview of the police-court reporter to the details of everyday life. The analogous theory in painting would, of course, rank a passable cyclorama above one of Raphael's cartoons.[1] Yet so widely is this view accepted that the mere fact of a digression condemns a novel to many a respectable young critic. It is an antiquated device, say these stripling moderns, worthy only of the rude untutored minds of Sterne or Thackeray. By way of contrast and reaction we have the new heresy of Mr Le Gallienne, who we conceive demands personality, a strutting obtrusive personality, as the sole test of literary value.[2] Certainly the peculiar delight of this delightful little book is not in the truth of the portraiture—does not every advertising suburban photographer exhibit your Mrs Mumford and her guest with equal fidelity at every railway station?—nor in the plausible quick sequence of events, but in the numerous faint flashes of ironical comment in the phrasing that Mr Gissing has allowed himself. So far the Le Gallienne view justifies itself.

Gissing, Crane and Joyce

We congratulate Mr Gissing unreservedly on thus breaking with an entirely misleading, because entirely one-sided, view of the methods of fiction. Thus liberated, his possibilities widen. Mr Gissing has an enviable past as a novelist; a steady conquest of the reviewers is to his credit. He has shown beyond all denial an amazing gift of restraint, a studious avoidance of perceptible wit, humour, or pathos that appealed irresistibly to their sympathies. Now if he will let himself go, which he may do with impunity, and laugh and talk and point with his finger and cough to hide a tear, and generally assert his humanity, he may even at last conquer the reading public.

NOTES

1 A 'cyclorama', in Wells's complex comparison of literary and painterly 'methods', is 'a picture of a landscape or scene arranged on the inside of a cylindrical surface, the spectator standing in the middle'. (O.E.D.) Raphael's 'cartoons', a series of paintings on New Testament themes acquired by Charles I, had by the time Wells was writing been moved from Hampton Court and been put on exhibit at the Victoria and Albert Museum.
2 Compare 'The Lost Quest'.

H. G. Wells's Literary Criticism
'THE NOVELS OF MR GEORGE GISSING'

Wells and Gissing were now regular correspondents, and this essay (Contemporary Review 72: August 1897, pp 192–201) drew an immediate response from its subject. That Gissing read Wells's analysis with mixed feelings is clear from his letter (7 August 1897; Gettmann, p 47): 'Of course I read with peculiar interest, and at times with peculiar feeling; but the sum of all is that I believe you have seen justly and spoken as it behoved you to do'. Gissing went on to dispute Wells's interpretation of the final scene of The Whirlpool.

In the general acceptation and in the spirit of most reviewing, a cheerful alacrity of story, together with certain grammatical observances, are apparently the end of the novelist's art. It is, no doubt, the most obvious function of the novel of commerce, that it should fill, if possible without resort to split infinitives, the gaps where the texture of unadventurous lives thins out to the blankly uneventful. But if the novel is to be treated as literature, it must rise unmistakably above this level of bogus gossip entertainingly told. Tried by the lower standard, it is doubtful if the novels of Mr Gissing would procure him a favourable verdict; it is said they are 'depressing'—a worse fault surely even than 'unreadableness'. But in the study, at any rate, they are not so lightly dismissed. Whatever their value as pastime, it is undeniable that so soon as Mr Gissing's novels are read with a view to their structural design and implications they become very significant literature indeed.

The earlier novelists seem to have shaped their stories almost invariably upon an illustrative moral intention, and to have made a typical individual, whose name was commonly the title of the novel, the structural skeleton, the sustaining interest of the book. He or she was presented in no personal spirit; Tom Jones came forward in the interests of domestic tolerance, and the admirable Pamela let the light of restraint shine before her sex. Beauty of form does not seem to have been sought by the earlier novelists—suffice it if the fabric cohered. About the central character a system of reacting personages and foils was arranged, and the whole was woven together by an ingenious and frequently complicated 'plot'. The grouping is at its simplest and best in the gracefully constructed novels of Jane Austen. As the novel developed in length under the influence of periodical publication, the need of some sustaining structure of ampler dimensions than the type individual led to the complication of 'plot' to hold the bulk together. Plot grew at last to be the curse of English fiction. One sees it in its most instructive aspect in the novels of Dickens, wherein personages, delightfully drawn, struggle like herrings in a net amidst the infinite reticulations of vapid intrigue. Who forgets Mr Smallweed, and who remembers what he had to do with Lady Dedlock's secret?[1] And in the novels of Wilkie Collins the plot in its direst form tramples stark and terrible. But in the novels of Dickens there also appears another structural influence. As Poe admirably demonstrated, the 'plot' of *Barnaby Rudge* collapsed under its weight of characters, and the Gordon riots were swept across the complications of the story.[2] The new structural conception was the grouping of characters and incidents, no longer about a lost will, a hidden murder, or a mislaid child, but about some social influence or some far-reaching movement of humanity. Its first great exponent was Victor Hugo, as Stevenson insists in one of his all too rare essays,[3] and in the colossal series of Balzac each novel aims to render a facet in the complex figure of a modern social organization. Zola's *Lourdes* [1894] and *Rome* [1896], and Tolstoi's *War and Peace* [1865–72] are admirable examples of this impersonal type of structure. This new and broader conception of novel construction finds its most perfect expression in several of the works of Turgenev, in *Smoke* [1867], for instance, and *Virgin Soil* [1877], each displaying a group of typical individuals at the point of action of some great social force, the social force in question and not the 'hero' and 'heroine' being the real operative interest of the story.[4]

No English novelists of the first rank have arisen to place beside the great Continental masters in this more spacious development of structural method. The unique work of Mr Meredith and the novels of Mr Hardy are essentially novels of persons, freed from the earlier incubus of plot. Diana and Ethelberta, Sir Willoughby Patterne and Jude,[5] are strongly marked individuals and only casually representative. In the novels of Disraeli—in *Sybil* [1845], for example—political forces appear, but scarcely as operative causes, and George Eliot and Mrs. Humphry Ward veil a strongly didactic disposition under an appearance of social study rather than give us social studies. Within the last few years, however, three English novelists at least have arisen, who have set themselves to write novels which are neither studies of character essentially, nor essentially series of incidents, but deliberate attempts to present in typical groupings distinct phases of our social order. And of these the most important is certainly Mr George Gissing.

The *Whirlpool* [1897], for instance, Mr Gissing's latest novel, has for its structural theme the fatal excitement and extravagance of the social life of London; Rolfe, Carnaby, Alma, Sybil, Redgrave, and Mrs Strangeways are, in the first place, floats spinning in the eddy. The book opens with the flight of the insolvent Wager, leaving his children to the landlady's tender mercies, and broadens to the vivid contrast of the suicide of Frothingham in his office, while his home is crowded with a multitudinous gathering of the semi-fashionable. The interlacing threads of the story weave steadily about this theme. Rolfe marries Alma, and for a couple of years they live an ostentatiously simple life in Wales, only to feel the fatal attraction grow stronger, and come circling back at last towards the vortex. Carnaby and his wife wander abroad seeking phantasmal fortunes for a space, but the fortune does not come and the exile becomes unendurable. Sooner or later the great eddy of strenuous vanity drags them all down (saving only Rolfe) to shame and futility, to dishonour and misery, or to absolute destruction. The design has none of the spare severity that makes the novels of Turgenev supreme, but the breadth and power of its conception are indisputable. It is, perhaps, the most vigorously designed of all the remarkable series of novels Mr Gissing has given us. But the scheme of his *Emancipated* [1890] is scarcely less direct, presenting as it does, in an admirably contrived grouping, the more or less complete release from religious and moral restraints of a number of typical characters. *In the Year of Jubilee* [1894] is more subtly and less consistently planned. The picture of lower middle-class barbarism, relieved by the appreciative comments of Mr Samuel Barmby, voracious reader of a latter-day press, was conceived in a fine vein of satire, but the development of the really very unentertaining passions of the genteel Tarrant robs the book of its unity and it breaks up into a froth of intrigue about a foolish will and ends mere novel of a very ordinary kind. But Samuel Barmby, with his delightful estimate of progress by statistics, the savage truthfulness in the treatment of the French sisters, the description of Nancy's art furnishing, the characters of Horace Lord and Crewe, atone for a dozen Tarrants.

So far as the structural scheme goes there is an increased conventionality of treatment as we pass to Mr Gissing's earlier novels, to *Thyrza* [1887], *Demos* [1886], and *The Nether World* [1889], and from these the curious may descend still lower to the amiable renunciations in *A Life's Morning* [1888]. *The Unclassed* [1884] has its width of implication mainly in its name; it is a story of by no means typical persons, and with no evident sense of the larger issues. But *The Nether World*, for instance, albeit indisputably 'plottésque', and with such violent story mechanisms in it as the incredible Clem Peckover and that impossible ancient, Snowdon, does in its title, and here and there in a fine passage, betray already an inkling of the spacious quality of design the late works more and more clearly display. Witness the broad handling of such a passage as this:

With the first breath of winter there passes a voice half-menacing, half-mournful, through all the barren ways and phantom-haunted refuges of the nether world. Too quickly has vanished the brief season when the sky is clement, when a little food suffices, and the chances of earning that little are more numerous than at other times; this wind that gives utterance to its familiar warning is the *avant-courier* [vaunt-courier] of cold and hunger and solicitude that knows not sleep. Will the winter be a hard one? It is the question that concerns this world before all others, that occupies alike the patient work-folk who have yet their home unbroken, the strugglers foredoomed to loss of such scant needments as the summer gifted them withal, the hopeless and the self-abandoned and the lurking creatures of prey. To all of them the first chill breath from a lowering sky has its voice of admonition: they set their faces, they sigh, or whisper a prayer, or fling out a curse, each according to his nature. [*The Nether World*, 28:247]

The treatment of the work of Mr Gissing as a progress, an adolescence, is inevitable. In the case of no other important writer does one perceive quite so clearly the steady elimination of immaturities. As a matter of fact his first novels must have been published when he was ridiculously young. I cannot profess research in this matter, but a raid upon dates brings to light the fact that a novel—it is unnecessary to give the curious the title—was published before 1881.[6] It was long, so long that a year, at least, must have gone in the writing of it. And a convenient compendium of literary details informs me that in this year of grace 1897 Mr Gissing is thirty-nine years old. This helps one to observe, what is still apparent without this chronological assistance, that he has been learning life and his art simultaneously. Very few novels indeed, of any literary value, have been written by men below thirty. Work essentially imaginative or essentially superficial a man of three and twenty may do as well as a man of forty; romance of all sorts, the fantastic story, the idealistic novel, even the novel of manners; all these are work for the young, perhaps even more than the old. But to see life clearly and whole, to see and represent it with absolute self-detachment, with absolute justice, above all with evenly balanced sympathy, is an ambition permitted only to a man full grown. It is the consequence of, it is the compensation for, the final strippings of disillusionment. 'There am I among the others', the novelist must say, 'so little capable, a thing of flimsy will, undisciplined desires and fitful powers, shaped by these accidents and driving with the others to my appointed end'. And until that serene upland of despair, that wide and peaceful view point is reached, men must needs be partisans, and whatever their resolves may be, the idealizing touch, the partiality, the inevitable taint of justification, will mar their handiwork.

Through all the novels of Mr Gissing, fading with their progress, indeed, and yet still evident even in the latest, runs this quality of bias, that intervention. Very few of them are without a 'most favoured' character. In the *Whirlpool* Rolfe plays the chief sympathetic part. Contrasted with the favoured characters of the earlier works he is singularly inert, he flickers into a temporary vitality to marry, and subsides; his character persists unchanging through a world of change. The whole design is an attraction, a disastrous vortex, but he survives without an effort; he remains motionless and implies fundamental doubts. He reflects, he does not react. He has, in fact, all the distinctive inhumanities of what one might call the 'exponent character', the superior commentary. If he errs he errs with elaborate conscientiousness; in all the petty manifestations of humanity, irritability, glimpses of vanity, casual blunders and stupidities, such details as enrich even the most perfect of real human beings, he is sadly to seek. Beside such subtle, real and significant characters as the brilliantly analysed Alma, Hugh Carnaby and his wife, Buncombe, Felix Dymes and Morphew, he gives one something of the impression one would receive on getting into an omnibus and discovering a respectably dressed figure of wax among the passengers. But Rolfe is but the survivor of a primordial race in the Gissing universe; like the ornithorhyncus[7] he represents a vanishing order. Personages of this kind grow more important, more commanding, more influential in their inhuman activities, as one passes towards the earlier works, and to compare Rolfe to Waymark (of *The Unclassed*) and that eloquent letter-writer, Egremont, in *Thyrza*, is to measure a long journey towards the impersonal in art. In *The Nether World* there are among such indubitable specimens of the kindly race of men as Pennyloaf and the Byasses, not only 'good characters' but 'bad' also. The steady emancipation is indisputable.

In one little book at least, *The Paying Guest*, published about a twelvemonth ago, the exponent personage has no place; so that is, indeed, in spite of its purely episodical character, one of the most satisfactory of Mr Gissing's books. It presents in a vein of quiet satire, by no means unfeeling, and from a standpoint entirely external, the meagre pretentiousness of a small suburban villa, the amaz-

H. G. Wells's Literary Criticism

ing want of intelligence which cripples middle-class life. It is compact of admirable touches. The villa was at Sutton, so conveniently distant from London that 'they had a valid excuse for avoiding public entertainments—an expense so often imposed by mere fashion' [1:6]. And while the negotiations for the Paying Guest were in progress, 'at this moment a servant entered with tea, and Emmeline, sorely flurried, talked rapidly of the advantages of Sutton as a residence. She did not allow her visitor to put in a word till the door closed again' [1:20–21]. These are haphazard specimens of the texture. Their quality is the quality of Jane Austen, and whenever in the larger books the youthful intensity of exposition, the stress of deliberate implication relaxes, the same delicate subtlety of humour comes to the surface. Nearest to *The Paying Guest*, in this emancipation from the idealizing stress, come that remarkable group of three figures, *Eve's Ransom*, and the long novel of *New Grub Street*.

Apart from their aspect as a diminishing series of blemishes, of artistic disfigurements, the 'exponent' characters of Mr Gissing deserve a careful consideration. If they are, in varying proportion, ideal personages, unstudied invention that is, they are, at any rate, unconventional ideal persons, created to satisfy the author rather than his readers. Taken collectively, they present an interesting and typical development, they display the personal problem with a quality of quite unpremeditated frankness. In that very early novel, *The Unclassed*, the exponent character is called Waymark, but, indeed, Egremont, Quarrier, Ross Mallard, Tarrant, and Rolfe are all, with a varying qualification of irony, successive Waymarks. At the outset we encounter an attitude of mind essentially idealistic, hedonistic, and polite, a mind coming from culture to the study of life, trying life, which is so terrible, so brutal, so sad and so tenderly beautiful, by the clear methodical measurements of an artificial refinement, and expressing even in its earliest utterance a note of disappointment. At first, indeed, the illusion dominates the disappointment. *The Unclassed* is still generous beyond the possibilities of truth. It deals with the 'daughters of joy', the culinary garbage necessary, as Mr Lecky[8] tells us, to the feast of English morality; and it is a pathetic endeavour to prove that these poor girls are—

young ladies. Jane Snowdon, the rescued drudge in *The Nether World*, Mr Gissing's parallel to the immortal Marchioness, falls short of conviction from the same desire to square reality to the narrow perfections of a refined life. She is one of nature's young ladies, her taste is innate. She often laughs, but 'this instinct of gladness had a very different significance from the animal vitality which prompted the constant laughter of Bessie Byass; it was but one manifestation of a moral force which made itself nobly felt in many another way' [*The Nether World* 16:139]. The implicit classification of this sentence is the essential fallacy of Mr Gissing's earlier attitude:—there are two orders of human beings. It is vividly apparent in *Thyrza*. It is evident in a curious frequency of that word 'noble' throughout all his works. The suburban streets are ignoble, great London altogether is ignoble, the continent of America also, considered as a whole. This nobility is a complex conception of dignity and space and leisure, of wide, detailed, and complete knowledge, of precision of speech and act without flaw or effort; it is, indeed, the hopeless ideal of a scholarly refinement.

As one passes to the later novels the clearness of vision increases, and the tone of disappointment deepens. *The Emancipated* is a flight to Italy to escape that steady disillusionment. People say that much of Mr Gissing's work is 'depressing', and to a reader who accepts his postulates it is indisputable that it is so. The idealized 'noble' women drop out of these later works altogether, the exponent personages no longer marry and prosper, but suffer, and their nobility tarnishes. Yet he clings in the strangest way to his early standards of value, and merely widens his condemnation with a widening experience. In *Eve's Ransom* and *New Grub Street* the stress between an increasingly truthful vision of things and the odd, unaltered conception that life can only be endurable with leisure, with a variety of books, agreeable furniture, service, costume, and refined social functions, finds its acute expression. The exponent character—a very human one—in *New Grub Street*, Reardon, is killed by that conflict, and the books ends in irony.

"Happiness is the nurse of virtue", said Jasper.
"And independence the root of happiness," answers Amy.
"True. 'The glorious privilege of being independent'—yes, Burns

understood the matter. Go to the piano, dear, and play me something. If I don't mind I shall fall into Whelpdale's vein, and talk about my 'blessedness'. Ha! Isn't the world a glorious place?"

"For rich people."

"Yes, for rich people. How I pity the poor devils!—Play anything. Better still if you will sing, my nightingale!"

So Amy first played and then sang, and Jasper lay back in dreamy bliss [37:469].

So ends *New Grub Street* with the ideal attained—at a price. But that price is still only a partial measure of the impracticability of the refined ideal. So far, children have played but a little part in Mr Gissing's novels. In *The Whirlpool*, on the other hand, the implication is always of the children, children being neglected, children dying untimely, children that are never born. *The Whirlpool* is full of the suggestion of a view greatly widened, and to many readers it will certainly convey the final condemnation of a 'noble' way of life which, as things are, must necessarily be built on ignoble expedients. Mrs Abbott's room, 'A very cosy room, where, amid books and pictures, and by a large fire, the lady of the house sat reading Ribot' [i:3:27], would surely have been the room of one of the most exemplary characters in the days before *New Grub Street*. But the new factor comes in with, 'She had had one child; it struggled through a few months of sickly life, and died of convulsions during its mother's absence at a garden party' [i:3:28]. In the opening chapter, moreover, Rolfe speaks of children, putting the older teaching into brutal phrases:

They're a burden, a hindrance, a perpetual source of worry and misery. Most wives are sacrificed to the next generation—an outrageous absurdity. People snivel over the death of babies; I see nothing to grieve about. If a child dies, why, the probabilities are it *ought* to die; if it lives, it lives, and you get the survival of the fittest. [i:2:13]

The fashionable, delightful, childless Sybil 'hates housekeeping' [i:2:12]. And Alma, pursuing the phantom of a career as a musical genius, leaves for the future one little lad, 'slight, and with little or no colour in his cheeks, a wistful, timid smile on his too-intelligent face' [iii:13:451]. In the early novels it would seem that the worst evil Mr Gissing could conceive was crudity, passion, sordidness and pain.

But the *Whirlpool* is a novel of the civilized, and a countervailing evil is discovered—sterility. This brilliant refinement spins down to extinction, it is the way of death. London is a great dying-place, and the old stupidities of the homely family are, after all, the right way. That is *The Whirlpool*'s implication, amounting very nearly to a flat contradiction of the ideals of the immature *Emancipated*. The widowed Mrs Abbott, desolate and penitent, gets to work at the teaching of children. And finally we come on this remarkable passage:

> It was a little book called *Barrack-Room Ballads*. Harvey read [in] it here and there, with no stinted expression of delight, occasionally shouting his appreciation. Morton, pipe in mouth, listened with a smile, and joined more moderately in the reader's bursts of enthusiasm.
> "Here's the strong man made articulate," cried Rolfe at length. "It's no use; he stamps down one's prejudice [--what?]. It's the voice of the reaction. Millions of men, natural men, revolting against the softness and sweetness of civilization; men all over the world, hardly knowing what they want and what they don't want; and here comes one who speaks for them—speaks with a vengeance."
> "Undeniable."
> "But——"
> "I was waiting for the *but*," said Morton, with a smile and a nod.
> "The brute savagery of it! The very lingo—how appropriate it is! The tongue of Whitechapel blaring lust of life in the track of English guns. He knows it; the man is a great artist; he smiles at the voice of his genius. It's a long time since the end of the Napoleonic wars. We must look to our physique, and make ourselves ready. Those Lancashire operatives, laming and killing each other at football, turning a game into a battle. Women turn to cricket—tennis is too soft—and to-morrow they'll be bicycling by the thousands; they must breed a stouter race. We may reasonably hope, old man, to see our boys blown into small bits by the explosive that hasn't got its name yet."
> "Perhaps," replied Morton meditatively. "And yet there are considerable forces on the other side."
> "Pooh! The philosopher sitting on the safety-valve. He has breadth of beam, good, sedentary man, but when the moment comes—— The Empire; that's beginning to mean something. The average Englander has never grasped the fact that there was such a thing as a British Empire. By God! we are the British Empire, and we'll just show 'em what *that* means!"
> "I'm reading the campaigns of Belisarius," said Morton, after a pause.
> "What has that to do with it?"
> "Thank heaven, nothing whatever."
> "I bore you," said Harvey, laughing. "Morphew is going to New

Zealand. I had a letter from him this morning. Here it is. 'I heard yesterday that H. W. is dead. She died a fortnight ago, and a letter from her mother has only just reached me in a roundabout way. I know you don't care to hear from me, but I'll just say that I'm going out to New Zealand. I don't know what I shall do there, but a fellow has asked me to go with him, and it's better than rotting here. It may help me to escape the devil yet; if so, you shall hear. Good-bye!'"
  He thrust the letter back into his pocket.
  "I rather thought the end would be pyrogallic acid."
  "He has the good sense to prefer ozone," said Morton. [iii:13:451][9]

Of course Rolfe here is not Mr Gissing, but quite evidently his speeches are not a genuinely objective study of opinions expressed. The passage is essentially a lapse into 'exposition'. The two speakers, Morton and Rolfe, become the vehicles of a personal doubt, taking sides between the old ideal of refined withdrawal from the tumult and struggle for existence, and the new and growing sense of the eternity and universality of conflict; it is a discussion, in fact, between a conception of spacious culture and a conception of struggle and survival. In his previous books Mr Gissing has found nothing but tragedy and the condemnation of life in the incompatibility between the refined way of life and life as it is. But here, in the mouth of a largely sympathetic character, is a vigorous exposition of the acceptance, the vivid appreciation of things as they are.

Enough has been written to show that *The Whirlpool* is a very remarkable novel, not only in its artistic quality, but in its presentation of a personal attitude. The clear change in the way of thinking that Mr Gissing's Rolfe is formulating (while the Whirlpool should be devouring him) is no incidental change of one man's opinion, it is a change that is sweeping over the minds of thousands of educated men. It is the discovery of the insufficiency of the cultivated life and its necessary insincerities; it is a return to the essential, to honourable struggle as the epic factor in life, to children as the matter of morality and the sanction of the securities of civilization.

To those who are familiar with Mr Gissing's work, the conviction that this character of Rolfe marks a distinct turning-point in his development will be inevitable. That his next work will be more impersonal than any that have gone before, that the characteristic insistence on what is really a personal discontent will be to some extent alleviated, seems to me, at any rate, a safe prophecy. Mr Gissing has written a series of extremely significant novels, perhaps the only series of novels in the last decade whose interest has been strictly contemporary. And even this last one, it seems to me, has still the quality of a beginning. It is by reason of his contemporary quality, by virtue of my belief that, admirable as his work has been, he is still barely ripening and that his best has still to come, that I have made this brief notice rather an analysis of his peculiarities and the tendencies of his development than the essay I could write with ease and sincerity in his praise.

NOTES

1 For Smallweed's part in the discovery of Lady Dedlock's secret (that she has borne an illegitimate child), see chapter 52 of *Bleak House* (1852–3).
2 Poe's long review of Dickens's novel originally appeared in *Graham's Magazine* for February 1842.
3 'Victor Hugo's Romances', in *Familiar Studies of Men and Books* (1882).
4 Compare 'The Novel of Types'.
5 Characters in Meredith's *Diana of the Crossways* (1885) and Hardy's *The Hand of Ethelberta* (1876), Meredith's *The Egoist* (1879) and Hardy's *Jude the Obscure* (1895).
6 *Workers in the Dawn* (1880).
7 The duck-billed platypus.
8 William Edward Hartpole Lecky (1838–1903) argued for moral progress and the advance of reason against superstition in his *History of Rationalism* (1865) and *History of European Morals* (1869). His *magnum opus* was his *History of England in the Eighteenth Century* (1878–90).
9 From the passage that he quotes, Wells has dropped three sentences after 'Napoleonic wars', one after 'a battle', six after 'Empire', seven after 'laughing', and another seven after 'roundabout way'.

H. G. Wells's Literary Criticism
'THE NEW AMERICAN NOVELISTS'

In this review (SR 82: 5 September 1896, pp 262–3) Wells considers George's Mother *by Stephen Crane together with* In the Heart of the Hills *by Sherwin Cody (1868–1959).*

Until the languages differentiate, it is necessarily an unscientific method to draw hard-and-fast lines between groups of American and English writers. Yet there are educational differences between the States and this country that are distinctly traceable in the workmanship of the younger writers. The system of the English public school and university, essentially a survival, finds no real counterpart in America; and the consequent predominance of Latin and Greek learning, the tradition of secluded scholarship, the want of intelligent appreciation of commerce and manufacture, the academic habit of criticizing deductively from admitted classics, are less conspicuous in the intellectual life of the States. And in the past English periodical literature and criticism were largely, and are so still to a distinctive extent, under the control of the graduate of Oxford and Cambridge. Through these influences a large amount of the enterprise of our younger men is directed along the line of imitation, the sham antique, the historical novel: the exhausted tradition of Scott dominates many of them, even fatally. From the point of view of artistic development the literary culture of the Universities is almost worse than no culture at all, since it establishes a barrier against all imperfect novelty, and all novelty is necessarily more or less imperfect. The influence of Tolstoi, for instance, of Ibsen, or of Turgenev, is robbed of half its potentialities in this country by the slim self-satisfaction engendered by the academic training. Turgenev, perhaps more than Tolstoi, has influenced us in England, and that chiefly through the French studio and the French critic. His methods are particularly in evidence in the work of Messrs George Gissing and George Moore.[1] It would be hard to find the suggestions of Tolstoi dominant among contemporary English work.

But in the last decade American criticism has become

noticeably emancipated from its subservience to the English academic tradition, and the more extensive use of scientific study in higher education there has resulted in a broader and more intelligent view of method and construction. To turn from the amiable fatuities of Mr Lang in such an English magazine as *Longman's*[2] to the altogether less graceful and incomparably saner writing of Mr Boy[e]sen[3] is to turn from the old learning to the new. Clearly there has been an enormous amount of mental activity among the ambitious young men across the Atlantic, and in Mr Crane and Mr Cody we have the first-fruits of the growth. Mr Crane, albeit much more of a theoretical product than critics here have recognized, is evidently a young man of very exceptional ability; Mr Cody is even more typical in that his mental stature is not conspicuously above that of the common man. And they are both indebted to Tolstoi to an extent out of all comparison with any English writer.

The distinction of Tolstoi from the purely descriptive or scientific school of which Turgenev is the prince and Mr George Gissing the most prominent English exponent lies in the extraordinary use in narrative of sustained descriptions of the mental states of his characters. Great lengths of story are told in a kind of monologue in the third person. Mr Crane outdoes his master in this direction in the present book almost as much as in *The Red Badge of Courage*, which has already been reviewed in these columns.[4] And in Mr Cody, too, to a lesser extent, this peculiarity of Tolstoi prevails. But reading Mr Cody, one comes upon the danger of the method. Nothing is so profoundly interesting, nothing appeals so vividly to the sympathetic imagination, as mental processes written with a masterly grip of the mind described. But without that masterly grip, or with that grip relaxed for a time! Witness Mr Cody's version of the mental processes of a town boy who has quarrelled with his father, and left him:

Alec had often heard how his father, Alexander senior, had gone to the city a poor boy, with only a dollar in his pocket and no immediate prospect of more, how he had worked and starved, and finally succeeded and grown rich. Now a brilliant idea came to him. Why should not he, Alexander junior, a poor city boy, come to the country with only two dollars in his pocket, and make his fortune? Fortune is a curious thing. You never know where it will turn up, and often it fails under the most propitious circumstances.

As he lay there in the rosy light of dawn, Alec saw fortunes in farming: the cattle and sheep he had passed were walking mines of gold; country store- and hotel-keeping was an enormous business. At any rate, he was going to tackle the question with energy, and exhaust its possibilities. Yesterday he would have been glad to know where he was to get his next meal. But the episode of Maud's dollar bill had put him on his mettle. Besides, without his knowing it, a new element had entered his mind. The dim figure of a woman lurked in the background of his thoughts and pricked him on. He pitied her, and it angered him that he was so helpless to help her. [6:74]

That phrase 'the rosy light of dawn' gives Mr Cody's quality very completely. With the remark that he contrives to keep a story, of such texture as this, interesting from start to finish, we may dismiss him. He has served to illustrate the Tolstoi form in a cheap material, and that is his sole purpose here.

But in Mr Crane's work not only is the method present, but the matter is admirably sound; young George getting drunk, for instance, in this passage:

Of a sudden Kel[c]ey felt the buoyant thought that he was having a good time. He was all at once an enthusiast, as if he were at a festival of a religion. He felt that there was something fine and thrilling in this affair, isolated from a stern world, and from which the laughter arose like incense. He knew that old sentiment of brotherly regard for those about him. He began to converse tenderly with them.

He was not sure of his drift of thought, but he knew that he was immensely sympathetic. He rejoiced at their faces, shining red and wrinkled with smiles. He was capable of heroism[s].

His pipe irritated him by going out frequently. He was too busy in amiable conversations to attend to it. When he arose to go for a match he discovered that his legs were a trifle uncertain under him. They bended, and did not precisely obey his intent.

At the table he lit a match, and then, in laughing at a joke made near him, forgot to apply it to the bowl of his pipe. He succeeded with the next match, after annoying trouble. He swayed so that the match would appear first on one side of the bowl and then on the other. At last he happily got it directly over the tobacco. He had burned his fingers. He inspected them, laughing vaguely. [9:93–95]

The story in *George's Mother* is this youngster's progress along the primose way, to headaches, fights, and the freedom of the streets. From first to last it goes with immense vigour and sympathy. But the story must be read for its power to be understood, quotation fails for the simple reason that it is bare story and nothing beyond. There are no purple passages, no decorations, no digressions.

In the suppression of the author's personality both these writers are as rigorous as the earlier Mr George Gissing, and there these disciples of Tolstoi join hands with our inheritors of Turgenev. There is no 'style', no 'Charm'; from the standpoint of Mr Le Gallienne such books as Mr Crane's cannot be literature.[5] There it is that these new novelists break most conspicuously from the tradition of the English succession of Fielding, Smollett, Sterne, Goldsmith, Jane Austen, Dickens, Thackeray, Mrs Gaskell, and Mr Meredith. Suppression of the author's personality means, among other things, a renunciation of satire, irony, laughter, and tears. One may doubt if any wide or enduring popular triumphs will reward the abstinence of this new school so long as it persists in the rigour of its method. Yet Falstaff shows that the charm of personality in a derivative form is still possible to a strictly dramatic method. It is well that in criticism the widening separation of novels into the severely descriptive on the one hand and the personal, the novel tinged with essay, on the other, should be clearly recognized. Practically they are already two distinct artistic forms. The great writers relying upon their own personality naturally do not establish schools, they merely engender a pest of imitators. If to-day there is a school of English writers in America following Tolstoi, and a school here representing Turgenev, and none to be ascribed to Dickens save such a weakling as Mr James,[6] and none to Mr Meredith save a few thieves of the phrase, it lies in that consideration.

Apart from their distinctive qualities, English readers will welcome both these books as an indication of the growth of a real and independent critical method across the Atlantic, side by side and directing really original work. That emancipation from the hampering gentilities of the English scholar, one may remember—American readers perhaps stand in need of the reminder—was the dream of Poe.[7]

NOTES

1 See 'The Paying Guest'.
2 Andrew Lang wrote a literary gossip column ('At the Sign of the Ship') for *Longman's Magazine* (from January 1886 through October 1905).
3 Hjalmar Hjorth Boyesen (1848–95), Professor of Germanic languages and literature at Columbia University, author of numerous articles on Scandinavian and Germanic literature, sometime proponent of the 'realist' position of Turgenev and William Dean Howells.
4 A review of *The Red Badge*—possibly the work of Frank Harris, certainly not by Wells—appeared in SR 81: 11 January 1896, pp 44–5.
5 See 'The Lost Quest'.
6 Montague Rhodes James (1862–1936) began publishing in magazines in the 1890s the ghost stories of his later issued in book form.
7 In Poe's review of poems by Joseph Rodman Drake and Fitz-Greene Halleck (*Southern Literary Messenger*, 2: April 1836).

Gissing, Crane and Joyce

'STEPHEN CRANE. FROM AN ENGLISH STANDPOINT'

This essay appeared in the North American Review *(171: August 1900, pp 233–42). Crane (b. 1871) had died on 5 June, aged twenty-eight (not thirty as Wells states).*

THE untimely death at thirty of Stephen Crane robs English literature of an interesting and significant figure, and the little world of those who write, of a stout friend and a pleasant comrade. For a year and more he had been ailing. The bitter hardships of his Cuban expedition had set its mark upon mind and body alike, and the slow darkling of the shadow upon him must have been evident to all who were not blinded by their confidence in what he was yet to do. Altogether, I knew Crane for less than a year, and I saw him for the last time hardly more than seven weeks ago. He was then in a hotel at Dover, lying still and comfortably wrapped about, before an open window and the calm and spacious sea. If you would figure him as I saw him, you must think of him as a face of a type very typically American, long and spare, with very straight hair and straight features and long, quiet hands and hollow eyes, moving slowly, smiling and speaking slowly, with that deliberate New Jersey manner he had, and lapsing from speech again into a quiet contemplation of his ancient enemy. For it was the sea that had taken his strength, the same sea that now shone, level waters beyond level waters, with here and there a minute, shining ship, warm and tranquil beneath the tranquil evening sky. Yet I felt scarcely a suspicion then that this was a last meeting. One might have seen it all, perhaps. He was thin and gaunt and wasted, too weak for more than a remembered jest and a greeting and good wishes. It did not seem to me in any way credible that he would reach his refuge in the Black Forest only to die at the journey's end. It will be a long time yet before I can fully realize that he is no longer a contemporary of mine; that the last I saw of him was, indeed, final and complete.

Though my personal acquaintance with Crane was so

H. G. Wells's Literary Criticism

soon truncated, I have followed his work for all the four years it has been known in England. I have always been proud, and now I am glad, that, however obscurely, I also was in the first chorus of welcome that met his coming.[1] It is, perhaps, no great distinction for me; he was abundantly praised; but, at least, I was early and willing to praise him when I was wont to be youthfully jealous of my praises. His success in England began with *The Red Badge of Courage* [1895], which did, indeed, more completely than any other book has done for many years, take the reading public by storm. Its freshness of method, its vigour of imagination, its force of colour and its essential freedom from many traditions that dominate this side of the Atlantic, came—in spite of the previous shock of Mr Kipling—with a positive effect of impact. It was a new thing, in a new school. When one looked for sources, one thought at once of Tolstoi;[2] but, though it was clear that Tolstoi had exerted a powerful influence upon the conception, if not the actual writing, of the book, there still remained something entirely original and novel. To a certain extent, of course, that was the new man as an individual; but, to at least an equal extent, it was the new man as a typical young American, free at last, as no generation of Americans have been free before, of any regard for English criticism, comment or tradition, and applying to literary work the conception and theories of the cosmopolitan studio with a quite American directness and vigour. For the great influence of the studio on Crane cannot be ignored; in the persistent selection of the essential elements of an impression, in the ruthless exclusion of mere information, in the direct vigour with which the selected points are made, there is Whistler even more than there is Tolstoi in *The Red Badge of Courage*. And witness this, taken almost haphazard:

At nightfall the column broke into regimental pieces, and the fragments went into the fields to camp. Tents sprang up like strange plants. Camp fires, like red, peculiar blossoms, dotted the night. * * * From this little distance the many fires, with the black forms of men passing to and fro before the crimson rays, made weird and satanic effects. [2:23]

And here again; consider the daring departure from all academic requirements, in this void countenance:

Gissing, Crane and Joyce

> A warm and strong hand clasped the youth's languid fingers for an instant, and then he heard a cheerful and audacious whistling as the man strode away. As he who had so befriended him was thus passing out of his life, it suddenly occurred to the youth that he had not once seen his face. [12:108]

I do not propose to add anything here to the mass of criticism upon this remarkable book. Like everything else which has been abundantly praised, it has occasionally been praised 'all wrong'; and I suppose that it must have been said hundreds of times that this book is a subjective study of the typical soldier in war. But Mr George Wyndham, himself a soldier of experience, has pointed out in an admirable preface to a re-issue of this and other of Crane's war studies, that the hero of the *Red Badge* is, and is intended to be, altogether a more sensitive and imaginative person than the ordinary man. He is the idealist, the dreamer of boastful things brought suddenly to the test of danger and swift occasions and the presence of death. To this theme Crane returned several times, and particularly in a story called 'Death and the Child' [1898] that was written after the Greek war. That story is considered by very many of Crane's admirers as absolutely his best. I have carefully re-read it in deference to opinions I am bound to respect, but I still find it inferior to the earlier work. The generalized application is, to my taste, a little too evidently underlined; there is just that touch of insistence that prevails so painfully at times in Victor Hugo's work, as of a writer not sure of his reader, not happy in his reader and seeking to drive his implication (of which also he is not quite sure) home. The child is not a natural child; there is no happy touch to make it personally alive; it is THE CHILD, something unfalteringly big; a large, pink, generalized thing, I cannot help but see it, after the fashion of a Vatican cherub. The fugitive runs panting to where, all innocent of the battle about it, it plays; and he falls down breathless to be asked, 'Are you a man'? [*The Open Boat and Other Stories*, p 206]. One sees the intention clearly enough; but in the later story it seems to me there is a new ingredient that is absent from the earlier stories, an ingredient imposed on Crane's natural genius from without—a concession to the demands of a criticism it had been wiser, if less modest, in him to disregard—criticism that missed this quality of generalization and demanded it, even though it had to be artificially and deliberately introduced.

Following hard upon the appearance of *The Red Badge of Courage* in England came reprints of two books, *Maggie* [1893; rpt. 1896] and *George's Mother* [1896], that had already appeared in America six years earlier.[3] Their reception gave Crane his first taste of the peculiarities of the new public he had come upon. These stories seem to me in no way inferior to the *Red Badge*, and at times there are passages, the lament of Maggie's mother at the end of *Maggie*, for example, that it would be hard to beat by any passage from the later book. But on all hands came discouragement or tepid praise. The fact of it is, there had been almost an orgie of praise—for England, that is; and ideas and adjectives and phrases were exhausted. To write further long reviews on works displaying the same qualities as had been already amply discussed in the notices of the *Red Badge* would be difficult and laborious; while to admit an equal excellence and deny an equal prominence would be absurd. But to treat these stories as early work, to find them immature, dismiss them and proceed to fresher topics, was obvious and convenient. So it was, I uncharitably imagine, that these two tales have been overshadowed and are still comparatively unknown. Yet, they are absolutely essential to a just understanding of Crane. In these stories, and in these alone, he achieved tenderness and a compulsion of sympathy for other than vehement emotions, qualities that the readers of *The Third Violet* [1897] and *On Active Service* [1899], his later love stories, might well imagine beyond his reach.

And upon the appearance of these books in England came what, in my present mood, I cannot but consider as the great blunder and misfortune of Crane's life. It is a trait of the public we writers serve, that to please it is to run the gravest risk of never writing again. Through a hundred channels and with a hundred varieties of seduction and compulsion, the public seeks to induce its favourite to do something else—to act, to lecture, to travel, to jump down volcanoes or perform in music halls, to do anything, rather than to possess his soul in peace and to pursue the work he was meant to do. Indeed, this modern public is as violently experimental with its writers as a little child with a kitten. It is animated, above all things, by an insatiable desire to plunge its victim into novel surroundings, and watch how he feels. And since Crane had demonstrated, beyond all cavil, that he could sit at home and, with nothing but his wonderful brain and his wonderful induction from recorded things, build up the truest and most convincing picture of war; since he was a fastidious and careful worker, intensely subjective in his mental habit; since he was a man of fragile physique and of that unreasonable courage that will wreck the strongest physique; and since, moreover, he was habitually a bad traveller, losing trains and luggage and missing connections even in the orderly circumstances of peace, it was clearly the most reasonable thing in the world to propose, it was received with the applause of two hemispheres as a most right and proper thing, that he should go as a war correspondent, first to Greece and then to Cuba. Thereby, and for nothing but disappointment and bitterness, he utterly wrecked his health. He came into comparison with men as entirely his masters in this work as he was the master of all men in his own; and I read even in the most punctual of his obituary notices the admission of his journalistic failure. I have read, too, that he brought back nothing from these expeditions. But, indeed, even not counting his death, he brought back much. On his way home from Cuba he was wrecked,[4] and he wrote the story of the nights and days that followed the sinking of the ship with a simplicity and vigour that even he cannot rival elsewhere.

'The Open Boat' [1897] is to my mind, beyond all question, the crown of all his work. It has all the stark power of the earlier stories, with a new element of restraint; the colour is as full and strong as ever, fuller and stronger, indeed; but those chromatic splashes that at times deafen and confuse in *The Red Badge*, those images that astonish rather than enlighten, are disciplined and controlled. 'That and "Flanagan"', he told me, with a philosophical laugh, 'was all I got out of Cuba'. I cannot say whether they were worth the price, but I am convinced that these two things are as immortal as any work of any living man. And the way 'The Open Boat' begins, no stress, plain—even a little grey and flattish:

H. G. Wells's Literary Criticism

None of them knew the colour of the sky. Their eyes glanced level, and were fastened upon the waves that swept toward them. These waves were of the hue of slate, save for the tops, which were of foaming white, and all of the men knew the colour[s] of the sea. The horizon narrowed and widened, and dipped and rose, and at all times its edge was jagged with waves that seemed thrust up in points like rocks.

Many a man ought to have a bath-tub larger than the boat which here rode upon the sea. These waves were most wrongfully and barbarously abrupt and tall, and each froth-top was a problem in small-boat navigation.

The cook squatted in the bottom, and looked with both eyes at the six inches of gunwale which separated him from the ocean. His sleeves were rolled over his fat forearms, and the two flaps of his unbuttoned vest dangled as he bent to bail out the boat. Often he said, "Gawd! That was a narrow clip". As he remarked it, he invariably gazed eastward over the broken sea.

The oiler, steering with one of the two oars in the boat, sometimes raised himself suddenly to keep clear of the water that swirled in over the stern. It was a thin little oar and it seemed often ready to snap.

The correspondent, pulling at the other oar, watched the waves and wondered why he was there. [*The Open Boat* . . . , pp 3–4]

From that beginning, the story mounts and mounts over the waves, wave frothing after wave, each wave a threat, and the men toil and toil and toil again; by insensible degrees the day lights the waves to green and olive, and the foam grows dazzling. Then as the long day draws out, they come toward the land. . . .[5]

In the meantime the oiler rowed, and then the correspondent rowed, and then the oiler rowed. Grey-faced and bowed forward, they mechanically, turn by turn, plied the leaden oars. The form of the lighthouse had vanished from the southern horizon, but finally a pale star appeared, just lifting from the sea. The streaked saffron in the west passed before the all-merging darkness, and the sea to the east was black. The land had vanished, and was expressed only by the low and dread[*drear*] thunder of the surf. [*The Open Boat* . . . , p 22]

'The Open Boat' gives its title to a volume containing, in addition to that and 'Flanagan', certain short pieces. One of these others, at least, is also to my mind a perfect thing, 'The Wise Men', [1898]. It tells of the race between two bartenders in the city of Mexico, and I cannot imagine how it could possibly have been better told. And in this volume, too, is that other masterpiece—the one I deny—'Death and the Child'.

Now I do not know how Crane took the reception of this

book, for he was not the man to babble of his wrongs; but I cannot conceive how it could have been anything but a grave disappointment to him. To use the silly phrase of the literary shopman, 'the vogue of the short story' was already over; rubbish, pure rubbish, provided only it was lengthy, had resumed its former precedence again in the reviews, in the publishers' advertisements and on the library and book-sellers' counters. The book was taken as a trivial by-product, its author was exhorted to abandon this production of 'brilliant fragments'—anything less than fifty thousand words is a fragment to the writer of literary columns—and to make that 'sustained effort', that architectural undertaking, that alone impresses the commercial mind. Of course, the man who can call 'The Open Boat' a brilliant fragment would reproach Rodin for not completing the edifice his brilliant fragments of statuary are presumably intended to adorn, and would sigh, with the late Mr Ruskin for the day when Mr Whistler would 'finish' his pictures.[6] Moreover, he was strongly advised—just as they have advised Mr Kipling—to embark upon a novel. And from other quarters, where a finer wisdom might have been displayed, he learned that the things he had written were not 'short stories' at all; they were 'sketches' perhaps, 'anecdotes'—just as they call Mr Kipling's short stories 'anecdotes'; and it was insinuated that for him also the true, the ineffable 'short story' was beyond his reach. I think it is indisputable that the quality of this reception, which a more self-satisfied or less sensitive man than Crane might have ignored, did react very unfavourably upon his work. They put him out of conceit with these brief intense efforts in which his peculiar strength was displayed.

It was probably such influence that led him to write *The Third Violet*. I do not know certainly, but I imagine, that the book was to be a demonstration, and it is not a successful demonstration, that Crane could write a charming love story. It is the very simple affair of an art student and a summer boarder, with the more superficial incidents of their petty encounters set forth in a forcible, objective manner that is curiously hard and unsympathetic. The characters act, and on reflection one admits they act, *true*, but the play of their emotions goes on behind the curtain of the style, and all the enrichments of imaginative appeal that make love beautiful are omitted. Yet, though the story as a whole fails to satisfy, there are many isolated portions of altogether happy effectiveness, a certain ride behind an ox cart, for example. Much more surely is *On Active Service* an effort, and in places a painful effort, to fit his peculiar gift to the uncongenial conditions of popular acceptance. It is the least capable and least satisfactory of all Crane's work.

While these later books were appearing, and right up to his last fatal illness, Crane continued to produce fresh war pictures that show little or no falling off in vigour of imagination and handling; and, in addition, he was experimenting with verse. In that little stone-blue volume, *War is Kind* [1899], and in the earlier *Black Riders* [1895], the reader will find a series of acute and vivid impressions and many of the finer qualities of Crane's descriptive prose, but he will not find any novel delights of melody or cadence or any fresh aspects of Crane's personality. There remain some children's stories to be published and an unfinished romance. With that the tale of his published work ends, and the career of one of the most brilliant, most significant and most distinctively American of all English writers comes to its unanticipated *finis*.

It would be absurd, here and now, to attempt to apportion any relativity of importance to Crane, to say that he was greater than A. or less important than B. That class-list business is, indeed, best left forever to the newspaper plebiscite and the library statistician; among artists, whose sole, just claim to recognition and whose sole title to immortality must necessarily be the possession of unique qualities, that is to say, of unclassifiable factors, these gradations are absurd. Suffice it that, even before his death, Crane's right to be counted in the hierarchy of those who have made a permanent addition to the great and growing fabric of English letters was not only assured, but conceded. To define his position in time, however, and in relation to periods and modes of writing will be a more reasonable undertaking; and it seems to me that, when at last the true proportions can be seen, Crane will be found to occupy a position singularly cardinal. He was a New Englander of Puritan lineage,[7] and the son of a long tradition of literature. There had been many Cranes who wrote before him. He has shown me a shelf of books, for the most part the pious and theological works of various antecedent Stephen Cranes. He had been at some pains to gather together these alien products of his kin. For the most part they seemed little, insignificant books, and one opened them to read the beaten *clichés*, the battered outworn phrases, of a movement that has ebbed. Their very size and binding suggested a dying impulse, that very same impulse that in its prime had carried the magnificence of Milton's imagery and the pomp and splendours of Milton's prose. In Crane that impulse was altogether dead. He began stark—I find all through this brief notice I have been repeating that in a dozen disguises, 'freedom from tradition', 'absolute directness' and the like—as though he came into the world of letters without ever a predecessor. In style, in method and in all that is distinctively *not* found in his books, he is sharply defined, the expression in literary art of certain enormous repudiations. Was ever a man before who wrote of battles so abundantly as he has done, and never had a word, never a word from first to last, of the purpose and justification of the war? And of the God of Battles, no more than the battered name; 'Hully Gee'?—the lingering trace of the Deity! And of the sensuousness and tenderness of love, so much as one can find in *The Third Violet*! Any richness of allusion, any melody or balance of phrase, the half quotation that refracts and softens and enriches the statement, the momentary digression that opens like a window upon beautiful or distant things, are not merely absent, but obviously and sedulously avoided. It is as if the racial thought and tradition had been razed from his mind and its site ploughed and salted. He is more than himself in this; he is the first expression of the opening mind of a new period, or, at least, the early emphatic phase of a new initiative—beginning, as a growing mind must needs begin, with the record of impressions, a record of a vigour and intensity beyond all precedent.

H. G. Wells's Literary Criticism
NOTES

1 See above, p 137; and also 'The New American Novelists'.
2 Compare 'The New American Novelists'.
3 Crane probably began writing *George's Mother* before *The Red Badge* (see John Berryman's *Stephen Crane* [1950; rpt. New York: World Publishing Co., 1962], pp 85, 134); but it was accepted for publication only after his war novel proved a success.
4 Crane survived the wreck of the *Commodore* on its way *to* Cuba.
5 A long quotation made up of passages from pp 19, 21, and 22 of *The Open Boat* . . . has been omitted.
6 John Ruskin (d. 1900) levelled this charge against James McNeill Whistler in *Fors Clavigera* (1871–84). It resulted in a celebrated libel suit, which Whistler won (the judge awarded him one farthing for damages). For Whistler's account, see *The Gentle Art of Making Enemies* (1890).
7 It seems unlikely that Crane, who was proud of his New Jersey ancestry (see Berryman, *op. cit.*, p 7), would have misled Wells into thinking him a New Englander.

Gissing, Crane and Joyce

'JAMES JOYCE'

Wells's review of A Portrait of the Artist as a Young Man *(Nation 20: 24 February 1917, pp 710, 712; a slightly abbreviated version appeared in the* New Republic, *10: 10 March 1917, pp 158–60) was the first fiction review he had published in several years. Beginning with the state of literary art in 1916, Wells ends with a pugnacious view of the Irish question (which was soon to lead to the 'Troubles' of partition and civil war). In between these extremes, he shows himself the only early reviewer, apart from Ezra Pound, who was able to do justice to the magnitude and originality of Joyce's novel.*

An eminent novelist[1] was asked recently by some troublesome newspaper what he thought of the literature of 1916. He answered publicly and loudly that he had heard of no literature of 1916; for his own part, he had been reading 'science'. This was kind neither to our literature nor our scientific activities. It was not intelligent to make an opposition between literature and science. It is not more legitimate than to oppose literature and 'classics', or literature and history, and as a matter of fact there were some admirable pieces of scientific literature published last year, Professor Wood Jones's *Arboreal Man*, for example. Good writing about the actualities of the war too has been abundant; that was only to be expected; it is an ungracious thing in the home critic to sit at a confused feast and bewail its poverty when he ought to be sorting out his discoveries. Criticism may analyse, it may appraise and attack, but when it comes to the mere grumbling of veterans no longer capable of novel perceptions, away with it! There is indeed small justification for grumbling at the writing of the present time. Quite apart from the books and stories about the war, a brilliant literature in itself, from that artless assured immortal, Arthur Green (*The Story of a Prisoner of War* [1916]), up to Mr Philip Gibbs[2] and the already active historians, there is a great amount of fresh and experimental writing that cannot be ignored by anyone still alive to literary interests. There are, for instance, Miss

H. G. Wells's Literary Criticism

Richardson's (*Pointed Roofs* and *Backwater*) amusing experiments[3] in writing as the Futurists paint, and Mr Caradoc Evans's invention (in *My People* [1915] and *Capel Sion* [1917]) of a new method of grimness, a pseudo-Welsh idiom that is in its grotesque force as pleasing to the intelligent story-reader as it must be maddening to every sensitive Welsh patriot. Nor have I seen anywhere anything like adequate praise for the romantic force and beauty of Mr Thomas Burke's *Limehouse Nights* [1917]. In the easier 'nineties, when Henley was alive and discovering was in fashion,[4] that book would have made a very big reputation indeed. Even more considerable is *A Portrait of the Artist as a Young Man*, by James Joyce, published rather obscurely by 'The Egoist', Ltd., because nobody else will issue it on this side of the Atlantic. It is a book to buy and read and lock up, but it is not a book to miss. Its claim to be literature is as good as the claim of the last book of *Gulliver's Travels*.

It is no good trying to minimize a characteristic that seems to be deliberately obtruded. Like Swift and another living Irish writer,[5] Mr Joyce has a cloacal obsession. He would bring back into the general picture of life aspects which modern drainage and modern decorum have taken out of ordinary intercourse and conversation. Coarse, unfamiliar words are scattered about the book, unpleasantly, and it may seem to many, needlessly. If the reader is squeamish upon these matters, then there is nothing for it but to shun this book, but if he will pick his way, as one has to do at times on the outskirts of some picturesque Italian village with a view and a church and all sorts of things of that sort to reward one, then it is quite worth while. And even upon this unsavoury aspect of Swift and himself, Mr Joyce is suddenly illuminating. He tells at several points how his hero Stephen is swayed and shocked and disgusted by harsh and loud *sounds*, and how he is stirred to intense emotion by music and the rhythms of beautiful words. But no sort of smell affects him like that. He finds olfactory sensations interesting or aesthetically displeasing, but they do not make him sick or excited, as sounds do. This is a quite understandable turnover from the more normal state of affairs. Long ago I remember pointing out in a review the difference in the sensory basis of the stories of Robert Louis Stevenson and Sir J. M. Barrie;[6] the former visualized and saw his story primarily as picture, the latter mainly heard it. We shall do Mr Joyce an injustice if we attribute a normal sensory basis to him, and then accuse him of deliberate offence. His work is not to be put out of court on this score.

But that is by the way. The value of Mr Joyce's book has little to do with its incidental insanitary condition. Like some of the best novels in the world, it is the story of an education; it is by far the most living and convincing picture that exists of an Irish Catholic upbringing. The writing is great writing. It is a mosaic of jagged fragments that does altogether render with extreme completeness the growth of a rather secretive, imaginative boy in Dublin. The technique is startling, but on the whole it succeeds. Like Mr Shaw and many other Irish writers, Mr Joyce is a bold experimentalist with paragraph and punctuation. He breaks away from scene to scene without a hint of the change of time and place; at the end he passes suddenly from the third person to the first; and he uses no inverted commas to mark off his speeches. The first trick I found sometimes tiresome here and there but then my own disposition, perhaps acquired at the blackboard, is to mark off and underline rather fussily, and I do not know whether I was so much put off the thing myself as anxious, which after all was not my business, about its effect on those others; the second trick, I will admit, seems entirely justified in this particular instance by its success; the third reduces Mr Joyce to a free use of dashes. One conversation in this book is a superb success, the one in which Mr Dedalus carves the Christmas turkey; I write with all due deliberation that Sterne himself could not have done it better; but most of the talk flickers blindingly with these dashes, one has the same wincing feeling of being flicked at that one used to have in the early cinema shows. I think Mr Joyce has failed to discredit the inverted commas.

The interest of the book depends entirely upon its quintessential and unfailing reality. One believes in Stephen Dedalus as one believes in few characters in fiction. And the peculiar lie of the interest for the intelligent reader is the convincing revelation it makes of the limitations of a great mass of Irishmen. Mr Joyce tells us unsparingly of the adolescence of this youngster under conditions that have passed almost altogether out of English life. There is an immense shyness, a profound secrecy, about matters of sex, with its inevitable accompaniment of nightmare revelations and furtive scribblings in unpleasant places, and there is a living belief in a real hell. The description of Stephen listening without a doubt to two fiery sermons on that tremendous theme, his agonies of fear—not disgust at dirtiness such as unorthodox children feel, but just fear—his terror-inspired confession of his sins of impurity to a strange priest in a distant part of the city, is like nothing in any boy's experience who has been trained under modern conditions. Compare its stuffy horror with Conrad's account of how, in analogous circumstances, Lord Jim wept.[7] And a second thing of immense significance to the English reader is the fact that everyone in this story, every human being, accepts as a matter of course, as a thing in nature like the sky and the sea, that the English are to be hated. There is no discrimination in that hatred, there is no gleam of recognition that a considerable number of Englishmen have displayed a very earnest disposition to put matters right with Ireland, there is an absolute absence of any idea of a discussed settlement, any notion of helping the slow-witted Englishman in his three-cornered puzzle between North and South. It is just hate, a cant cultivated to the pitch of monomania, an ungenerous violent direction of the mind. That is the political atmosphere in which Stephen Dedalus grows up, and in which his essentially responsive mind orients itself. I am afraid it is only too true an account of the atmosphere in which a number of brilliant young Irishmen have grown up. What is the good of pretending that the extreme Irish 'patriot' is an equivalent and parallel of the English or American Liberal? He is narrower and intenser than any English Tory. He is the most antiquated bigot in Western Europe. He will be the natural ally of the Tory in delaying our social and economic reconstruction after the war. He will play into the hands of the Tories by threatening an outbreak and providing the bogey of excuse for a militarist reaction in England. It is time we faced the truth of that. No reason in that why we should not do justice to Ireland, but excellent reason for bearing in mind that these bright green young people from across the Channel are something quite different from ourselves in training and tradition, and are absolutely set against helping us. No single book has ever shown how different they are, as completely as this most memorable novel.

NOTES

1 Probably Arnold Bennett.
2 Sir Philip Gibbs (1877–1962) was author of *The Soul of the War* (1915) and of a series of war histories, beginning with *The Battle of the Somme* (1917).
3 Dorothy Richardson (1873–1957) was the first English writer to use the 'stream-of-consciousness' method, in novels such as *Pointed Roofs* (1915) and *Backwater* (1916).
4 See 'On Lang and Buchan', n 2.
5 Most likely this is George Moore, who is reported to have said of the *Portrait*: 'why, I did the same thing, but much better, in *The Confessions of a Young Man* [1888]' (from Barrett H. Clark's *Intimate Portraits*, quoted by Richard Ellmann in *James Joyce* [Oxford University Press, New York, 1959], p 544).
6 In 'Margaret Ogilvy' (SR 83: 23 January 1897, p 94), Wells had argued that Stevenson, like Dickens and George Moore, allows the reader to picture his characters; but 'Mr [James] Barrie is hard to visualize'.
7 Presumably this refers to Jim's confession in chapter 12 of *Lord Jim* (1900).

H. G. Wells's Literary Criticism
EXPERIMENTAL SCIENCE VS. EXPERIMENTAL ART

The first meeting between Wells and Joyce did not take place until 1928. Immediately afterwards, Joyce gave instructions for Wells to be sent the issues of transition *containing the early instalments of* Work in Progress. *He then asked Wells's help in persuading the public to accept the new book. Joyce was in no way offended by Wells's refusal,[1] which took the form of the following letter, dated from his Provençal home at Lou Pidou (23 November 1928).*

I've been studying you and thinking over you a lot. The outcome is that I don't think I can do anything for the propaganda of your work. I've an enormous respect for your genius dating from your earliest books and I feel now a great personal liking for you but you and I are set upon absolutely different courses. Your training has been Catholic, Irish, insurrectionary; mine, such as it was, was scientific, constructive and, I suppose, English. The frame of my mind is a world wherein a big unifying and concentrating process is possible (increase of power and range by economy and concentration of effort), a *progress* not inevitable but interesting and possible. That game attracts and holds me. For it, I want language and statement as simple and clear as possible. You began Catholic, that is to say you began with a system of values in stark opposition to reality. Your mental existence is obsessed by a monstrous system of contradictions. You may believe in chastity, purity and the personal God and that is why you are always breaking out into cries of cunt, shit and hell. As I don't believe in these things except as quite personal values my mind has never been shocked to outcries by the existence of waterclosets and menstrual bandages—and undeserved misfortunes. And while you were brought up under the delusion of political suppression I was brought up under the delusion of political responsibility. It seems a fine thing for you to defy and break up. To me not in the least.

Now with regard to this literary experiment of yours. It's a considerable thing because you are a very considerable man and you have in your crowded composition a mighty genius for expression which has escaped discipline. But I don't think it gets anywhere. You have turned your back on common men, on their elementary needs and their restricted time and intelligence and you have elaborated. What is the result? Vast riddles. Your last two works have been more amusing and exciting to write than they will ever be to read. Take me as a typical common reader. Do I get much pleasure from this work? No. Do I feel I am getting something new and illuminating as I do when I read Anrep's dreadful translation of Pavlov's badly written book on Conditioned Reflexes?[2] No. So I ask: Who the hell is this Joyce who demands so many waking hours of the few thousands I have still to live for a proper appreciation of his quirks and fancies and flashes of rendering?

All this from my point of view. Perhaps you are right and I am all wrong. Your work is an extraordinary experiment and I would go out of my way to save it from destructive or restrictive interruption. It has its believers and its following. Let them rejoice in it. To me it is a dead end.

My warmest good wishes to you Joyce. I cant follow your banner any more than you can follow mine. But the world is wide and there is room for both of us to be wrong.

NOTES

1 See Ellmann, *op. cit.*, p 621. The text of Wells's letter reprinted here follows that given by Ellmann, pp 620–1.
2 G. V. Anrep's translation, *Conditioned Reflexes*, was published in 1927. Wells's position is comparable to that of Rebecca West, who discusses Joyce and Pavlov at length in *The Strange Necessity* (1928).

5 *H. G. Wells and Henry James*

Wells and James struck up a friendship in the summer of 1898 (see *ExA* 8:4). By that time Wells was familiar with at least some of the older man's work. He had been witness to James's discomfiture the night that *Guy Domville* opened at George Alexander's theatre (see 'The Importance of Being Earnest', n 4). He had also written about *Terminations* (1895), a gathering of James's short stories, in the pages of the *Saturday Review*. For his part, James soon set out to acquaint himself with his young friend's accomplishments in fiction. He scrupulously read the volumes that Wells provided him with; and by and large he found them praiseworthy. 'Your spirit is huge, your fascination irresistible, your resources infinite', he declares in one of his earliest surviving letters to Wells (20 November 1899: E&R, p 62); and in another from the same period, he thanks him for sending 'me your book—I mean the particular masterpiece entitled *The Time Machine*' (29 January 1900: E&R p 63). To be sure, his correspondence with Wells, when scrutinized in retrospect, does reveal signs of James's increasing impatience over the young novelist's persistent disregard for the exigencies of his art. None the less, he sustains a tone of admiration that Wells, on his side, reciprocates.

It may seem strange that two writers who have so little in common—who, indeed, appear to be so totally at odds in temperament and outlook—should mutually profess their high regard for one another's achievements. Yet to doubt that James was sincere would be tantamount to accusing him of duplicity. Nor is it possible to explain Wells's abiding obsession with James without recognizing his profound esteem for the Master of Rye. Years after James's death, Wells continued to treat him as his chief antagonist in an ongoing debate about The Novel. It is true that those passages in his autobiography which are addressed, as it were, to James indicate that their relations had by then become for Wells a bitter and rankling memory. But even in

H. G. Wells and Henry James

giving vent to—and perhaps exorcizing—his resentment, Wells paid tribute to the novelist whose 'stories are woven with a peculiar humorous, faintly fussy, delicacy, that gives them a flavour like nothing else in the language' (*ExA* 8:2).

1

Despite their frequent literary disagreements, Wells's relations with James remained amicable for more than a decade. The first real strain on their friendship came in 1911. Wells at the time was in a self-defensive mood. He had recently been having difficulties finding a publisher for *The New Machiavelli* (1911). Moreover, he was still incensed at the critical reception that his books had been accorded of late, and especially at the charges of immorality that had been levelled against *Ann Veronica* (1909; see *ExA* 7:4). He therefore looked upon an invitation to speak at a meeting of the Times Book Club as a sought-for opportunity to explain himself. He did so in a talk called 'The Scope of the Novel', the text of which subsequently appeared in the *Fortnightly Review* for November 1911 (and in the *Atlantic Monthly* the following January) under the title 'The Contemporary Novel'.

'The Contemporary Novel' represents Wells's fullest attempt to bring together and systematize many of the ideas that he had put forward as a reviewer of fiction in the 1890s. In it, he argues for the novel as above all—and inherently—'a powerful instrument of moral suggestion'. It perforce 'leaves impressions, not simply of things seen, but of acts judged and made attractive or unattractive'. This does not mean that the novelist's job is to teach or to preach—in the manner, say, of Richard Le Gallienne or Robert Hichens (see 'The Lost Quest' and 'Flickers of Imagination . . .'). But at a time when traditional values are being questioned and 'The importance of the individual instance as against the generalization' is being reasserted, the novelist, dealing as he does in 'individualities', has both the occasion and the responsibility to 'discuss, point out, plead [for], and display' possible courses of thought and conduct. And if he is to fulfil that obligation, he must have complete freedom in matters of subject and treatment.

Wells thus makes a case for allowing the novelist virtually

unlimited scope. It is also, and necessarily, a case against 'the restrictions imposed upon [the novel] by the fierce pedantries of those who would define a general form for it'. In particular, Wells rejects the demand for authorial detachment and upholds instead his own preference for fiction 'saturated in the personality of the author' (see 'The Paying Guest' and 'The New American Novelists'). He likewise opposes the idea that the novelist should aim at a single impression or effect. These and similar prescriptions, Wells contends, have little to do with what the novel has been or with what it is in the process of becoming. Fielding, Thackeray, and Dickens, Romain Rolland, Joseph Conrad, and Arnold Bennett, are among the names that resonate throughout Wells's remarks as a reminder of how diverse—and how 'personal'—its greatness may be.

Although he nowhere mentions the name of his principal antagonist, there can be no doubt that Wells designed 'The Contemporary Novel' as a rejoinder to James. That intent is unmistakable in Wells's pointed, if subtle, reference to Flaubert. His praise of Flaubert recalls the tenor of the famous essay in which James reveals an attachment for the author of *Madame Bovary* that even surpasses his deeply felt affinities with Hawthorne and Balzac.[1] But it is the Flaubert of *Bouvard et Pécuchet*—an encyclopaedic effort that Flaubert did not live long enough to finish—that Wells seizes upon. He claims 'this gay, sad miracle of intellectual abundance' not only as one more proof that the novel is, by its nature, 'a discursive thing', but also as evidence that 'Flaubert is really the Continental emancipator of the novel from the restrictions of form'. He then gives tribute to Flaubert's eighteenth-century counterpart, 'the Master to whom we of the English persuasion, we of the discursive school, must for ever recur': the author of *Tristram Shandy*. He challenges anyone to deny Sterne 'to be the subtlest and greatest *artist*—I lay stress upon that word artist—that Great Britain has ever produced in all that is essentially the novel'. The immediate context and double emphasis suggest that Wells was directing his challenge especially at James.

If this essay gave James one cause for being displeased with his friend, their disagreement over the Academic

Committee gave him another. When asked to join, James had accepted membership on the Committee; and he repeatedly urged Wells to follow his example and do 'the simple, civil, social *easiest* thing' (James to Wells, 20 March 1912: E&R, p 158). But Wells, having publicly voiced his fears about the tyrannical power that such a body might exercise (see above, pp 13–14), adamantly refused to serve. Writing to Edmund Gosse after his last exchange with Wells on the subject, James conceded that he '*had* decently to decline, and I think it decent of him to have felt that'. However, James agreed that this was the right decision only because he had concluded that Wells 'has cut loose from literature clearly—practically altogether' (James to Gosse, 26 March 1912: E&R, pp 163–4 n).

2

The next and ultimate phase in Wells's falling out with James began after a lapse of two years. During that time, their extant correspondence shows James more forward than he had hitherto been in expressing reservations about Wells's fiction. Yet he continues to confess 'that I find myself unable, and still more unwilling, to approach you, or to take leave of you, in any projected light of criticism' (18 October 1912: E&R, p 168). Barely six months before committing his essay on 'The Younger Generation' to print, James was still echoing his enthusiastic outbursts of earlier years, when he had saluted Wells as 'the most interesting "literary man" of your generation—in fact, the only interesting one' (19 November 1905: E&R, p 103). In a letter dated 21 September 1913, James, after paying respects to 'the high intensity with which your talent keeps itself interesting', adds: 'I jib altogether and utterly at the "fiction of the day" and find no company but yours and that, in a degree, of one or two others possible' (E&R, pp 172–3). One cannot pass from effusions of this kind to a perusal of 'The Younger Generation' without feeling something of the surprise and anger that Wells must have felt when the first part of James's essay appeared in *The Times Literary Supplement* for 19 March 1914.[2] James's polemic is often spoken of as if it were an even-handed attack on novelists who had come into prominence more or less around the turn of the century. Had it been such, Wells might conceivably have suffered it in silence. He would, after all, have found nothing totally new or startling in the strictures against *Marriage* that supply the main basis for James's charges against him in 'The Younger Generation'; nor would he have had good reason to think James perfidious for making public a critique whose gist he had already communicated in private (James to Wells, 18 October 1912: E&R, pp 166–7). Of course, he would not have been happy with the turn that James now gave to erstwhile compliments like 'what primarily flies in my face in *these* things of yours is *you* and your so amazingly active and agile intellectual personality' (8 November 1906: E&R, pp 113–4)—which James in 'The Younger Generation' (re)phrases in a most uncomplimentary way:

It is literally Mr Wells's own mind, and the experience of his own mind . . . that suffices for his exhibition of grounds of interest. The more he knows and knows, or at any rate learns and learns . . . the greater is our impression of his holding it good enough for us, such as we are, that he shall but turn out his mind and its contents upon us by any free familiar gesture and as from a high window forever open. (E&R, pp 189–90)

What Wells could least have expected, however, was to see himself singled out for special opprobrium.

Although James in the course of his diatribe mentions the names of ten writers, he discusses at any length little more than half their number: Joseph Conrad, Edith Wharton, Hugh Walpole, Compton Mackenzie, Arnold Bennett, and H. G. Wells. (Gilbert Cannan he dismisses in short order; D. H. Lawrence he ostentatiously ignores). For Conrad he has measured, and for Mrs Wharton virtually unbounded, praise. Walpole and Mackenzie he treats ambiguously as novelists who may yet expiate their literary sins. Arnold Bennett, on the other hand, he puts among the unredeemable—and Wells along with him. Each in his own way, James avers, is an arch-exponent of the 'saturation' theory of the novel: 'They squeeze out to the utmost the plump and more or less juicy orange of a particular acquainted state and let this affirmation of energy, however directed or undirected, constitute for them the "treatment" of the theme'

H. G. Wells and Henry James

('The Younger Generation', in E&R, pp 182–3). Bennett's 'canvas is covered, ever so closely and vividly covered, by the exhibition, of innumerable small facts and aspects' (ibid, p 187). Wells, as James implies in the passage quoted above, 'saturates' his books by emptying into them the contents of his mental chamber pot.

There is a sense of understatement in the letter that Wells sent to Hugh Walpole, shortly after James's death, in which he speaks of the 'old man' as having been 'a little treacherous to me' (quoted in E&R, p 8). He unquestionably did not enjoy any aspect of James's performance. He would not have applauded the pillorying of Arnold Bennett, a lifelong friend whose work he admired; and he certainly resented the fact that James, by giving a satiric twist to his own demand that the novel be 'saturated in the personality of the author' ('The Contemporary Novel'), had put him in the same pillory, as one of the principal offenders against Literary Art.

Wells replied in kind. His response, though not immediately forthcoming, was *Boon*. He had been working intermittently on it for over a decade. In the spring of 1914, with 'The Younger Generation' fresh in his mind, he returned to it. The manuscript that he had in hand at the time differed significantly from the book that he had completed by December. In the former, James's presence was quite incidental (see E&R, p 36). In the final version, however, James had come to occupy a place of prominence. Wells, in fact, devotes most of one long chapter to him. The parody in 'Of Art, of Literature, of Mr Henry James', while not unaffectionate, is devastatingly thorough. Wells begins by satirizing James's manner of speaking, proceeds to a general critique of his literary stance, and concludes with *The Spoils of Mr Blandish*, a send-up of the Jamesian novel and of what Wells, twenty years earlier, had characterized as the author's 'ground-glass style' (see 'Three *Yellow-Book* Story-Tellers').

'Of Art, of Literature, of Mr Henry James' has always been regarded as a personal attack on James. It has less frequently been recognized, or taken seriously, as literary criticism. Yet Wells's image of James as a caged hippopotamus desperately trying to pick up a pea, while as a retaliatory gesture it may appear disproportionate to the derogatory metaphors in 'The Younger Generation' that provoked it, serves to make a telling point about James's fiction—a point subsequently exemplified in *The Spoils of Mr Blandish*. Hyperbolically, derisively, and unflatteringly—that is, in a fashion usual in literary parodies of its kind—it exhibits that author moving with cumbrous and circumlocutory grace around and around his seemingly miniscule subject. Wells minimizes—perhaps deliberately—James's 'processional meaning'; but he otherwise reveals (to use his term) the 'essential' James.

Wells saw to it that James got a copy of *Boon*: he left one for him at the Reform Club. This has generally been interpreted as an act of malevolent effrontery. But to suppose that he was actuated solely or consciously by malice is unlikely, not to say uncharitable. Had that been the case, he would not have abjectly apologized—as he afterwards did (see E&R, pp 263–4). His motives may indeed have been ambivalent; indubitably, they were complex. They surely included an intent to avow authorship of a book that had been published pseudonymously. Wells may also have meant by his gesture of forthrightness to remind James that James had not been quite so above-board in his dealings with him. Not inconceivably, he might even have imagined that James would take *Boon* in the spirit in which he had accepted Max Beerbohm's parody, 'The Mote in the Middle Distance'.[3] If so, he was quite wrong. James was not at all amused.

The day after receiving *Boon*, he wrote to say that it 'has naturally not filled me with fond elation' (6 July 1915: E&R, p 261). Wells answered apologetically that '*Boon* is just a waste-paper basket' (8 July 1915: E&R, p 264). 'Your comparison . . . ,' James retorted, 'strikes me as the reverse of felicitous, for what one throws into that receptacle is exactly what one *doesn't* commit to publicity and make the affirmation of one's estimate of one's contemporaries by' (10 July 1915: E&R, p 265). Thus, over *Boon*, their friendship came to an end.

3

Almost three years to the day after James's death, Arnold Bennett, solicited to act as intermediary, wrote to ask Wells for James's letters. 'Admirers and fanatics of H. J.', he told Wells, 'regard his letters in this affair as the greatest statement of his artistic "case" that he ever gave'. 'The publication of the correspondence . . . as it stands', Wells replied, 'might entirely misrepresent my attitude towards our "art"' (Wilson, pp 203–4). His fear has proved to be totally justified. His definition of the 'essence' of his differences with James—'I had rather be called a journalist than an artist' (8 July 1915: E&R, p 264)—has left the perhaps ineradicable impression that theirs was a debate between the Literary Artist and the Philistine 'Bounder'. Ignoring the fact that 'journalist' does not for Wells include 'hack' among its synonyms, most historians of the quarrel have, understandably enough, sided with James. The issues in dispute have accordingly been represented as rather simple and easily resolvable (in James's favour, of course). But in reality they were complex, entangled, and intractable. Furthermore, Wells and James did not fully articulate those issues in their correspondence—or, for that matter, in the documents immediately pertinent to their quarrel. Nor are their pronouncements always directly to the point. Most of what Wells says in his 'Digression about Novels' (*ExA* 7:5), for instance, is only obliquely relevant to the questions on which he and James took opposing sides. The same can be said of James's words, 'It is art that *makes* life, makes interest, makes importance, . . . and I know of no substitute for the force and beauty of its process' (letter to Wells, 10 July 1915: E&R, p 267). By them, James eloquently confirms his commitment to Literature . . . and leaves undefined the crucial term whose meaning he and Wells could never agree upon: 'art'.

In calling himself a 'journalist', Wells was seeking to differentiate his own stance from that of James. He did not mean to sever any and all connections with literary art. He did mean to express his belief that a writer must, first and above all, be responsive to the historical moment in which he finds himself situated. Throughout the greater part of his life, Wells retained a profound faith in literature as a 'countervailing force' in history,[4] as a 'powerful instrument' for giving voice to and educating and shaping 'the mind of the race' (see 'The Contemporary Novel' and *Boon*). That faith underlies *his* conscious and lifelong commitment to fiction, and is reflected elsewhere in the sociological orientation of some of his literary criticism (for examples, see 'Popular Writers and Press Critics' and 'About Sir Thomas More'). On the other hand, he came to have equally profound doubts as to whether a writer could—or even should—aspire to achieve something absolutely permanent. His doubts arose from the intimation that the aesthetic demands for ensuring literary permanence were at odds with the socio-moral responsibilities of the novelist. His sense that these were conflicting imperatives became more and more insistent in the course of his argument with James. If permanence in Literature required the kind of selectivity—in Wells's view, the narrowness—that James espoused and practised, then Wells preferred an unconstricted timeliness.

It is usually assumed that in repudiating Jamesian formalism, Wells also repudiated literary form. This is not the case. As he put it, he rejected the 'intensive' in favour of the 'extensive' novel (see *ExA* 7:5). Though he deeply admired—and, be it added, profoundly appreciated—what James was doing in his later works, he himself saw no universal necessity for the kind of 'unity' and 'homogeneity' that James required of a novel. Wells, in rejecting Jamesian strictures, approved instead of a centrifugal and inclusive approach, one that did not constrain the novelist to 'omit everything that demands digressive treatment or collateral statement' (see *Boon*). If in his allegiance to literature as a social force—a force, that is, affecting man's mental environment—Wells was influenced by the example of Swift, of Blake, and of Dickens, here he takes as his models chiefly Fielding and Sterne, Thackeray and (again) Dickens, Turgenev and Tolstoi.

Clearly related to, and underlying, their disagreement over the 'intensive' versus the 'extensive' novel was another, which neither James nor Wells ever seems to have

H. G. Wells and Henry James

been aware of as such. That further difference has to do with the way in which each writer conceived—and conceived of—a novel. The difference, that is, bears upon both literary theory and creative processes. T. S. Eliot perhaps hints at one aspect of it when, having remarked that James 'had a mind so fine that no idea could violate it', he goes on to speak of James's novels as 'maintaining a point of view . . . untouched by the parasite idea'.[5] They do so because James thought of them in terms of point of view. In them, point of view determines form, oftentimes to an extreme degree. Indeed, James can be credited with the conscious discovery of that relationship. Certainly his emphasis on point of view as the essence of novelistic form—an emphasis manifest in both his theory and practice of fiction—distinguishes him as the progenitor of formalist criticism of the novel. His habit of mind made him sensitive to the merits of Balzac and Flaubert. It also left him unsympathetic to those of, say, Dickens or Tolstoi. To read James on *Bleak House*, for example, is to realize how insensitive he could be when he came to a novel whose point of view is wholly secondary to the conception directing it. Wells, at the other extreme, thought of a novel primarily in terms of its governing conception. That is why he frequently shows himself to be careless of point of view (as James, of course, was the first to recognize). That is also why he is so often equally careless in matters of style. He himself says as much, albeit with facetious exaggeration, in a letter to Bennett in 1904: 'Stile [*sic*] my dear chap in this sense of petty word mongering has no place in English literature. The stile of my general design, the stile of my thought—C'est moi!' (Wilson, p 115). Similarly, it is his attention to the 'general design' of a fiction that enables him to admire, and write perceptively about, the accomplishments of authors as diverse as Meredith, Turgenev, Hardy, Conrad, Stevenson, Crane, Gissing, and Joyce.

In regard to some of the issues on which they disagreed, James and Wells took logically irreconcilable positions. But the incompatibility of their respective approaches to the conceiving of a novel was, logically speaking, an accident, was contingent upon differences of temperament and outlook. Governing conception and point of view do not of necessity stand as opposing priorities: in *Tom Jones*, for instance, they have patently co-determined one another. For James and Wells, however, the two were not equal considerations. James continued to insist on his sense of novelistic form as a function of point of view, while Wells continued to experiment with the conceptual shape of fiction.[6] Wells found it difficult to formulate a theoretical basis for those experiments. He never proceeded with quite the same assurance that James had. Despite his generally iconoclastic stance, despite also his pioneering efforts in the direction of a sociology of literature, he was reluctant to break away totally from certain established attitudes towards fiction (see 'On Science Fiction, Utopian Fiction, and Fantasy'). He perhaps came closest to doing so in his preface to *Babes in the Darkling Wood* (1940). Addressing again the issue of 'Whether I am a Novelist' (*ExA* 7:5), he identifies himself as a proponent of 'the novel of ideas' and as heir to 'a great tradition, the tradition of discussing human problems in dialogue form'. His posture still has in it some of the defensiveness consequent upon his falling out with James. But for the first time, he openly and seriously questions the assumption that had made his debate with James—and for years afterwards, with himself—possible. He wonders aloud, that is, whether something called The Novel exists.

NOTES

1 James's *Hawthorne* appeared in 1879; his two essays on Balzac (1902, 1913) were collected in *Notes on Novelists* (1914).
2 Part Two was printed in *The Times Literary Supplement* for April 1914.
3 Beerbohm's parody was first published in SR and then reprinted in *A Christmas Garland* (1912). David Daiches, in *Max* (Constable, London, 1964), p 317, cites testimony indicating that James was amused by it.
4 Wells uses this phrase in 'The Making of Men at Cambridge', a signed review of E. F. Benson's *The Babe, B. A.* (SR 83: 13 February 1897, p 174).
5 T. S. Eliot, 'In Memory of Henry James', *The Egoist*, 5: January 1918, p [1]–2. Rebecca West (Wells's mistress at the time) had expressed similar sentiments in the opening chapter of *Henry James* (1915).
6 See William J. Scheick's 'The Fourth Dimension in Wells's Novels of the 1920's', *Criticism*, 20 (1978), pp 167–90.

H. G. Wells and Henry James
'THREE *YELLOW-BOOK* STORY-TELLERS'

The Saturday Review *for 1 June 1895 (79:730–1) carried Wells's notice of three books of short stories:* Grey Roses *by Henry Harland (1861–1905),* Terminations *by Henry James (1843–1916), and* Monochromes *by Ella D'Arcy (1851–1939). Most of the stories in these volumes had previously appeared in the pages of the* Yellow Book *(1894–8), of which Harland was the literary editor and John Lane the publisher.*

There came to hand almost simultaneously three volumes of short stories, most of which have appeared in Mr Lane's yellow quarterly. Mr Harland's work one may take as typical of the *Yellow Book* school. There are popular misconceptions abroad. A persuasion exists that this group of writers, like the sculpture in the caves of Elephanta,[1] insists overmuch upon sex. But that at any rate is not *the* characteristic. People muddle up these story-tellers with George Egerton, who, so far as our cursory acquaintance with the periodical in question goes, has never been a contributor.[2] Happily we find an implicit exposition of the entire *Yellow Book* Theory of Literature in one of the stories by Mr Harland, the editor of the school, and its quotation will serve to correct a common misconception.

In the meanwhile, some of us had read his books: chromo-lithographs, struck in the primary colours; pasteboard complications of passion and adventure, with the conservative entanglement of threadbare marionettes—a hero, tall, with golden brown moustaches and blue eyes; a heroine, with "sunny locks"; then a swarthy villain, for the most part a nobleman, and his Spanish-looking female accomplice, who had an uncomfortable habit of delivering her remarks "from between clenched teeth," and generally "in a blood-chilling hiss"—the narrative set forth in a sustained *fortissimo*, and punctuated by the timely exits of the god from the machine. Never a felicity, never an impression. I fancy he had made his notes of human nature whilst observing the personages of a melodrama at a provincial theatre. He loved the obvious sentiment, the obvious and but approximate word. ['A Re-Incarnation,' in *Grey Roses*, p 101]

To understand the true *Yellow Book* school properly one must keep that passage in mind. It describes all that a novel should not be, according to Mr Harland's standards, and Mr

Harland is the editor of the *Yellow Book*. Imagine now a young man or a young woman, highly educated, highly ambitious, very painstaking, and of quite mediocre intellect, sitting down to write a story; imagine the conscientious rejection of the obvious sentiment, of the obvious and but appropriate word; imagine the pen stayed at the end of a page or so—'time for a felicity', says the author, or 'Dear me!—not an impression for quite a dozen pages', and you have the clue to the entire business. In a flash Mr Harland and his following are explained. Everyone has wondered at the subtle resemblance and the subtle difference between the fiction of the *Family Herald*[3] and this new development. It is only *Family Herald*—copper gilt. . . .[4]

Of the same school—we speak loosely—but of a different calibre is Mr Henry James. He, too, dreads the 'obvious', but his particular weakness is not felicity but melody. Mr Harland, at times, almost conceals the feeble meaning of his stories by his studious avoidance of the obvious word. Mr Henry James, on the other hand, has eyes for human beings, and his singular distaste for the obvious is a thing to be regretted. We could be enthusiastic over these stories were we not exasperated by the thorns and briars of style we have traversed to appreciate them. There is such a thing as a pellucid style, a transparent window upon the author's thought. But Mr Henry James has a ground-glass style. By close application you can just discern through it, men and women as trees walking. Nevertheless, they are living men and women. The 'Death of the Lion' is hazy, but it leaves an impression of indisputable reality, and the 'Altar of the Dead', here first printed, has a fanciful strangeness that we scarcely hesitate to call beautiful. But reading 'The Coxon Fund' is like walking about the city on Sunday in a dense fog. Rare characters loom upon one dimly and pass, muttering incoherent nothings; vague action goes on in the penumbra; Saltram, the principal person in the drama, is especially elusive. You want to get close to him, to look into his face; you want to say to him, 'Mr Caliph, I believe?' and you never get the chance. The peculiar exasperation of Mr James's style is not so much the avoidance of the obvious word as of the obvious construction. He has a positive distaste for the simple sentence, and he cannot avoid tangling his dependent clauses. His paragraphs remind one of a skein of wool after a kitten has played with it. One sees the thread of the narrative occasionally. Sometimes he gets clever ambiguities, sometimes his ambiguities are not even clever. Often he is subtle; but always he is involved. Possibly it is a passion for cadences. Here are two passages, taken haphazard, that will serve as examples of his characteristic offence. Alone these are not perhaps so very formidable, but page after page of nothing else is as wearying as beautiful black-letter. And everything he says here could be said as fully and with infinitely better effect in English of the normal pattern.

> Others of the faithful, and in the rest of the church, came and went, appealing sometimes, when they disappeared, to a vague or to a particular recognition; but this unfailing presence was always to be observed when he arrived and still in possession when he departed. ['Altar of the Dead', p 219]

> She lived, as she said, in a mere slum, with an old aunt, a person in connection with whom she spoke of the engrossment of humdrum duties and regular occupations. She was not, the mourning niece, in her first youth, and her vanished freshness had left something behind which, for Stransom, represented the proof that it had been tragically sacrificed. Whatever she gave him the assurance of she gave it without references. [ibid. p 224]

Of course, if one wanted to read Mr James aloud without any reference to his meaning, his English would be charming enough. . . .[5]

NOTES

1 The chief cave-temples (sixth-eighth centuries A.D.) on the island of Elephanta (in Bombay harbour) contain sculptures dedicated to Siva, the Hindu god who, as creator and preserver, presides over procreativity.
2 'George Egerton' (see 'The Novel of Types', n 2) did contribute one story to the *Yellow Book*—the month after this review of Wells's appeared.
3 See 'A Servants' Hall Vision', n 7.
4 Wells goes on to illustrate the resemblances between Harland's stories and those of the *Family Herald*.
5 In the brief concluding paragraph of the review, Wells hails Ella D'Arcy as a promising beginner.

H. G. Wells's Literary Criticism
'THE CONTEMPORARY NOVEL'

This essay is Wells's most extensive statement of his theory of the novel. The text as it appeared under the present title in periodicals on both sides of the Atlantic and in An Englishman Looks at the World *(1914; pp 148–69) would seem to be a slightly retrenched version of an address to the Times Book Club in May 1911 on 'The Scope of the Novel' (see p 179 and E&R, p 131n). Unless otherwise noted, the ellipsis points are the author's.*

Circumstances have made me think a good deal at different times about the business of writing novels, and what it means, and is, and may be; and I was a professional critic of novels long before I wrote them. I have been writing novels, or writing about novels, for the last twenty years. It seems only yesterday that I wrote a review—the first long and appreciative review he had—of Mr Joseph Conrad's *Almayer's Folly* in the *Saturday Review*.[1] When a man has focussed so much of his life upon the novel, it is not reasonable to expect him to take too modest or apologetic a view of it. I consider the novel an important and necessary thing indeed in that complicated system of uneasy adjustments and readjustments which is modern civilization. I make very high and wide claims for it. In many directions I do not think we can get along without it.

Now this, I know, is not the usually received opinion. There is, I am aware, the theory that the novel is wholly and solely a means of relaxation. In spite of manifest facts, that was the dominant view of the great period that we now in our retrospective way speak of as the Victorian, and it still survives to this day. It is the man's theory of the novel rather than the woman's. One may call it the Weary Giant theory. The reader is represented as a man, burthened, toiling, worn. He has been in his office from ten to four, with perhaps only two hours' interval at his club for lunch; or he has been playing golf; or he has been waiting about and voting in the House; or he has been fishing; or he has been disputing a point of law; or writing a sermon; or doing one of a thousand other of the grave important things which constitute the substance of a prosperous man's life. Now at last comes the little precious interval of leisure, and the Weary Giant takes up a book. Perhaps he is vexed: he may have been bunkered, his line may have been entangled in the trees, his favourite investment may have slumped, or the judge have had indigestion and been extremely rude to him. He wants to forget the troublesome realities of life. He wants to be taken out of himself, to be cheered, consoled, amused—above all, amused. He doesn't want ideas, he doesn't want facts; above all, he doesn't want—*Problems*. He wants to dream of the bright, thin, gay excitements of a phantom world—in which he can be hero—of horses ridden and lace worn and princesses rescued and won. He wants pictures of funny slums, and entertaining paupers, and laughable longshoremen, and kindly impulses making life sweet. He wants romance without its defiance, and humour without its sting; and the business of the novelist, he holds, is to supply this cooling refreshment. That is the Weary Giant theory of the novel. It ruled British criticism up to the period of the Boer war—and then something happened to quite a lot of us, and it has never completely recovered its old predominance. Perhaps it will; perhaps something else may happen to prevent its ever doing so. . . .[2]

And if the novel is to be recognized as something more than a relaxation, it has also, I think, to be kept free from the restrictions imposed upon it by the fierce pedantries of those who would define a general form for it. Every art nowadays must steer its way between the rocks of trivial and degrading standards and the whirlpool of arbitrary and irrational criticism. Whenever criticism of any art becomes specialized and professional, whenever a class of adjudicators is brought into existence, those adjudicators are apt to become as a class distrustful of their immediate impressions, and anxious for methods of comparison between work and work, they begin to emulate the classifications and exact measurements of a science, and to set up ideals and rules as data for such classification and measurements. They develop an alleged sense of technique, which is too often no more than the attempt to exact a laboriousness of method, or to insist upon peculiarities of method which impress the professional critic not so much as being merits as being meritorious. This sort of thing has gone very far with the critical discussion both of the novel and the play. You have all heard that impressive dictum that some particular theatrical display, although moving, interesting, and continually entertaining from start to finish, was for occult technical reasons 'not a play', and in the same way you are continually having your appreciation of fiction dashed by the mysterious parallel condemnation, that the story you like 'isn't a novel'. The novel has been treated as though its form was as well-defined as the sonnet. Some year or so ago, for example, there was a quite serious discussion, which began, I believe, in a weekly paper devoted to the interests of various nonconformist religious organizations,[3] about the proper length for a novel. The critic was to begin his painful duties with a yard measure. The matter was taken up with profound gravity by the *Westminster Gazette*,[4] and a considerable number of literary men and women were circularized and asked to state, in the face of *Tom Jones, The Vicar of Wakefield, The Shabby-Genteel Story,* and *Bleak House*,[5] just exactly how long the novel ought to be. Our replies varied according to the civility of our natures, but the mere attempt to raise the question shows, I think, how widespread among the editorial, paragraph-writing, opinion-making sort of people is this notion of prescribing a definite length and a definite form for the novel. In the newspaper correspondence that followed, our friend the weary giant made a transitory appearance again. We were told the novel ought to be long enough for him to take up after dinner and finish before his whisky at eleven.

That was obviously a half-forgotten echo of Edgar Allan Poe's discussion of the short story. Edgar Allan Poe was very definite upon the point that the short story should be finished at a sitting.[6] But the novel and short story are two entirely different things, and the train of reasoning that made the American master limit the short story to about an hour of reading as a maximum, does not apply to the longer work. A short story is, or should be, a simple thing; it aims at producing one single, vivid effect; it has to seize the attention at the outset, and never relaxing, gather it together more and more until the climax is reached. The limits of the human capacity to attend closely therefore set a limit to it; it must explode and finish before interruption occurs or fatigue sets in. But the novel I hold to be a discursive thing; it is not a single interest, but a woven tapestry of interests; one is drawn on first by this affection and curiosity, and then by that; it is something to return to, and I do not see that we can possibly set any limit to its extent. The distinctive value of the novel among written works of art is in characterization, and the charm of a well-conceived character lies, not in knowing its destiny, but in watching its proceedings. For my own part, I will confess that I find all the novels of Dickens, long as they are, too short for me. I am sorry they do not flow into one another more than they do. I wish Micawber and Dick Swiveller and Sairey Gamp turned up again in other novels than their own, just as Shakespeare ran the glorious glow of Falstaff through a group of plays.[7] But Dickens tried this once when he carried on the Pickwick Club into *Master Humphrey's Clock* [1840–1]. That experiment was unsatisfactory, and he did not attempt anything of the sort again. Following on the days of Dickens, the novel began to contract, to subordinate characterization to story and description to drama; considerations of a sordid nature, I am told, had to do with that; something about a guinea and a half and six shillings with which we will not concern ourselves[8]—but I rejoice to see many signs to-day that that phase of narrowing and restriction is over, and that there is every encouragement for a return towards a laxer, more spacious form of novel-writing. The movement is partly of English origin, a revolt against those more exacting and cramping conceptions of artistic perfection to which I will recur in a moment, and a return to the lax freedom of form, the rambling discursiveness, the right to roam, of the earlier English novel, of *Tristram Shandy* [1759–67] and of *Tom Jones*; and partly it comes from abroad, and derives a stimulus from such bold and original enterprises as that of Monsieur Rolland in his *Jean Christophe* [1903–12]. Its double origin involves a double nature; for while the English spirit is towards discursiveness and variety, the new French

H. G. Wells's Literary Criticism

movement is rather towards exhaustiveness. Mr Arnold Bennett has experimented in both forms of amplitude. His superb *Old Wives' Tale* [1908], wandering from person to person and from scene to scene, is by far the finest 'long novel' that has been written in English in the English fashion in this generation, and now in *Clayhanger* [1910] and its promised collaterals, he undertakes that complete, minute, abundant presentation of the growth and modification of one or two individual minds, which is the essential characteristic of the Continental movement towards the novel of amplitude. While the *Old Wives' Tale* is discursive, *Clayhanger* is exhaustive; he gives us both types of the new movement in perfection.

I name *Jean Christophe* as a sort of archetype in this connection, because it is just at present very much in our thoughts by reason of the admirable translation [1910] Mr Cannan is giving us; but there is a greater predecessor to this comprehensive and spectacular treatment of a single mind and its impressions and ideas, or of one or two associated minds, that comes to us now *via* Mr Bennett and Mr Cannan from France. The great original of all this work is that colossal last unfinished book of Flaubert, *Bouvard et Pécuchet* [1881]. Flaubert, the bulk of whose life was spent upon the most austere and restrained fiction—Turgenev was not more austere and restrained—broke out at last into this gay, sad miracle of intellectual abundance. It is not extensively read in this country; it is not yet, I believe, translated into English; but there it is—and if it is new to the reader I make him this present of the secret of a book that is a precious wilderness of wonderful reading. But if Flaubert is really the Continental emancipator of the novel from the restrictions of form, the master to whom we of the English persuasion, we of the discursive school, must for ever recur is he, whom I will maintain against all comers to be the subtlest and greatest *artist*—I lay stress upon that word artist—that Great Britain has ever produced in all that is essentially the novel, Laurence Sterne. . . .

The confusion between the standards of a short story and the standards of the novel which leads at last to these—what shall I call them?—*Westminster Gazettisms?*—about the correct length to which the novelist should aspire, leads also to all kinds of absurd condemnations and exactions upon matters of method and style. The underlying fallacy is always this: the assumption that the novel, like the story, aims at a single, concentrated impression. From that comes a fertile growth of error. Constantly one finds in the reviews of works of fiction the complaint that this, that or the other thing, in a novel is irrelevant. Now it is the easiest thing, and most fatal thing, to become irrelevant in a short story. A short story should go to its point as a man flies from a pursuing tiger: he pauses not for the daisies in his path, or to note the pretty moss on the tree he climbs for safety. But the novel by comparison is like breakfasting in the open air on a summer morning; nothing is irrelevant if the writer's mood is happy, and the tapping of the thrush upon the garden path, or the petal of apple-blossom that floats down into my coffee, is as relevant as the egg I open or the bread and butter I bite. And all sorts of things that inevitably mar the tense illusion which is the aim of the short story—the introduction, for example, of the author's personality—any comment that seems to admit that, after all, fiction is fiction, a change in manner between part and part, burlesque, parody, invective, all such things are not necessarily wrong in the novel. Of course, all these things may fail in their effect; they may jar, hinder, irritate, and all are difficult to do well; but it is no artistic merit to evade a difficulty any more than it is a merit in a hunter to refuse even the highest of fences. Nearly all the novels that have, by the lapse of time, reached an assured position of recognized greatness, are not only saturated in the personality of the author, but have in addition quite unaffected personal outbreaks.[9] The least successful instance, the one that is made the text against all such first-personal interventions, is, of course, Thackeray. But I think the trouble with Thackeray is not that he makes first-personal interventions, but that he does so with a curious touch of dishonesty. I agree with the late Mrs. Craigie that there was something profoundly vulgar about Thackeray.[10] It was a sham thoughtful, sham man-of-the-world pose he assumed; it is an aggressive, conscious, challenging person astride before a fire, and a little distended by dinner and a sense of social and literary precedences, who uses the first person in Thackeray's novels. It isn't the real Thackeray; it isn't a frank man who looks you in the eyes and bares his soul and demands your sympathy. That is a criticism of Thackeray, but it isn't a condemnation of intervention.

I admit that for a novelist to come in person in this way before his readers involves grave risks; but when it is done without affectations, starkly as a man comes in out of the darkness to tell of perplexing things without—as, for instance, Mr Joseph Conrad does for all practical purposes in his *Lord Jim* [1900]—then it gives a sort of depth, a sort of subjective reality, that no such cold, almost affectedly ironical detachment as that which distinguishes the work of Mr John Galsworthy, for example, can ever attain. And in some cases the whole art and delight of a novel may lie in the author's personal interventions; let such novels as *Elizabeth and her German Garden*, and the same writer's *Elizabeth in Rügen*, bear witness.[11]

Now, all this time I have been hacking away at certain hampering and limiting beliefs about the novel, letting it loose, as it were, in form and purpose; I have still to say just what I think the novel is, and where, if anywhere, its boundary-line ought to be drawn. It is by no means an easy task to define the novel. It is not a thing premeditated. It is a thing that has grown up into modern life, and taken upon itself uses and produced results that could not have been foreseen by its originators. Few of the important things in the collective life of man started out to be what they are. Consider, for example, all the unexpected aesthetic values, the inspiration and variety of emotional result which arises out of the cross-shaped plan of the Gothic cathedral, and the undesigned delight and wonder of white marble that has ensued, as I have been told, through the ageing and whitening of the realistically coloured statuary of the Greeks and Romans. Much of the charm of the old furniture and needlework, again, upon which the present time sets so much store, lies in acquired and unpremeditated qualities. And no doubt the novel grew up out of simple story-telling, and the universal desire of children, old and young alike, for a story. It is only slowly that we have developed the distinction of the novel from the romance, as being a story of human beings, absolutely credible and conceivable, as distinguished from human beings frankly endowed with the glamour, the wonder, the brightness, of a less exacting and more vividly eventful world. The novel is a story that demands, or professes to demand, no make-believe. The novelist undertakes to present you people and things as real as any that you can meet in an omnibus. And I suppose it is conceivable that a novel might exist which was just purely a story of that kind and nothing more. It might amuse you as one is amused by looking out of a window into a street, or listening to a piece of agreeable music, and that might be the limit of its effect. But almost always the novel is something more than that, and produces more effect than that. The novel has inseparable moral consequences. It leaves impressions, not simply of things seen, but of acts judged and made attractive or unattractive. They may prove very slight moral consequences, and very shallow moral impressions in the long run, but there they are, none the less, its inevitable accompaniments. It is unavoidable that this should be so. Even if the novelist attempts or affects to be impartial, he still cannot prevent his characters setting examples; he still cannot avoid, as people say, putting ideas into his readers' heads. The greater his skill, the more convincing his treatment, the more vivid his power of suggestion. And it is equally impossible for him not to betray his sense that the proceedings of this person are rather jolly and admirable, and of that, rather ugly and detestable. I suppose Mr Bennett, for example, would say that he should not do so; but it is as manifest to any disinterested observer that he greatly loves and admires his Card, as that Richardson admired his Sir Charles Grandison, or that Mrs Humphry Ward considers her Marcella a very fine and estimable young woman.[12] And I think it is just in this, that the novel is not simply a fictitious record of conduct, but also a study and judgement of conduct, and through that of the ideas that lead to conduct, that the real and increasing value—or perhaps to avoid controversy I had better say the real and increasing importance—of the novel and of the novelist in modern life comes in.

It is no new discovery that the novel, like the drama, is a

powerful instrument of moral suggestion. This has been understood in England ever since there has been such a thing as a novel in England. This has been recognized equally by novelists, novel-readers, and the people who wouldn't read novels under any condition whatever. Richardson wrote deliberately for edification, and *Tom Jones* is a powerful and effective appeal for a charitable, and even indulgent, attitude towards loose-living men. But excepting Fielding and one or two other of those partial exceptions that always occur in the case of critical generalizations, there is a definable difference between the novel of the past and what I may call the modern novel. It is a difference that is reflected upon the novel from a difference in the general way of thinking. It lies in the fact that formerly there was a feeling of certitude about moral values and standards of conduct that is altogether absent to-day. It wasn't so much that men were agreed upon these things—about these things there have always been enormous divergences of opinion—as that men were emphatic, cocksure, and unteachable about whatever they did happen to believe to a degree that no longer obtains. . . .[13]

. . . . [T]o-day, while we live in a period of tightening and extending social organization, we live also in a period of adventurous and insurgent thought, in an intellectual spring unprecedented in the world's history. There is an enormous criticism going on of the faiths upon which men's lives and associations are based, and of every standard and rule of conduct. And it is inevitable that the novel, just in the measure of its sincerity and ability, should reflect and co-operate in the atmosphere and uncertainties and changing variety of this seething and creative time.

And I do not mean merely that the novel is unavoidably charged with the representation of this wide and wonderful conflict. It is a necessary part of the conflict. The essential characteristic of this great intellectual revolution amidst which we are living to-day, that revolution of which the revival and restatement of nominalism under the name of pragmatism is the philosophical aspect, consists in the reassertion of the importance of the individual instance as against the generalization. All our social, political, moral problems are being approached in a new spirit, in an inquiring and experimental spirit, which has small respect for abstract principles and deductive rules. We perceive more and more clearly, for example, that the study of social organization is an empty and unprofitable study until we approach it as a study of the association and inter-reaction of individualized human beings inspired by diversified motives, ruled by traditions, and swayed by the suggestions of a complex intellectual atmosphere. And all our conceptions of the relationships between man and man, and of justice and rightfulness and social desirableness, remain something misfitting and inappropriate, something uncomfortable and potentially injurious, as if we were trying to wear sharp-edged clothes made for a giant out of tin, until we bring them to the test and measure of realized individualities.

And this is where the value and opportunity of the modern novel comes in. So far as I can see, it is the only medium through which we can discuss the great majority of the problems which are being raised in such bristling multitude by our contemporary social development. Nearly every one of those problems has at its core a psychological problem, and not merely a psychological problem, but one in which the idea of individuality is an essential factor. Dealing with most of these questions by a rule or a generalization is like putting a cordon round a jungle full of the most diversified sort of game. The hunting only begins when you leave the cordon behind you and push into the thickets. . . .[14]

. . . . Bumble is a magnificent figure of the follies and cruelties of ignorance in office—I would have every candidate for the post of workhouse master pass a severe examination upon *Oliver Twist* [1837–8]—but it is not only caricature and satire I demand. We must have not only the fullest treatment of the temptations, vanities, abuses, and absurdities of office, but all its dreams, its sense of constructive order, its consolations, its sense of service, and its nobler satisfactions. You may say that is demanding more insight and power in our novels and novelists than we can possibly hope to find in them. So much the worse for us. I stick to my thesis that the complicated social organization of to-day cannot get along without the amount of mutual understanding and mutual explanation such a range of characterization in our novels implies. The success of civilization amounts ultimately to a success of sympathy and understanding. If people cannot be brought to an interest in one another greater than they feel to-day, to curiosities and criticisms far keener, and co-operations far subtler, than we have now; if class cannot be brought to measure itself against, and interchange experience and sympathy with class, and temperament with temperament, then we shall never struggle very far beyond the confused discomforts and uneasiness of to-day, and the changes and complications of human life will remain as they are now, very like the crumplings and separations and complications of an immense avalanche that is sliding down a hill. And in this tremendous work of human reconciliation and elucidation, it seems to me it is the novel that must attempt most and achieve most.

You may feel disposed to say to all this: We grant the major premises, but why look to the work of prose fiction as the main instrument in this necessary process of, so to speak, sympathizing humanity together? Cannot this be done far more effectively through biography and autobiography, for example? Isn't there the lyric; and, above all, isn't there the play? Well, so far as the stage goes, I think it is a very charming and exciting form of human activity, a display of actions and surprises of the most moving and impressive sort; but beyond the opportunity it affords for saying startling and thought-provoking things—opportunities Mr Shaw, for example, has worked to the utmost limit—I do not see that the drama does much to enlarge our sympathies and add to our stock of motive ideas. And regarded as a medium for startling and thought-provoking things, the stage seems to me an extremely clumsy and costly affair. One might just as well go about with a pencil writing up the thought-provoking phrase, whatever it is, on walls. The drama excites our sympathies intensely, but it seems to me it is far too objective a medium to widen them appreciably, and it is that widening, that increase in the range of

H. G. Wells and Henry James

understanding, at which I think civilization is aiming. The case for biography, and more particularly autobiography, as against the novel, is, I admit, at the first blush stronger. You may say: Why give us these creatures of a novelist's imagination, these phantom and fantastic thinkings and doings, when we may have the stories of real lives, really lived—the intimate record of actual men and women? To which one answers: 'Ah, if one could! But it is just because biography does deal with actual lives, actual facts, because it radiates out to touch continuing interests and sensitive survivors, that it is so unsatisfactory, so untruthful. Its inseparable falsehood is the worst of all kinds of falsehood—the falsehood of omission. Think what an abounding, astonishing, perplexing person Gladstone must have been in life, and consider Lord Morley's *Life of Gladstone*, cold, dignified—not a life at all, indeed, so much as embalmed remains; the fire gone, the passions gone, the bowels carefully removed.[15] All biography has something of that post-mortem coldness and respect, and as for autobiography—a man may show his soul in a thousand half-conscious ways, but to turn upon oneself and explain oneself is given to no one. It is the natural liars and braggarts, your Cellinis and Casanovas,[16] men with a habit of regarding themselves with a kind of objective admiration, who do best in autobiography. And, on the other hand, the novel has neither the intense self-consciousness of autobiography nor the paralysing responsibilities of the biographer. It is by comparison irresponsible and free. Because its characters are figments and phantoms, they can be made entirely transparent. Because they are fictions, and you know they are fictions, so that they cannot hold you for an instant so soon as they cease to be true, they have a power of veracity quite beyond that of actual records. Every novel carries its own justification and its own condemnation in its success or failure to convince you that *the thing was so*. Now history, biography, blue-book, and so forth, can hardly ever get beyond the statement that the superficial fact was so.

You see now the scope of the claim I am making for the novel; it is to be the social mediator, the vehicle of understanding, the instrument of self-examination, the parade of morals and the exchange of manners, the factory of customs, the criticism of laws and institutions and of social dogmas and ideas. It is to be the home confessional, the initiator of knowledge, the seed of fruitful self-questioning. Let me be very clear here. I do not mean for a moment that the novelist is going to set up as a teacher, as a sort of priest with a pen, who will make men and women believe and do this and that. The novel is not a new sort of pulpit; humanity is passing out of the phase when men *sit under* preachers and dogmatic influences. But the novelist is going to be the most potent of artists, because he is going to present conduct, devise beautiful conduct, discuss conduct, analyse conduct, suggest conduct, illuminate it through and through. He will not teach, but discuss, point out, plead, and display. And this being my view you will be prepared for the demand I am now about to make for an absolutely free hand for the novelist in his choice of topic and incident and in his method of treatment; or rather, if I may presume to speak for other novelists, I would say it is not so much a demand we make as an intention we proclaim. We are going to write, subject only to our limitations, about the whole of human life. We are going to deal with political questions and religious questions and social questions. We cannot present people unless we have this free hand, this unrestricted field. What is the good of telling stories about people's lives if one may not deal freely with the religious beliefs and organizations that have controlled or failed to control them? What is the good of pretending to write about love, and the loyalties and treacheries and quarrels of men and women, if one must not glance at those varieties of physical temperament and organic quality, those deeply passionate needs and distresses from which half the storms of human life are brewed? We mean to deal with all these things, and it will need very much more than the disapproval of provincial librarians, the hostility of a few influential people in London, the scurrility of one paper, and the deep and obstinate silence of another,[17] to stop the incoming tide of aggressive novel-writing. We are going to write about it all. We are going to write about business and finance and politics and precedence and pretentiousness and decorum and indecorum, until a

H. G. Wells and Henry James

thousand pretences and ten thousand impostures shrivel in the cold, clear air of our elucidations. We are going to write of wasted opportunities and latent beauties until a thousand new ways of living open to men and women. We are going to appeal to the young and the hopeful and the curious, against the established, the dignified, and defensive. Before we have done, we will have all life within the scope of the novel.

NOTES

1 Wells did write appreciatively of *Almayer's Folly* (1895), but only briefly. His 'long . . . review' dealt with *An Outcast of the Islands* (q.v.).
2 Two paragraphs generally concerned with the 'revolt against that tired giant' have been omitted.
3 The noncomformist paper was the *British Weekly*. Wells, according to a letter of August (?) 1909 now in the possession of the Yale University Library, apparently refused to contribute to the *British Weekly*'s symposium.
4 Untraced.
5 Novels by Fielding (1749), Goldsmith (1766), Thackeray (1840), and Dickens (1852–3), respectively.
6 Poe made this point in a review of Hawthorne's *Twice-Told Tales* (*Graham's Magazine*, May 1842).
7 Micawber appears in *David Copperfield* (1849–50), Dick Swiveller in *The Old Curiosity Shop* (1840–1), and Mrs Gamp in *Martin Chuzzlewit* (1843–4). Falstaff's 'glorious glow' of course illuminates the last three plays of Shakespeare's Second Tetralogy and *The Merry Wives of Windsor*.
8 Thanks to the popularity of Sir Walter Scott, the price of books of fiction escalated to 31s. 6d. in the second quarter of the nineteenth century; but the 6s. reprint caused prices to decrease steadily from the 1860s on (see Altick, *op. cit.*, pp 263, 298ff.).
9 Compare 'The Paying Guest'.
10 On Mrs Craigie ('John Oliver Hobbes'), see 'The Method of Mr George Meredith', n 2. Wells's exact reference has not been discovered.
11 Two books (1898, 1904) by Elizabeth Mary, Countess Russell (d. 1941), with whom Wells was having an affair at the time (see Gordon N. Ray, *H. G. Wells and Rebecca West* [Yale University Press, New Haven, 1974], pp 13 and 17).
12 Bennett's Card is Edward Henry Machin, hero of *The Card* (1911)

H. G. Wells's Literary Criticism

and (later) *The Regent* (1913). Sir Charles Grandison (1754) and Marcella (1894) are the principal figures in the novels that bear their names.

13 The editors have left out two pages of the *Englishman* text (pp 160–2) in which Wells expatiates on this last point.
14 Here (pp 163–5 in *An Englishman* . . .) Wells gives examples.
15 The three-volume *Life of Gladstone* (1903) by John Morley (1838–1923) was the official biography of the great Victorian statesman.
16 Benvenuto Cellini (1500–71) and Giovanni Giacomo Casanova (1725–98) both wrote sensation-filled autobiographies.
17 The *Fortnightly* text (n.s. 90: November 1911, p 873) names the *Spectator* and the *Westminster Gazette*. The *Spectator* had denounced *Ann Veronica* as 'A Poisonous Book' (20 November 1909), and Wells had replied with an indignant letter to the editor (4 December 1909). See CH, pp 169–74.

H. G. Wells and Henry James
'OF ART, OF LITERATURE, OF MR HENRY JAMES'

Boon, *a literary farrago loosely patterned on W. H. Mallock's* The New Republic *(1877) and, still more distantly, on the satiric fictions of Thomas Love Peacock (1785–1866), appeared in 1915. Purportedly a 'Selection from the Literary Remains of George Boon . . . Prepared for Publication by Reginald Bliss', the book has little in the way of narrative coherence. What holds its components together is their common theme: 'the mind of the race' (also the title of Boon's unfinished* Magnum opus; *see pp 15—16 above). The sections of* Boon *reprinted here (pp 89—96, 99–108 of the first edition) are from the chapter devoted primarily to James (pp 84–128).*

Meanwhile Boon's plan was to make Mr George Moore and Mr Henry James wander off from the general dispute, and he invented a dialogue that even at the time struck me as improbable, in which both gentlemen pursue entirely independent trains of thought.

Mr Moore's conception of the projected symposium was something rather in the vein of the journeyings of Shelley, Byron, and their charming companions through France to Italy, but magnified to the dimensions of an enormous pilgrimage, enlarged to the scale of a stream of refugees. 'What, my dear James', he asked, 'is this mind of humanity at all without a certain touch of romance, of adventure? Even Mallock appreciated the significance of *frou-frou*;[1] but these fellows behind here . . . [.]'

To illustrate his meaning better, he was to have told, with an extraordinary and loving mastery of detail, of a glowing little experience that had been almost forced upon him at Nismes by a pretty little woman from Nebraska and the peculiar effect it had, and particularly the peculiar effect that the coincidence that Nebraska and Nismes begin with an 'N' and end so very differently, had had upon his imagination. . . .

Meanwhile Mr James, being anxious not merely to state but also to ignore, laboured through the long cadences of his companion as an indefatigable steam-tug might labour endlessly against a rolling sea, elaborating his own particular point about the proposed conference.

'Owing it as we do', he said, 'very, very largely to our friend Gosse,[2] to that peculiar, that honest but restless and, as it were, at times almost malignantly ambitious organizing energy of our friend, I cannot altogether—altogether, even if in any case I should have taken so extreme, so devastatingly isolating a step as, to put it violently, *stand out*; yet I must confess to a considerable anxiety, a kind of distress, an apprehension, the terror, so to speak, of the kerbstone, at all this stream of intellectual trafficking, of going to and fro, in a superb and towering manner enough no doubt, but still essentially going to and fro rather than in any of the completed senses of the word *getting there*, that does so largely constitute the aggregations and activities we are invited to traverse. My poor head, such as it is and as much as it can and upon such legs—save the mark!—as it can claim, must, I suppose, play its inconsiderable part among the wheels and the rearings and the toots and the whistles and all this uproar, this—Mm, Mm!—let us say, this *infernal* uproar, of the occasion; and if at times one has one's doubts before plunging in, whether after all, after the plunging and the dodging and the close shaves and narrow squeaks, one does begin to feel that one is getting through, whether after all one *will* get through, and whether indeed there is any getting through, whether, to deepen and enlarge and display one's doubt quite openly, there is in truth any sort of ostensible and recognizable other side attainable and definable at all, whether to put this thing with a lucidity that verges on the brutal, whether our amiable and in most respects our adorable Gosse isn't indeed preparing here and now, not the gathering together of a conference but the assembling, the *meet*, so to speak, of a wild-goose chase of an entirely desperate and hopeless description'.

At that moment Mr George Moore was saying: 'Little exquisite shoulders without a touch of colour and with just that suggestion of rare old ivory in an old shop window in some out-of-the-way corner of Paris that only the most patent abstinence from baths and the brutality of soaping—'

H. G. Wells and Henry James

Each gentleman stopped simultaneously.

Ahead the path led between box-hedges to a wall, and above the wall was a pine-tree, and the editor of the *New Age* was reascending the pine-tree in a laborious and resolute manner, gripping with some difficulty in his hand a large and very formidable lump of unpleasantness. . . .[3]

With a common impulse the two gentlemen turned back towards the house.

Mr James was the first to break the momentary silence. 'And so, my dear Moore, and so—to put it shortly—without any sort of positive engagement or entanglement or pledge or pressure—I *came*. And at the proper time and again with an entirely individual detachment and as little implication as possible I shall *go*. . . .'

Subsequently Mr James was to have buttonholed Hallery's American,[4] and in the warm bath of his sympathy to have opened and bled slowly from another vein of thought.

'I admit the abundance of—what shall I say?—*activities* that our friend is summoning, the tremendous wealth of matter, of material for literature and art, that has accumulated during the last few decades. No one could appreciate, could savour and watch and respond, more than myself to the tremendous growing clangour of the mental process as the last half-century has exhibited it. But when it comes to the enterprise of gathering it together, and not simply just gathering it together, but gathering it *all* together, then surely one must at some stage ask the question, *Why* all? Why, in short, attempt to a comprehensiveness that must be overwhelming when in fact the need is for a selection that shall not merely represent but elucidate and lead. Aren't we, after all, all of us after some such indicating projection of a leading digit, after such an insistence on the outstanding essential in face of this abundance, this saturation, this fluid chaos that perpetually increases? Here we are gathering together to celebrate and summarize literature in some sort of undefined and unprecedented fashion, and for the life of me I find it impossible to determine what among my numerous associates and friends and—to embrace still larger quantities of the stuff in hand—my contemporaries is considered to be the literature in question. So confused now are we between matter and treatment, between what is stated and documented and what is prepared and presented, that for the life of me I do not yet see whether we are supposed to be building an ark or whether by immersion and the meekest of submersions and an altogether complete submission of our distended and quite helpless carcasses to its incalculable caprice we are supposed to be celebrating and, in the whirling uncomfortable fashion of flotsam at large, indicating and making visible the whole tremendous cosmic inundation. . . .'

'You see,' Boon said, 'you can't now talk of literature without going through James. James is unavoidable. James is to criticism what Immanuel Kant is to philosophy—a partially comprehensible essential, an inevitable introduction. If you understand what James is up to and if you understand what James is not up to, then you are placed. You are in the middle of the critical arena. You are in a position to lay about you with significance. Otherwise. . . .

'I want to get this Hallery of mine, who is to be the hero of "The Mind of the Race", into a discussion with Henry James, but that, you know, is easier said than imagined. Hallery is to be one of those enthusiastic thinkers who emit highly concentrated opinion in gobbets, suddenly. James—isn't. . . .'

Boon meditated upon his difficulties. 'Hallery's idea of literature is something tremendously comprehensive, something that pierces always down towards the core of things, something that carries and changes all the activities of the race. This sort of thing.'

He read from a scrap of paper—

'"The thought of a community is the life of that community, and if the collective thought of a community is disconnected and fragmentary, then the community is collectively vain and weak. That does not constitute an incidental defect but essential failure. Though that community have cities such as the world has never seen before, fleets and hosts and glories, though it count its soldiers by the army corps and its children by the million, yet if it hold not to the reality of thought and formulated will beneath these outward things, it will pass, and all its glories will pass, like smoke before the wind, like mist beneath the sun; it will become at last only one more vague and fading dream upon the scroll of time, a heap of mounds and pointless history, even as are Babylon and Nineveh."'

'I've heard that before somewhere,' said Dodd.[5]

'Most of this dialogue will have to be quotation,' said Boon.

'He makes literature include philosophy?'

'Everything. It's all the central things. It's the larger Bible to him, a thing about which all the conscious direction of life resolves. It's alive with passion and will. Or if it isn't, then it ought to be. . . . And then as the antagonist comes this artist, this man who seems to regard the whole seething brew of life as a vat from which you skim, with slow, dignified gestures, works of art. . . . Works of art whose only claim is their art. . . . Hallery is going to be very impatient about art.'

'Ought there to be such a thing as a literary artist?' someone said.

'Ought there, in fact, to be Henry James?' said Dodd.

'I don't think so. Hallery won't think so. You see, the discussion will be very fundamental. There's contributory art, of course, and a way of doing things better or worse. Just as there is in war, or cooking. But the way of doing isn't the end. First the end must be judged—and then if you like talk of how it is done. Get there as splendidly as possible. But get there. James and George Moore, neither of them take it like that. They leave out getting there, or the thing they get to is so trivial as to amount to scarcely more than an omission. . . .'

Boon reflected. 'In early life both these men poisoned their minds in studios. Thought about pictures even might be less studio-ridden than it is. But James has never discovered that a novel isn't a picture. . . . That life isn't a studio. . . .

'He wants a novel to be simply and completely *done*. He wants it to have a unity, he demands homogeneity. . . . Why *should* a book have that? For a picture it's reasonable, because you have to see it all at once. But there's no need to see a book all at once. It's like wanting to have a whole county done in one style and period of architecture. It's like insisting that a walking tour must stick to one valley. . . .

'But James *begins* by taking it for granted that a novel is a work of art that must be judged by its oneness. Judged first by its oneness. Some one gave him that idea in the beginning of things and he has never found it out. He doesn't find things out. He doesn't even seem to want to find things out. You can see that in him; he is eager to accept things— elaborately. You can see from his books that he accepts etiquettes, precedences, associations, claims. That is his peculiarity. He accepts very readily and then—elaborates. He has, I am convinced, one of the strongest, most abundant minds alive in the whole world, and he has the smallest penetration. Indeed, he has no penetration. He is the culmination of the Superficial type. Or else he would have gone into philosophy and been greater even than his wonderful brother [6] . . . But here he is, spinning about, like the most tremendous of water-boatmen—you know those insects?—kept up by surface tension. As if, when once he pierced the surface, he would drown. It's incredible. A water-boatman as big as an elephant. I was reading him only yesterday *The Golden Bowl* [1904]; it's dazzling how never for a moment does he go through.'

'Recently he's been explaining himself,' said Dodd.

'His *Notes on Novelists* [1914]. It's one sustained demand for the picture effect. Which is the denial of the sweet complexity of life, of the pointing this way and that, of the spider on the throne. Philosophy aims at a unity and never gets there. . . . That true unity which we all suspect, and which no one attains, if it is to be got at all it is to be got by penetrating, penetrating down and through. The picture, on the other hand, is forced to a unity because it can see only one aspect at a time. I am doubtful even about that. Think of Hogarth or Carpaccio.[7] But if the novel is to follow life it must be various and discursive. Life is diversity and entertainment, not completeness and satisfaction. All actions are half-hearted, shot delightfully with wandering thoughts —about something else. All true stories are a felt of irrelevances. But James sets out to make his novels with the

H. G. Wells and Henry James

presupposition that they can be made continuously relevant. And perceiving the discordant things, he tries to get rid of them. He sets himself to pick the straws out of the hair of Life before he paints her. But without the straws she is no longer the mad woman we love. He talks of "selection", and of making all of a novel definitely *about* a theme. He objects to a "saturation" that isn't oriented. And he objects, if you go into it, for no clear reason at all. Following up his conception of selection, see what in his own practice he omits. In practice James's selection becomes just omission and nothing more. He omits everything that demands digressive treatment or collateral statement. For example, he omits opinions. In all his novels you will find no people with defined political opinions, no people with religious opinions, none with clear partisanships or with lusts or whims, none definitely up to any specific impersonal thing. There are no poor people dominated by the imperatives of Saturday night and Monday morning, no dreaming types—and don't we all more or less live dreaming? And none are ever decently forgetful. All that much of humanity he clears out before he begins his story. It's like cleaning rabbits for the table.

'But you see how relentlessly it follows from the supposition that the novel is a work of art aiming at pictorial unities!

'All art too acutely self-centred comes to this sort of thing. James's denatured people are only the equivalent in fiction of those egg-faced, black-haired ladies, who sit and sit, in the Japanese colour-prints, the unresisting stuff for an arrangement of blacks. . . .

'Then with the eviscerated people he has invented he begins to make up stories. What stories they are! Concentrated on suspicion, on a gift, on possessing a "piece" of old furniture, on what a little girl may or may not have noted in an emotional situation. These people cleared for artistic treatment never make lusty love, never go to angry war, never shout at an election or perspire at poker; never in any way *date*. . . . And upon the petty residuum of human interest left to them they focus minds of Jamesian calibre. . . .

'The only living human motives left in the novels of

Henry James are a certain avidity and an entirely superficial curiosity. Even when relations are irregular or when sins are hinted at, you feel that these are merely attitudes taken up, gambits before the game of attainment and over-perception begins. . . . His people nose out suspicions, hint by hint, link by link. Have you ever known living human beings do that? The thing his novel is *about* is always there. It is like a church lit but without a congregation to distract you, with every light and line focused on the high altar. And on the altar, very reverently placed, intensely there, is a dead kitten, an egg-shell, a bit of string. . . . Like his "Altar of the Dead",[8] with nothing to the dead at all. . . . For if there was they couldn't all be candles and the effect would vanish. . . . And the elaborate, copious emptiness of the whole Henry James exploit is only redeemed and made endurable by the elaborate, copious wit. Upon the desert his selection has made Henry James erects palatial metaphors. . . . The chief fun, the only exercise, in reading Henry James is this clambering over vast metaphors. . . .

'Having first made sure that he has scarcely anything left to express, he then sets to work to express it, with an industry, a wealth of intellectual stuff that dwarfs Newton. He spares no resource in the telling of his dead inventions. He brings up every device of language to state and define. Bare verbs he rarely tolerates. He splits his infinitives and fills them up with adverbial stuffing. He presses the passing colloquialism into his service. His vast paragraphs sweat and struggle; they could not sweat and elbow and struggle more if God Himself was the processional meaning to which they sought to come. And all for tales of nothingness. . . . It is leviathan retrieving pebbles. It is a magnificent but painful hippopotamus resolved at any cost, even at the cost of its dignity, upon picking up a pea which has got into a corner of its den. Most things, it insists, are beyond it, but it can, at any rate, modestly, and with an artistic singleness of mind, pick up that pea. . . .'

NOTES

1 The first section of this chapter of *Boon* is set in the very same garden

H. G. Wells and Henry James

wherein Mr Laurence tells Miss Merton about 'the romance and adventure' of his now-dead uncle (in Mallock's *New Republic*).

2 Edmund Gosse (1849–1928) is described earlier in *Boon* as 'the official British man of letters' (p 76).

3 In Wells's fiction, A. R. Orage (1873–1928), after being 'refused admission' to the premises, 'gets into a point of vantage in a small pine-tree . . ., and from this he contributes a number of comments that are rarely helpful, always unamiable, and frequently in the worst possible taste' (p 86). Wells in 1912 had considered suing Orage for having made unauthorized changes in an article of his printed in the *New Age* (see Norman and Jeanne Mackenzie, *H. G. Wells* [Simon and Schuster, New York, 1973], p 277).

4 Identified elsewhere in *Boon* only as 'a quiet Harvard sort of man speaking meticulously accurate English' (p 85).

5 Edward Clodd (1840–1930), 'a leading member of the Rationalist Press Association, a militant agnostic, and a dear, compact man' (*Boon*, pp 44–5). The paragraph that Boon has just read is taken from the chapter of Wells's *Mankind in the Making* entitled 'Thought in the Modern State'.

6 William James (1842–1910), the Pragmatist philosopher, whom Wells greatly admired.

7 Vittore Carpaccio (c1460–1525/6) and William Hogarth (1697–1764) were both 'narrative' painters.

8 See 'Three *Yellow-Book* Story-Tellers'.

H. G. Wells's Literary Criticism
'THE NOVEL OF IDEAS'

In this preface to Babes in the Darkling Wood *(1940), Wells attempts to explain and justify the kind of fiction that that penultimate novel of his exemplifies. 'The Novel of Ideas', though not literally his last word on the subject (which he takes up again a year later in the foreword to* You Can't be too Careful), *is perhaps his most important.*

It is characteristic of most literary criticism to be carelessly uncritical of the terms it uses and violently partisan and dogmatic in its statements about them. No competent Linnaeus has ever sat down to sort out the orders and classes, genera and varieties, of fiction, and no really sane man ever will. They have no fixed boundaries; all sorts interbreed as shamelessly as dogs, and they pass at last by indefinite gradations into more or less honest fact telling, into 'historical reconstruction', the *roman à clef*, biography, history and autobiography. So the literary critic, confronted with a miscellany of bookish expression far more various than life itself, has an excellent excuse for the looseness of his vocabulary, if not for his exaltations and condemnations. Unhappily he insists on adopting types for his preference and he follows fashions. My early life as a naive, spontaneous writer was much afflicted by the vehement advocacy by Henry James II, Joseph Conrad, Edward Garnett and Ford Madox Hueffer, of something called *The* Novel, and by George Moore of something called *The* Short Story. There were all sorts of things forbidden for *The* Novel; there must be no explanation of the ideas animating the characters, and the author himself had to be as invisible and unheard-of as God; for no conceivable reason. So far as *The* Short Story went, it gave George Moore the consolation of calling Kipling's stories, and in fact any short stories that provoked his ready jealousy, 'anecdotes'. Novelists were arranged in order of merit that made the intelligent reader doubt his own intelligence, and the idea of 'Progress' was urged upon the imaginative writer. Conrad was understood to be in the van of progress; Robert Louis Stevenson had 'put the clock back', and so on. Quite inconspicuous young writers were able to believe that in some mysterious technical way they were leaving Defoe and Sterne far away behind them.

There has been no such 'progress' in human brains. Against this sort of thing, which for many reasons I found tiresome and unpalatable, I rebelled. I declared that a novel, as distinguished from the irresponsible plausibilities of romance or the invention in imaginative stories of hitherto unthought-of human circumstances, could be any sort of honest treatment of the realities of human behaviour in narrative form. Conduct was the novel's distinctive theme. It was and is and must be, if we are to have any definition of a novel. All writing should be done as well as it can be done, wit and vigour are as God wills, but pretentious artistry is a minor amateurism on the flank of literature.

This present story belongs to a school to which I have always been attracted, and in which I have already written several books. The merit of my particular contributions may be infinitesimal, but that does not alter the fact that they follow in a great tradition, the tradition of discussing fundamental human problems in dialogue form.

The dialogue, written or staged, is one of the oldest forms of literary expression. Very early, men realized the impossibility of abstracting any philosophy of human behaviour from actual observable flesh and blood. As soon can you tear a brain away from its blood and membranes: it dies. Abstract philosophy is the deadest of stuff; one disintegrating *hortus siccus* follows another; I am astounded at the implacable scholarly industry of those who still write Textbooks of Philosophy. And your psychological handbook is only kept alive by a stream of anecdote. The Socratic Dialogue on the other hand produces character after character to state living views, to have them ransacked by an interlocutor who is also a character subject to all the infirmities of the flesh. Plato's dramas of the mind *live* to this day. They may have inspired—it is a fancy of mine for which there is only very slight justification—that kindred Socratic novel, the Book of Job. For that magnificent creation my admiration is unstinted. I have made a close study of it; I have in fact not only studied it but modernized it, traced it over, character by character and speech, in *The Undying Fire* [1919]. The Book of Job has been compared to a Greek tragedy, to the *Prometheus Bound* of Aeschylus, for example, but I see it myself, naturally enough, from the angle of the writer. It was written to be read.

Manifestly the novel of ideas and the play of ideas converge. My friend George Bernard Shaw has lived a long, vivid life, putting the discussion of ideas on to the English stage,[1] to the infinite exasperation of generation after generation of dramatic critics, who insist upon puppets with heads of solid wood. Then they can get the drama of pure situation within the compass of overnight judgements. From opposite directions Shaw and I approach what is to us and, I submit, firmly and immodestly, to all really intelligent people, the most interesting thing in the world, the problems of human life and behaviour as we find them incarnate in persons. We have no claim to be pioneers, but by an inner necessity we were revivalists. *Hamlet* is evidently a dramatic dialogue about suicide in face of intolerable conditions, and *Julius Caesar* a treatment of political assassination. But by the time Shaw began dramatic criticism ideas had vanished from the English theatre for generations. Mallock and Peacock,[2] however, had kept the dialogue alive through the darkest period of the three volume novel.

I found myself, and I got to the dialogue novel, through a process of trial and error. The critical atmosphere was all against me. As I felt about rebelliously among the possibilities of fiction, I found certain of my characters were displaying an irresistible tendency to break out into dissertation. Many critical readers, trained to insist on a straight story, objected to these talkers; they said they were my self-projections, author's exponents. But in many cases these obtrusive individuals were not saying things I thought, but, what is a very different thing, things I wanted to put into shape by having them said. An early type of this sort of book was *Ann Veronica*. She is a young woman who soliloquizes and rhapsodizes incessantly, revealing the ideas of the younger intelligentsia round about 1910, which I had found very interesting indeed. Before then no one had realized there

H. G. Wells and Henry James

was an English intelligentsia. The book is not a dialogue, simply because no one answers Ann Veronica. It interested a number of people who did not realize fully what bad taste they showed in being interested.

I made a much nearer approach to the fully developed novel of ideas in *Mr Britling Sees It Through* [1916]. I was getting more cunning about the business. I made him a writer and I used the letters home of his son to say a number of things that could be said in no other way. In *Joan and Peter* [1918], I did what I think was a better book than *Mr Britling*; it is a dialogue about education, and I centred the discussion on the perplexities of the guardian who has to find a school for these young people. All my most recent books, *Brynhild* [1937], *Dolores* [1938] (apart from the scandalous misbehaviour of her dog and a few such uncontrollable incidents), *The Holy Terror* [1939], are primarily discussions carried on through living characters; it is for the discussion of behaviour they were written, and to cut out the talk would be like cutting a picture out of its frame.

And now I will come to the plan and purpose of this present book, which is the most comprehensive and ambitious dialogue novel I have ever attempted. I will try to explain certain devices I have had to adopt, and certain unavoidable necessities of the treatment. At the present time a profounder change in human thought and human outlook is going on than has ever occurred before. The great literary tradition I follow demands that this be rendered in terms of living human beings. It must be shown in both word and act. This I attempt here. So far as my observation and artistry as a novelist have enabled me to achieve it, there is not a single individual in this book that you might not meet and recognize in the street. If you have had any experience in writing fiction, I think you will find that you can take any of my characters out of this book and invent a meeting between them and the real people you know. But because of the very great burden of fresh philosophical matter that this novel has to carry, I have chosen my chief individuals from among the sort of people who would be closest to that matter.

. . . . Again and again, to do them justice, it has been

necessary to clarify, condense, expand or underline their words. Nevertheless, what is given here is what they imagined they were saying, and what indeed they meant. And I do not know of any way of writing the novel of ideas that can dispense with such magnified and crystallized conversations and meditations. . . .

That magnification and clarification applies in a greater or lesser degree to nearly all the talk in every novel of ideas. It is the exact opposite of that 'flow of consciousness' technique, with which Virginia Woolf, following in the footsteps of Dorothy Richardson, has experimented more or less successfully.[3] Thereby personalities are supposed to be stippled out by dabs of response—which after all have to be verbalized. Uncle Robert, when he discourses on a University Education, tells Stella a score of things that as a matter of fact he knew she knew. Later on he and Gemini perform a sort of duet of mutual information.[4] They explain the whole gist and bearing of the new and entirely revolutionary philosophy of behaviourism to one another, cheerfully, uncivilly and without embarrassment. I know of no better way of setting out this new way of thinking. To the best of my ability I contrive a situation that makes their talk as plausible as possible, and I keep rigorously true to their mental characters. In this fashion I may manage to get away with the understanding reader. But against the carping realist who objects that people do not talk like this, there is no reply, except that people know what they mean much better than they say it, and that the most unrighteous thing a reporter can do to a speaker or lecturer is to report him verbatim. So I put this dialogue novel of contemporary ideas before you with characters I claim to be none the less living because through my lens you see them larger and clearer than life.

NOTES

1 See 'H. G. Wells as Drama Critic for the *Pall Mall Gazette*'.
2 See the headnote to 'Of Art, of Literature, of Mr Henry James'.

H. G. Wells and Henry James

3 On Dorothy Richardson, see 'James Joyce', n 3. Virginia Woolf (1882–1941) embarked on her novelistic experiments in the 'flow of consciousness' technique in *Jacob's Room* (1922)—and at about the same time, defined her antagonism to Wells, Bennett, and Galsworthy as novelists in an essay entitled 'Modern Fiction'.
4 The main discussants in *Babes*.

6 On Science Fiction, Utopian Fiction, and Fantasy

Those books of his that Wells refers to sometimes as 'scientific romances', sometimes as 'fantasies', comprise almost a third of his total fictional output, and more than two-thirds of that output to the end of 1910. By them he first made his reputation as a writer. In them what Arnold Bennett spoke of as the 'philosophic quality'[1] that individuates his work manifests itself unmistakably. Yet his critical utterances reveal him to be of two minds concerning fiction of this sort, including—indeed, particularly—his own.

The ambivalence, especially prominent in his pronouncements of the 1930s, attains fullest expression in the preface to his *Scientific Romances*. As a statement of his guiding principles, and also for its insights about the nature of science fiction generally, this preface remains indispensable. It cannot, however, be regarded as a straightforward defence of its author's practice. While he insists upon the radical differences between his science fiction and Jules Verne's, and aligns himself with a tradition going back to Lucian and Apuleius, he continually resorts to a rhetoric of self-deprecation in arguing his case.

His opening remarks about Verne, together with his subsequent comparison of *The First Men in the Moon* (1900–1) to *De la terre à la lune* . . . (1865) and *Autour de la lune* (1870), suggest that he may be thinking of the Frenchman's accusation of thirty years earlier, that Wells's stories 'do not repose on very scientific bases'. 'There is no rapport between his work and mine', Verne had told a reporter for *T.P.'s Weekly* (in 1903):

> I go to the moon in a cannon-ball, discharged from a cannon. Here there is no invention. He goes to Mars in an airship, which he constructs of a metal which does away with the law of gravitation. 'Ça c'est très joli,' cried Monsieur Verne in an animated way, 'but show me this metal. Let him produce it'.[2]

On Science Fiction, Utopian Fiction, and Fantasy

Wells, in his 1933 preface, substantially agrees with Verne's point. As he puts it, Verne 'dealt almost always with actual possibilities of invention and discovery'; whereas such 'exercises of the imagination' as *The Invisible Man* and *The War of the Worlds* 'do not aim to project a serious possibility'. Their object is not to arrive at scientifically plausible 'forecasts' of things to come, but to render the 'fantastic' situation 'human and real'. 'The invention' in them 'is nothing in itself': it has the status of a pure 'hypothesis', which, if rigorously adhered to, allows the writer to acquire a 'new angle' for 'looking at human feelings and human ways'.

Wells's emphasis on the 'new angle' that his 'scientific fantasies' bring to the portrayal of human affairs may be said to look forward to recent theories about the 'speculative' and 'cognitively estranged' nature of science fiction.[3] At the same time, his call for rigour and realism in working out the consequences of the hypothetical 'invention' reaffirms principles that he had espoused as a reviewer of fiction for Frank Harris. In those days, he had demanded that writers of fantasy master 'the necessary trick of commonplace detail that renders horrors'—or anything else quite out of the ordinary—'convincing' (see 'The Three Impostors'). 'Fantasy', he had warned, is not a license for the arbitrary; it does not mean 'anyhow': 'granted the fantastic assumption, the most strenuous consistency must be observed in its development'.[4] What made *Lilith*, in his view, 'fantastic to wildness and well-nigh past believing' was George MacDonald's refusal to abide by that 'elementary rule'. He nevertheless conceived of MacDonald's 'metaphysical fiction' as having a basic premise and overall intent rather like *The Time Machine*'s. Certainly he found *Lilith* far more congenial than Max Pemberton's *The Impregnable City* or any other book by Verne's imitators—or by Verne himself. Although a passage of 'realistic description' might count as a redeeming quality in a story like Pemberton's, the technological 'novelties' 'invented, . . . but unhappily not patented by Jules Verne' did not.

The 1933 preface, however, is not merely a systematic restatement of principles that Wells had been endorsing all along. He himself had written a number of books which he categorized, in his 1921 preface to *The Sleeper Awakes*, as 'fantasias of possibility'. These 'fantasias', which he usually thought of as forming a distinct group, are not represented in the volume of *Scientific Romances*. But this does not mean that he was invariably willing to concede the 'impossibility' of all the works in that collection. At one time, for instance, he had defended Moreau's experiments with 'the limits of individual plasticity' as practicable, at least in theory.[5] On occasion, he refers to *The Time Machine* as an example of the 'fiction of prophecy' (as in 'Fiction about the Future'). And in the 1933 preface itself, he implies that he considers *Food of the Gods* to be a kind of prophetic allegory.

By defining 'the anticipatory inventions of the great Frenchman' in opposition to 'fantasies' such as these, Wells strictly delimits the territory that he assigns to Verne. If Wells's 'scientific romances' have nothing to do with it, then the realm of 'practical possibility' over which he allows Verne dominion must consist only of 'forecasts' of 'things' that may come to be, not of their human—and social— consequences. In other words, it comprises what C. S. Lewis would later call 'the fiction of Engineers'.[6] It seems likely that Wells's intention here is to dissociate his own fiction not only from Verne's, but from that of the most recent group of Verne's disciples: the writers for the new science-fiction magazines, of whose existence he had recently become aware. For three years after the launching of *Amazing Stories* in 1926, he and his agents had been engaged in a querulous correspondence with Hugo Gernsback, the magazine's editor, over the fees for reprinting a large proportion of his early stories.[7] It is clear from the correspondence that Wells viewed Gernsback's whole operation with distaste; and Gernsback was an outspoken advocate of the type of 'anticipation' that Wells associates with Verne. Wells's discussion of the contrast between himself and 'the great Frenchman' is therefore rather more topical than it might at first appear to be.

Apart from its polemical features, the 1933 preface reflects Wells's disenchantment with his own 'inventions'. He had some time ago become convinced that at least one of his books presented 'a fantastic possibility no longer possible'

On Science Fiction, Utopian Fiction, and Fantasy

(see the 'Preface to *The Sleeper Awakes*'). He in effect takes that conclusion as the starting point for his argument about the 'fantasies' collected as his *Scientific Romances*. Admitting at the outset their 'impossibility', he goes on to downplay the philosophical and scientific aspects of his work.

The scientific component of his 'scientific romances' is far from incidental to the kind of integrity that he demands of 'fantasy'. Indeed, their cognitive or 'prophetic' intent derives from the way in which they incorporate and take over scientific theories and modes of thought. Arnold Bennett, perhaps at his friend's instigation and certainly with his approval, wrote in his essay on 'Herbert George Wells and his Work' of the 'philosophic quality' that separates Wells's stories from Verneian or 'pseudo-scientific romances'. Wells in his younger days inclined to stress that same quality. Though he publicly objected to *The British Barbarians* for being 'neither philosophy nor fiction' (see 'Mr Grant Allen's New Novel'), in a private letter he confided to its author: 'I believe that this field of scientific romance with a philosophical element which I am trying to cultivate, belongs properly to you'.[8] But in his 1933 preface, Wells slights that 'philosophical element'. He likewise minimizes the significance of the explanatory scientific content of his 'fantasies', deeming it nothing more than 'an ingenious use of scientific patter', an 'up to date' means for creating an air of plausibility that is no longer obtainable by recourse to the 'fetish stuff' of magic. His 'scientific romances', he now argues, 'are appeals for human sympathy quite as much as any "sympathetic" novel'; and are accordingly to be assessed by the standards of novelistic excellence, not those of philosophical or scientific insight. At the same time, he shows few signs of sharing the confident artistic estimate of his romances that is to be found in the pioneering essays of Bennett, Yevgeny Zamyatin, and others.[9] Although he notes the kinship of his stories to Swift's, Wells tends to play down their seriousness and their continuing interest. It is as if these 'fantasies' based upon an 'impossible hypothesis' had turned out—in their author's view—to be as ephemeral as Verneian science fiction after all. While they may not have the immediacy of his deliberately topical 'fantasias of possibility', their thematic content, he suggests, has been similarly determined by the historical moment in which each was written. On the other hand, dealing as they do with 'life in the mass and life in general as distinguished from life in the individual experience', they fall short of those standards by which he gauges the enduring interest of a realistic novel. Nor is Wells able to take refuge, in the 1933 preface, in any broad defiance of the idea of literary permanence. Rather, the self-deprecation of this essay reflects his brooding sense of failure both as a novelist and as a prophet.

In fiction, 'fantasy', and journalism Wells had done more than any other writer in the first third of the twentieth century to warn his contemporaries of the destructiveness that could be unleashed by modern civilization. His distress at the onset of the First World War had been succeeded by the conviction that its termination would present a unique opportunity for constructing a better and safer world. Yet by 1933 he had become convinced of the inevitability of the second major conflict in a generation. It is with the bitterness of a prophet who has been turned into a court jester that he now professes to be weary of 'talking in playful parables' and 'doing imaginative books that do not touch imaginations'.

Throughout his years of journalism and prophecy, Wells continued to hold to his hierarchical preference for the novel over any other kind of fiction. That preference is as evident in his pronouncements of the 1930s as it had been in the 1890s. In his autobiography he describes his bent as a young writer towards 'fantasy' as 'a sign of growing intelligence that I was realizing my exceptional ignorance of the contemporary world' (*ExA* 6:2). This would imply that the writing of 'fantasy' was a mere stage in his literary apprenticeship, rather than the discovery of a legitimate mode of social criticism and imaginative exploration in its own right.

Strange as it must seem, the author most responsible for defining the direction of science fiction in the twentieth century always regarded his 'scientific romances' as substitutes for the novel—and as inadequate substitutes at that. He never called any of them 'science fiction'. Nor did he otherwise differentiate them categorically from 'fantasy' or 'romance'. With or without the qualifying word 'scientific', he often employed the latter terms interchangeably: to his way of thinking, they were equivalent in being names for any fiction outside the strictly realistic mode. The 'scientific romance' or 'fantasy' might serve for embodying sociological 'criticism of life' and for discussing matters of social importance. But to do more than approximate 'the highest form of literary art' in those respects was, in his view, beyond the scope of romance or fantasy. Only the novelist could give life to ideas by incorporating them in fiction as 'living, breathing individuals' (see 'The Novel of Types').

Yet, despite his declared intention of abandoning 'the possibilities of fantasy', Wells as an artist remained as committed to them as he had ever been. Peculiarly enough, the most grandiose of his prophecies, *The Shape of Things to Come*, was published in the very year when he was gloomily announcing: 'The world in the presence of cataclysmal realities has no need for fresh cataclysmal fantasies'. In fact, every one of his dozen or so books of fiction from the 1930s and 40s could be placed under the heading of 'fantasy'; and if his two film-scripts be numbered among them, the majority must also be classed as science fiction. Even novels such as *The Bulpington of Blup* (1932), *Apropos of Dolores* (1938), and *Babes in the Darkling Wood* (1940) deal in various ways with the clash between the fantasizing mind and reality.

While he thus continued to preoccupy himself with 'fantasy' in one sense or another, Wells repeatedly expressed reservations concerning it. 'Fiction about the Future' indicates that he was conscious of, and troubled by, the discrepancy, but does nothing to resolve it. In this talk, broadcast over Australian radio in 1938, he claims that he has never succeeded in writing a novel about the future; he has confined himself to 'romances and pseudo-histories', which can be 'manage[d] with broad generalizations'. Once again he extols the novel over any other kind of fiction. And once again, but now with a poignancy not wholly disguised by his air of self-deprecating whimsy, he voices his misgivings as to the value of much of his work: no one 'who dreams of writing for posterity . . . will ever think twice of engaging in this ephemeral but amusing art, the fiction of prophecy—on which I have spent so much of my time'.

H. G. Wells's Literary Criticism

The key to Wells's final sense of his own achievement might be found at the beginning of his very much earlier essay, 'About Sir Thomas More' (1908). 'There are some writers who are chiefly interesting in themselves', he says, 'and some whom chance and the agreement of men have picked out as symbols and convenient indications of some particular group or temperament of opinions'. In his early and middle years, neither Wells nor his critics doubted that he was one of those who are 'chiefly interesting in themselves'. His confidence on this point reaches its high-water mark in *Tono-Bungay*, written at a time when he was expressing his desire 'to get on to the work that has always attracted me most, and render some aspects of this great spectacle of life and feeling in which I find myself in terms of individual experience and character'.[10] Yet he would subsequently look back on *Tono-Bungay* as the nearest he had come to a 'deliberate attempt upon The Novel' (*ExA* 5:5). As he approached his seventieth year, he succumbed more and more to the conviction that his life's work was merely the symbol of 'some particular group or temperament of opinions'. Whether it proceeded from belated modesty, or world-weariness, or a sense of defeat, self-deprecation typifies Wells's utterances of his later years. In keeping with that attitude, he subtitled his autobiography 'Discoveries and Conclusions of a Very Ordinary Brain—Since 1866', and regularly treated his most original and characteristic writings as if they too were rather ordinary. Thus, while his essays on science fiction, utopian fiction, and fantasy are without doubt classic statements on their subjects, his estimate in them of the value of his own work should not be (and, in the event, has not been) taken as definitive.

NOTES

1 Bennett, 'Herbert George Wells and his Work', *Cosmopolitan Magazine*, 33 (August 1902), pp 465–71; reprinted in Wilson, pp 260–76.
2 'Jules Verne Revisited', by Robert H. Sherard, *T.P.'s Weekly*, 2 (9 October 1903), 589; reprinted in CH, pp 101–2. Ironically enough, Verne confuses *The First Men in the Moon* with Robert Cromie's *A Plunge into Space*, for the second (1891) edition of which Verne supplied a preface

introducing readers to his 'English disciple'. Wells, however, does not mention this, even though he would have (again?) come across the text of the interview in Geoffrey West's biography (see West, p 153n). It is also instructive to compare Wells's 1933 preface with Bennett's 1902 essay (see n 1 above).

3 See Damon Knight, *In Search of Wonder* (Advent Publishers, Chicago, 1967), pp 1–2; and Darko Suvin, 'On the Poetics of the Science Fiction Genre', *College English*, 34 (1972), pp 373–82, revised as pp 3–15 of *Metamorphoses of Science Fiction: On the Poetics and History of a Literary Genre* (Yale University Press, New Haven & London, 1979).

4 Wells enunciates this 'elementary rule' of the fantastic in a review of John Davidson's *The Pilgrimage of Strongsoul; and Other Stories* ('The Immature Fantastic', SR 82: 7 November 1896, p 500).

5 See 'Correspondence: "The Island of Dr Moreau"', SR 82: 7 November 1896, p 497, as well as 'The Limits of Individual Plasticity', SR 79: 19 January 1895, pp 89–90.

6 C. S. Lewis, 'On Science Fiction', in *Of Other Worlds: Essays and Stories*, ed. Walter Hooper (Harcourt, Brace, and World, New York, 1967), pp 59–73.

7 Gernsback's unpublished letters to Wells, with Wells's marginalia, are in the Wells Collection at the University of Illinois.

8 This undated reply to a letter from Allen (11 June 1895) is quoted by David Y. Hughes (see 'Mr Grant Allen's New Novel', n 1).

9 For Bennett's illuminating but too-often-neglected essay, see n 1 above; Zamyatin's 1922 tribute to Wells as the writer who established science fiction as a mode of social criticism appears in CH, pp 258–74; *A Soviet Heretic: Essays* by Yevgeny Zamyatin, ed. and trans. Mirra Ginsburg (University of Chicago Press, Chicago & London, 1970), pp 259–70, contains a later (1924) version of the same essay.

10 'Mr Wells Explains Himself', *loc. cit.*, p 342.

H. G. Wells's Literary Criticism
ON MAX PEMBERTON

Sir Max Pemberton (1863–1950) wrote more than three dozen works of fiction, most of them adventure stories. The Impregnable City *is an early example, replete with science-fictional gadgets. Wells (SR 80: 3 August 1895, p 150) thought it inferior to* The Little Huguenot, *a conventional tale of adventure by the same author.*

Mr Max Pemberton and Mr William Le Queux have presented the world with their portraits in the forefront of their volumes,[1] a pretty fancy, intimating a sense of the personal interest their work has aroused, which wins upon the humour of the reviewer. Mr Max Pemberton is not, as we had rashly anticipated, a composite photograph, there is not the faintest touch of either Stevenson, Jules Verne, Mr Rider Haggard, Mr Griffiths [sic],[2] or Mr Stanley Weyman[3] in his face. For these one must search his works. His city is that impossible place in the South Pacific inhabited by philosophical Anarchists, and fitted with electric bells, submarine ships, and every modern convenience, to which Mr Griffiths has recently made an excursion. It was invented, we believe, but unhappily not patented, by Jules Verne. This time the coast of it is precipitous like a wall, and one reaches it by Mr Rider Haggard's rocky tunnel. Having arrived and refreshed oneself, one turns round with a confident air for the young woman of surpassing beauty, and the swift dart strikes home without the slightest delay. One Adam Monk gradually develops, as the story proceeds, into our dear departed friend, that mighty Alan of the whistling sword whom David Balfour knew, the resemblance completing itself when he and Max Pemberton stand side by side and fight a multitude of insurgent ruffians. But this tone is perhaps ungrateful. Mr Max Pemberton writes for boys and not for reviewers, and if he deals in a mixed pickle of incident rather than a dish of fresh invention, he may plead the narrow reading of the average boy. In that case the average boy may console him for the unappreciative reviewer. One thing at least we have found new and good in

On Science Fiction, Utopian Fiction, and Fantasy

the book, and that is the description of the cavernous valley in which the island stored its malcontents. It was suggested beyond doubt by the accounts of the stockades in which the Confederate States of America kept their prisoners of war, but none the less it is an exceedingly effective piece of description. But it does not to our mind redeem the offence of those conventional Anarchists warring on society with all the latest novelties and quite regardless of expense. Surely even the schoolboy is sick of them by this time. Mr Max Pemberton can do better things than that, as his other book, *The Little Huguenot*, witnesses. It is in quite a different vein altogether; Mr Stanley Weyman might reasonably claim the inspiration of it, but the sentiment of it is original, and honestly, well, and delicately done.

NOTES

1 This segment of Wells's 'Fiction' column includes a notice of *Stolen Souls* by the prolific William Le Queux (1864–1927).
2 A few weeks before this notice appeared, Wells had panned George Chetwyn Griffith's *The Outlaws of the Air*, which he recommended for 'those who can endure Mr Verne at his worst' (SR 79: 22 June 1895, p 839).
3 On Weyman, see 'On Lang and Buchan', n 7. See also 'The Lost Stevenson' and the two reviews of books by Haggard.

H. G. Wells's Literary Criticism
ON GEORGE MACDONALD

*George MacDonald (1824–1905) took up fiction as a means of publicizing those religious views of his that had got him dismissed from the Congregationalist ministry (in 1853) for heresy. Though he wrote a number of novels, he is chiefly remembered for his fantasies, which had a profound influence on C. S. Lewis, J. R. R. Tolkien, Charles Williams, and others. Even Wells (SR 80: 19 October 1895, p 513) saw in—or rather, read into—*Lilith *something with which he could sympathize.*

For wealth of fanciful imaginings few contemporary novelists can compare with Dr MacDonald. In *Lilith* he has returned to the vein of his delightful Phantasies,[1] and the book is a perfect jungle of exuberant extravagance, complicated with metaphysics, whilst allegory runs in and out of the tangle, and unexpected gay-coloured flowers of digression are seen amidst the thicket of story. The leading idea, a mathematical conception full of romantic possibilities that no one has cared to touch, has been lying unused for years, but to-day is the day of metaphysical fiction, and Dr MacDonald has been lucky to secure the first handling of it. Briefly the idea is this. Assuming there are more than three spatial dimensions, then in a space of four or more dimensions any number of three dimensional universes can be packed, just as in a space of three dimensions there is room for any number of plane or two dimensional universes. And one such three dimensional universe might be almost touching another at every point, just as one plane universe might be at an infinitesimal distance from another throughout its extent. Clearly once your born romancer has realized this infinite series of universes, his one desire is to invent a way into some of them. Once there you may do what you like, create such animals and plants as please you, and in all things follow the desire of your heart. In *Lilith* this long-sought way is attained ingeniously enough, and it is needless to say that the universe into which Dr MacDonald takes his readers is fantastic to wildness and well-nigh past believing. In fact, to be frankly just, it is altogether too fantastic. Dr

On Science Fiction, Utopian Fiction, and Fantasy

MacDonald's critical and constructive faculties are relatively too weak for his fertile imagination, and, as a consequence, he wastes to a large extent his unique opportunity of a realistic wonderland. His book passes into the insanity of dreams, declines to the symbolic and cryptic, ends in an allegorical tangle. Lilith, we humbly submit, had no business in it, nor Adam; the spots of the spotted panther and its war with the white confuse us, the lisping imperfections of the Little Ones irritate. There is imagination enough in this one book to last a common respectable author a lifetime. But for lack of pruning and restraint it seems, beside such work as Poe's like the many-breasted, many-armed Diana of Ephesus beside the Venus of Milo, an image that is depraved to the hieroglyphic level. Or we may take another view of it, and compare it to a confused theological discussion in carnival dress.

NOTES

1 This is either a misprint or a literary pun on the title of MacDonald's first book in the manner of *Lilith*, *Phantastes* (1858).

H. G. Wells's Literary Criticism
'ABOUT SIR THOMAS MORE'

This little essay, reprinted in An Englishman Looks at the World *(pp 183–7), originally served as the preface to a 1908 edition of More's* Utopia *(1516), in Ralph Robinson's 'classic' English rendition (1551). Perhaps surprisingly, Wells ignores the social satire in the first part of More's fiction, and thus overlooks the dialectical structure of the work as a whole. Yet he shows himself sensitive to the paradox of* Utopia*'s 'incidental scepticism', and presents a persuasive and sensible argument for More's capacity 'of conceiving a non-Christian community excelling all Christendom in wisdom and virtue'.*

There are some writers who are chiefly interesting in themselves, and some whom chance and the agreement of men have picked out as symbols and convenient indications of some particular group or temperament of opinions. To the latter it is that Sir Thomas More belongs. An age and a type of mind have found in him and his Utopia a figurehead and a token; and pleasant and honourable as his personality and household present themselves to the modern reader, it is doubtful if they would by this time have retained any peculiar distinction among the many other contemporaries of whom we have chance glimpses in letters and suchlike documents, were it not that he happened to be the first man of affairs in England to imitate the *Republic* of Plato. By that chance it fell to him to give the world a noun and an adjective of abuse, 'Utopian', and to record how under the stimulus of Plato's releasing influence the opening problems of our modern world presented themselves to the English mind[1] of his time. For the most part the problems that exercised him are the problems that exercise us to-day; some of them, it may be, have grown up and intermarried, new ones have joined their company, but few, if any, have disappeared, and it is alike in his resemblances to and differences from the modern speculative mind that his essential interest lies.

The portrait presented by contemporary mention and his own intentional and unintentional admissions, is of an

On Science Fiction, Utopian Fiction, and Fantasy

active-minded and agreeable-mannered man, a hard worker, very markedly prone to quips and whimsical sayings and plays upon words, and aware of a double reputation as a man of erudition and a wit. This latter quality it was that won him advancement at court, and it may have been his too clearly confessed reluctance to play the part of an informal table jester to his king that laid the grounds of that deepening royal resentment that ended only with his execution. But he was also valued by the king for more solid merits, he was needed by the king, and it was more than a table scorned or a clash of opinion upon the validity of divorce; it was a more general estrangement and avoidance of service that caused that fit of regal petulance by which he died.[2]

It would seem that he began and ended his career in the orthodox religion and a general acquiescence in the ideas and customs of his time, and he played an honourable and acceptable part in that time; but his permanent interest lies not in his general conformity but in his incidental scepticism, in the fact that underlying the observances and recognized rules and limitations that give the texture of his life were the profoundest doubts, and that, stirred and disturbed by Plato, he saw fit to write them down. One may question,[3] if such scepticism is in itself unusual, whether any large proportion of great statesmen, great ecclesiastics and administrators have escaped phases of destructive self-criticism, of destructive criticism of the principles upon which their general careers were framed. But few have made so public an admission as Sir Thomas More. A good Catholic undoubtedly he was, and yet we find him capable of conceiving a non-Christian community excelling all Christendom in wisdom and virtue; in practice his sense of conformity and orthodoxy was manifest enough, but in his *Utopia* he ventures to contemplate, and that not merely wistfully, but with some confidence, the possibility of an absolute religious toleration.

The *Utopia* is none the less interesting because it is one of the most inconsistent[4] of books. Never were the forms of Socialism and Communism animated by so entirely an Individualist soul. The hands are the hands of Plato, the wide-thinking Greek, but the voice is the voice of a humane, public-spirited, but limited and very practical English gentleman who takes the inferiority of his inferiors for granted, dislikes friars and tramps and loafers and all undisciplined and unproductive people, and is ruler in his own household. He abounds in sound practical ideas, for the migration of harvesters, for the universality of gardens and the artificial incubation of eggs, and he sweeps aside all Plato's suggestion of the citizen woman as though it had never entered his mind. He had indeed the Whig temperament, and it manifested itself down even to the practice of reading aloud in company, which still prevails among the more representative survivors of the Whig tradition. He argues ably against private property, but no thought of any such radicalism as the admission of those poor peons of his, with head half-shaved and glaring uniform against escape, to participation in ownership, appears in his proposals. His communism is all for the convenience of his Syphogrants and Tranibores,[5] those gentlemen of gravity and experience, lest one should swell up above the others. So too is the essential Whiggery of the limitation of the Prince's revenues. It is the very spirit of eighteenth-century Constitutionalism. And his Whiggery bears Utilitarianism instead of the vanity of a flower. Among his cities, all of a size, so that 'he that knoweth one knoweth all' (p 89), the Benthamite would have revised his sceptical theology and admitted the possibility of heaven.[6]

Like any Whig, More exalted reason above the imagination at every point, and so he fails to understand the magic prestige of gold, making that beautiful metal into vessels of dishonour to urge his case against it, nor had he any perception of the charm of extravagance, for example, or the desirability of various clothing. The Utopians went all in coarse linen and undyed wool—why should the world be coloured?—and all the economy of labour and shortening of the working day was to no other end than to prolong the years of study and the joys of reading aloud, the simple satisfactions of the good boy at his lessons, to the very end of life. 'In the institution of that weal publique this end is only and chiefly pretended and minded, that what time may possibly be spared from the necessary occupations and affairs of the commonwealth, all that the citizens should

On Science Fiction, Utopian Fiction, and Fantasy

withdraw from the bodily service to the free liberty of the mind and garnishing of the same. For herein they suppose the felicity of this life to consist' (p 105).

Indeed, it is no paradox to say that *Utopia*,[7] which has by a conspiracy of accidents become a proverb for undisciplined fancifulness in social and political matters, is in reality a very unimaginative work. In that, next to the accident of its priority, lies the secret of its continuing interest. In some respects it is like one of those precious and delightful scrapbooks people disinter in old country houses; its very poverty of synthetic power leaves its ingredients, the cuttings from and imitations of Plato, the recipe for the hatching of eggs, the stern resolutions against scoundrels and rough fellows, all the sharper and brighter. There will always be found people to read in it, over and above the countless multitudes who will continue ignorantly to use its name for everything most alien to More's essential quality.

NOTES

1 1908: 'the opening English mind'.
2 More (1478–1535) became Henry VIII's Lord Chancellor in 1529, but was later imprisoned and subsequently beheaded after his falling out with Henry on the matter of the king's divorce and break with Rome. By 'more general estrangement', Wells may have in mind the argument against serving the State that More has Raphael Hythloday put forward in Book I of *Utopia*.
3 1908: 'one may doubt'.
4 1908: 'one of the most profoundly inconsistent of books'.
5 The 200 syphogrants and twenty tranibores are officials elected annually to exercise the power and responsibility of decision-making in Utopia.
6 See Jeremy Bentham's *The Principles of Morals and Legislation* (1789), chapter 2, section 18.
7 1908: 'the *Utopia*'.

H. G. Wells's Literary Criticism
PREFACE TO *THE SLEEPER AWAKES*

Wells's revaluation of the book originally published under the title When the Sleeper Wakes *(1899) and here described as 'a nightmare of Capitalism triumphant' appeared as the 'Author's Preface' to a 1921 paperback issued by Collins.*

This book, *The Sleeper Awakes*, was written in that remote and comparatively happy year, 1898. It is the first of a series of books which I have written at intervals since that time; *The World Set Free* [1914] is the latest; they are all 'fantasias of possibility'; each one takes some great creative tendency, or group of tendencies, and develops its possible consequences in the future. *The War in the Air* [1908] did that for example with aviation, and is perhaps, as a forecast, the most successful of them all. The present volume takes up certain ideas already very much discussed in the concluding years of the last century, the idea of the growth of the towns and the depopulation of the country-side and the degradation of labour through the higher organization of industrial production. 'Suppose these forces to go on', that is the fundamental hypothesis of the story.

The 'Sleeper' is of course the average man, who owns everything—did he but choose to take hold of his possessions—and who neglects everything. He wakes up to find himself the puppet of a conspiracy of highly intellectual men in a world which is a practical realization of Mr Belloc's nightmare of the Servile States.[1] And the book resolves itself into as vigorous an imagination as the writer's quality permitted of this world of base servitude in hypertrophied cities.

Will such a world ever exist?

I will confess I doubt it. At the time when I wrote this story I had a considerable belief in its possibility, but later on, in *Anticipations* (1900), I made a very careful analysis of the causes of town aggregation and showed that a period of town dispersal was already beginning.[2] And the thesis of a gradual systematic enslavement of organized labour, presupposes an intelligence, a power of combination, and a *wickedness* in the class of rich financiers and industrial organisers, such as this class certainly does not possess, and probably cannot possess. A body of men who had the character and the largeness of imagination necessary to combine and overcome the natural insubordination of the worker would have a character and largeness of imagination too fine and great for any such plot against humanity. I was young in those days, I was thirty-two, I had met few big business men, and I still thought of them as wicked, able men. It was only later that I realized that on the contrary they were, for the most part, rather foolish plungers, fortunate and energetic rather than capable, vulgar rather than wicked, and quite incapable of world-wide constructive plans or generous combined action. 'Ostrog' in *The Sleeper Awakes*, gave way to reality when I drew Uncle Ponderevo in *Tono-Bungay* [1909]. The great city of this story is no more then than a nightmare of Capitalism triumphant, a nightmare that was dreamt nearly a quarter of a century ago. It is a fantastic possibility no longer possible. Much evil may be in store for mankind, but to this immense, grim organization of servitude, our race will never come.

NOTES

1 An allusion to *The Servile State* (1912) by Hilaire Belloc (1870–1953).
2 See 'The Probable Diffusion of Great Cities', chapter 2 of *Anticipations* (published in book form in 1901).

H. G. Wells's Literary Criticism
PREFACE TO *THE SCIENTIFIC ROMANCES*

The following text appeared as the introduction to The Scientific Romances of H. G. Wells *(1933; published in the United States as* Seven Famous Novels by H. G. Wells, *1934). It presents Wells's fullest critical statement about the nature and method of his science fiction.*

Mr Gollancz[1] has asked me to write a preface to this collection of my fantastic stories. They are put in chronological order, but let me say here right at the beginning of the book, that for anyone who does not as yet know anything of my work it will probably be more agreeable to begin with *The Invisible Man* [1897] or *The War of the Worlds* [1898]. *The Time Machine* [1895] is a little bit stiff about the fourth dimension and *The Island of Dr Moreau* [1896] rather painful.[2]

These tales have been compared with the work of Jules Verne and there was a disposition on the part of literary journalists at one time to call me the English Jules Verne.[3] As a matter of fact there is no literary resemblance whatever between the anticipatory inventions of the great Frenchman and these fantasies.[4] His work dealt almost always with actual possibilities of invention and discovery, and he made some remarkable forecasts. The interest he invoked was a practical one; he wrote and believed and told that this or that thing could be done, which was not at that time done. He helped his reader to imagine it done and to realize what fun, excitement or mischief would ensue. Many of his inventions have 'come true'. But these stories of mine collected here do not pretend to deal with possible things; they are exercises of the imagination in a quite different field. They belong to a class of writing which includes the *Golden Ass of Apuleius*, the *True Histories of Lucian*, *Peter Schlemil* and the story of *Frankenstein*.[5] It includes too some admirable inventions by Mr David Garnett, *Lady into Fox* [1922] for instance. They are all fantasies; they do not aim to project a serious possibility; they aim indeed only at the same amount of conviction as one gets in a good gripping dream. They have to hold the reader to the end by art and illusion and not by

On Science Fiction, Utopian Fiction, and Fantasy

proof and argument, and the moment he closes the cover and reflects he wakes up to their impossibility.

In all this type of story the living interest lies in their non-fantastic elements and not in the invention itself. They are appeals for human sympathy quite as much as any 'sympathetic' novel, and the fantastic element, the strange property or the strange world, is used only to throw up and intensify our natural reactions of wonder, fear or perplexity. The invention is nothing in itself and when this kind of thing is attempted by clumsy writers who do not understand this elementary principle nothing could be conceived more silly and extravagant. Anyone can invent human beings inside out or worlds like dumb-bells or a gravitation that repels. The thing that makes such imaginations interesting is their translation into commonplace terms and a rigid exclusion of other marvels from the story. Then it becomes human. 'How would you feel and what might not happen to you', is the typical question, if for instance pigs could fly and one came rocketing over a hedge at you? How would you feel and what might not happen to you if suddenly you were changed into an ass and couldn't tell anyone about it? Or if you became invisible? But no one would think twice about the answer if hedges and houses also began to fly, or if people changed into lions, tigers, cats and dogs left and right, or if everyone could vanish anyhow. Nothing remains interesting where anything may happen.

For the writer of fantastic stories to help the reader to play the game properly, he must help him in every possible unobtrusive way to *domesticate* the impossible hypothesis. He must trick him into an unwary concession to some plausible assumption and get on with his story while the illusion holds. And that is where there was a certain slight novelty in my stories when first they appeared. Hitherto, except in exploration fantasies, the fantastic element was brought in by magic. Frankenstein even, used some jiggery-pokery magic to animate his artificial monster. There was trouble about the thing's soul. But by the end of last century it had become difficult to squeeze even a momentary[6] belief out of magic any longer. It occurred to me that instead of the usual interview with the devil or a magician, an ingenious use of scientific patter might with advantage be substituted. That was no great discovery. I simply brought the fetish stuff up to date, and made it as near actual theory as possible.

As soon as the magic trick has been done the whole business of the fantasy writer is to keep everything else human and real. Touches of prosaic detail are imperative and a rigorous adherence to the hypothesis. Any *extra* fantasy outside the cardinal assumption immediately gives a touch of irresponsible silliness to the invention. So soon as the hypothesis is launched the whole interest becomes the interest of looking at human feelings and human ways, from the new angle that has been acquired. One can keep the story within the bounds of a few individual experiences as Chamisso does in *Peter Schlemil*, or one can expand it to a broad criticism of human institutions and limitations as in *Gulliver's Travels* [1726–27]. My early, profound and lifelong admiration for Swift, appears again and again in this collection, and it is particularly evident in a predisposition to make the stories reflect upon contemporary political and social discussions. It is an incurable habit with literary critics to lament some lost artistry and innocence in my early work and to accuse me of having become polemical in my later years. That habit is of such old standing that the late Mr Zangwill in a review in 1895 complained that my first book, *The Time Machine*, concerned itself with 'our present discontents'.[7] *The Time Machine* is indeed quite as philosophical and polemical and critical of life and so forth, as *Men like Gods* written twenty-eight years later. No more and no less. I have never been able to get away from life in the mass and life in general as distinguished from life in the individual experience, in any book I have ever written. I differ from contemporary criticism in finding them inseparable.

For some years I produced one or more of these 'scientific fantasies', as they were called, every year. In my student days we were much exercised by talk about a possible fourth dimension of space; the fairly obvious idea that events could be presented in a rigid four dimensional space time framework had occurred to me, and this is used as the magic trick for a glimpse of the future that ran counter to the placid assumption of that time that Evolution was a pro-human

On Science Fiction, Utopian Fiction, and Fantasy

force making things better and better for mankind. *The Island of Dr Moreau* is an exercise in youthful blasphemy. Now and then, though I rarely admit it, the universe projects itself towards me in a hideous grimace. It grimaced that time, and I did my best to express my vision of the aimless torture in creation. *The War of the Worlds* like *The Time Machine* was another assault on human self-satisfaction.

All these three books are consciously grim, under the influence of Swift's tradition. But I am neither a pessimist nor an optimist at bottom. This is an entirely indifferent world in which wilful wisdom seems to have a perfectly fair chance. It is after all rather cheap to get force of presentation by loading the scales on the sinister side. Horror stories are easier to write than gay and exalting stories. In *The First Men in the Moon* I tried an improvement on Jules Verne's shot, in order to look at mankind from a distance and burlesque the effects of specialization. Verne never landed on the moon because he never knew of radio and of the possibility of sending back a message. So it was his shot that came back.[8] But equipped with radio, which had just come out then, I was able to land and even see something of the planet.

The three later books[9] are distinctly on the optimistic side. *The Food of the Gods* is a fantasia on the change of scale in human affairs. Everybody nowadays realizes that change of scale; we see the whole world in disorder through it; but in 1904 it was not a very prevalent idea. I had hit upon it while working out the possibilities of the near future in a book of speculations called *Anticipations* (1901).

The last two stories are Utopian.[10] The world is gassed and cleaned up morally by the benevolent tail of a comet in one, and the reader is taken through a dimensional trap door with a weekend party of politicians, into a world of naked truth and deliberate beauty in the other. *Men like Gods* is almost the last of my scientific fantasies. It did not horrify or frighten, was not much of a success, and by that time I had tired of talking in playful parables to a world engaged in destroying itself. I was becoming too convinced of the strong probability of very strenuous and painful human experiences in the near future to play about with them much more. But I did two other sarcastic fantasies, not included here, *Mr Blettsworthy on Rampole Island* [1928] and *The Autocracy of Mr Parham* [1930], in which there is I think a certain gay bitterness, before I desisted altogether.

The Autocracy of Mr Parham is all about dictators, and dictators are all about us, but it has never struggled through to a really cheap edition. Work of this sort gets so stupidly reviewed nowadays that it has little chance of being properly read. People are simply warned that there are ideas in my books and advised not to read them, and so a fatal suspicion has wrapped about the later ones. 'Ware stimulants!' It is no good my saying that they are quite as easy to read as the earlier ones and much more timely.

It becomes a bore doing imaginative books that do not touch imaginations, and at length one stops even planning them. I think I am better employed now nearer reality, trying to make a working analysis of our deepening social perplexities in such labours as *The Work, Wealth and Happiness of Mankind* [1932] and *After Democracy* [1932]. The world in the presence of cataclysmal realities has no need for fresh cataclysmal fantasies. That game is over. Who wants the invented humours of Mr Parham in Whitehall, when day by day we can watch Mr Hitler in Germany? What human invention can pit itself against the fantastic fun of the Fates? I am wrong in grumbling at reviewers. Reality has taken a leaf from my book and set itself to supersede me.

NOTES

1 Victor Gollancz was the English publisher of the anthology; the preface to the American edition substitutes 'Mr Knopf'.
2 In addition to these four titles, the Gollancz volume contains four others (mentioned later on by Wells): *The First Men in the Moon* (1900–01), *The Food of the Gods* (1904), *In the Days of the Comet* (1907), and *Men like Gods* (1923). The Knopf edition excludes the latter title (which accounts for the textual differences—noted below—between the English and the American prefaces).
3 In a letter that Wells sent to Bennett in 1902, he complained of American reviewers to whom '"English Jules Verne" is my utmost glory' (Wilson, p 73).

On Science Fiction, Utopian Fiction, and Fantasy

4 Bennett makes a similar point in his 1902 essay on Wells; see Wilson, pp 261ff.
5 Apuleius's *Golden Ass* and Lucian of Samosata's *True History* (or *Histories*) both date from the second century A.D. Apuleius's satiric fantasy, like the book by David Garnett that Wells alludes to next, concerns the metamorphosis of a human being into an animal. *Peter Schlemihls wundersame Geschichte* (1814), by Adalbert von Chamisso (1781–1838), relates the adventures of a man who sells his shadow to the devil. Mary Shelley's *Frankenstein* (1818; rev. ed., 1831) is frequently discussed in histories of science fiction, as is Lucian's prose satire.
6 This reading is from the Knopf text; the Gollancz has 'monetary'.
7 Israel Zangwill (1864–1926) used this phrase in his column 'Without Prejudice', *Pall Mall Magazine*, 7 (September 1895), 153; reprinted in CH, pp 40–2.
8 In *Autour de la lune* (1870), the sequel to *De la terre à la lune* . . . (1865), three members of the Baltimore Gun Club circle the moon in a cannonball before returning to Earth (see above, pp 222–3).
9 Knopf: 'The two later books . . .'
10 At the end of the preceding paragraph, the Knopf edition has: 'The last story is Utopian'. The new paragraph in the Knopf text begins, '*Men like Gods*, written seventeen years after *In the Days of the Comet*, and not included in this volume, was almost the last of my scientific fantasies'.

H. G. Wells's Literary Criticism
'FICTION ABOUT THE FUTURE'

Wells broadcast these remarks on writing 'prophetic' fiction over Australian radio on 29 December 1938. The Sydney Daily Telegraph *and the* Adelaide Advertiser *reported the event on the following day, and the Melbourne* Leader *a week later. But the full text, based on a typescript in the University of Illinois Wells Collection, is here printed for the first time.*

I have been asked to give a talk on the Australian air on some subject connected with literature. It has occurred to me that you might be interested in a few things I have thought and observed about one peculiar sort of book-writing in which I have had some experience. This is *Fiction about the Future*. Almost my first published book[1] was *The Time Machine*, which went millions of years ahead, and since then I have made repeated excursions into the unknown, from *The Sleeper Awakes* in 1898 to *The Shape of Things to Come* in 1933, and it is still going on. The last one, the *Holy Terror* is due to wind up about twenty years from now.[2]

I doubt whether one can call anything of this sort literature in the sense that it aims to be something perfect and enduring. Maybe no literature is perfect and enduring, but there is something specially and incurably topical about all these prophetic books; the more you go ahead, the more you seem to get entangled with the burning questions of your own time. And all the while events are overtaking you. You may cast your tale a century or so ahead, and even then something may happen next week that will knock your most plausible reasoning crooked. For instance, who would have thought in 1900 of the possibility of mankind burrowing underground to escape from air raids? In that book of 1898[3] I put all my populations into vast towering cities and left the countryside desolate. Would any young man starting to write a futurist story now dare to do that in the face of the bomber aeroplane? When I wrote *Anticipations* in 1900, I was already giving up the idea of these crowded cities,[4] and by the time I wrote *The War in the Air* in 1908 and *The World Set Free* in 1914, I had completely reversed that concentra-

On Science Fiction, Utopian Fiction, and Fantasy

tion. You might even think there was something malicious about the future, as though it didn't like to be prophesied and dodged me about. I thought that anyhow I was pretty safe to take my *Time Machine* some millions of years ahead and show the sun cooled down to a red ball and the earth dried up and frozen. That was what science made of the outlook in 1893. But since then all sorts of mitigating considerations have arisen, and there is no reason, they tell us now, to suppose there will not be humanity, or the descendants of humanity, living in comfort and sunshine on this planet, for millions of years yet[5]—provided always they do not blow it to pieces in some great war-climax. You see you never can tell. So—since it has no permanent quality—I should be disposed to class *all* this futuristic stuff as journalism, less ephemeral only in degree than the news in the daily papers. We read and discuss it in our own time, because for the time being and in face of our problems it is interesting, and there's an end to it. If posterity reads it at all it will probably be to marvel at our want of knowledge, imagination and hope. And no doubt our posterity too will write their own futuristic stories and no doubt they too will be just as transitory as ours.

I think myself that the best sort of futurist story should be one that sets out to give you the illusion of reality. It ought to produce the effect of an historical novel, the other way round. It ought to read like fact. But alas, do any of us futurist writers ever get in sight of that much conviction? I'm afraid I must admit that none of us have ever succeeded in producing anything like the convincingness of hundreds of historical novels. No reader has ever *lived* in a futurist novel as we have all lived in the London of Dickens' *Barnaby Rudge* [1841] or the Paris of Hugo's *Notre Dame* [1831] or the Russia of Tolstoi's *War and Peace* [1863–9]. But then the historical romancer has a whole mass of history, ruins, old costumes, museum pieces, to work upon and confirm him; your minds are all ready furnished for him; the futurist writer has at most the bare germs of things to come and all your prejudices to surmount. He has to throw himself on your willingness to believe. You have to help him. He invites you to embark upon a collaboration in make-believe, or the whole thing fails. That is why so much *Fiction of the Future* degenerates into a rather silly admission of insincerity before the tale is half-way through. The writer's imagination gives *out*, he ceases to feel you can possibly believe in him, and so he begins to grimace and pretend that all along he was only making fun. He was being sarcastic, you must understand. That is the case, for example, in that incredibly dismal book, Mr Aldous Huxley's *Brave New World* [1932]. It becomes at last a sour grimace at human hope. Never was any pretence of making fun less funny. Every developing tendency to which a young man might devote himself is distorted and guyed. You had better not start out living constructively; you will only make things worse for yourself and everyone; you had better achieve detachment by the simple process of hanging yourself at once, and *that's that*.

But a lot of fiction about the future starts as a joke from the outset and does not attempt to be anything more. There is a shock of laughter in nearly every discovery. Every new discovery is necessarily *strange* to begin with, and if a writer keeps at the level of that first laugh, he will save himself a lot of trouble. Here, for example, is an idea from which it would be easy to produce a comic futurist story. Suppose—which is probably quite within the range of biological possibility—that a means is discovered for producing children—and feminine children only—without actual fathers. Most doctors and biologists now will tell you that that is at least a conceivable thing. Very well, take that. Don't ask whether people would avail themselves of that discovery, don't probe into the immensely interesting problems of individual or mass psychology that it would open up, but just suppose it done. Then you have the possibility of a comic, manless world. In order to be really and easily funny about it, you must ignore the fact that it would change the resultant human being into a creature mentally and emotionally different from ourselves. That would complicate things too much. You must carry over every current gibe at womanhood, jokes about throwing stones, not keeping secrets, lip-stick and vanity bags, into the story, and there you are. That's the Futurist Story at the lowest level.

But suppose now you chose to complicate things by

On Science Fiction, Utopian Fiction, and Fantasy

carrying out your hypothesis to the extent of trying to imagine how such a possibility would really work. Suppose you were psychologist enough to speculate how a girl would grow up to womanhood in a manless world, a girl for whom the marriage market did not exist, what sort of emotional releases would she discover, how would women tackle the complicated mechanisms of life, how would they hunt and drive the plough, what modification of political life would they make, would they care less for beauty than they do now or more, and so on. Well, you'd have to write a far graver story; you'd giggle less but you'd find a lot more interest and complication. That would be a much more difficult book to write; it would probably lose itself in dissertations and unrealities, but it would be a much finer thing to bring off if you could bring it off. And now suppose humanity refused to accept the great change without vast disputation and struggle. Then you'd come still nearer to living possibility. You'd probably have to narrow the story down to a small group of people—and see the rest of the world out of the window. You'd have then what I should call a futurist novel, the highest and most difficult form of futurist literature.

Now I will confess that in spite of my constant preoccupation with the future I have never attempted a novel, set in times to come. I could never satisfy myself with the first chapter. All I have written has been romances and pseudo-histories, or books of pure speculation like *Anticipations*. For that you can manage with broad generalizations. You can write of mighty embankments of thousands of feet high, stupendous aeroplanes, you can hint at great palaces of crystal and beautiful robes and adornments. It passes muster. But directly you come down to real persons seen close-up, you meet what is the final and conclusive defeat of futuristic imagination and that is—the small material details. That was brought home to me when we made a film that had a certain vogue some years ago, called *Things to Come*.[6] It was easy to write of a Dictator, splendidly clothed, seated at the head of his council, and then go on with the speeches. But when it came to the screen, you have to show him from top to toe. And how was he going to dress his hair? Would he be clean-shaven? We consulted a number of hairdressers but none of them had any clear views about the hairdressing of the year 2035. And what sort of clothes would he be wearing? That opened up endless trouble. We invoked dress-designers by the dozen; we went into the problem of novel materials. More new dress materials have been introduced into the world in the past thirty years, than in the previous three thousand, and still the novelties come. We couldn't even decide whether his garments would be held together by buckles or buttons or zips or safety-pins. In my lifetime I have seen the practical disappearance of the tape and the pin and hooks and eyes. Probably no man under 40 among my hearers has ever had to hook up his wife's dress. And was our Dictator going to sit down to a wooden table with a wooden chair? No. But all we could think of were slightly modernistic metal chairs and a glass table. We did our best, but in fact we could never get beyond contemporary modernism. As I remember that film, it began in the present time with an intense realism. At the end it culminated in scenes of the intensest detailed improbability. You see we had been trying to anticipate the inventions, discoveries, freaks and fancies of scores of millions of our descendants; obviously we could not have our scene right; but what we discovered was that we could not even make it plausible. No one would believe it was so. And also we realized something else. Suppose one of us or all of us had had a real prophetic vision—exact and full of detail—of the buildings, rooms, garments of a hundred years hence—and suppose we had actually put that on the screen, would it have been even as convincing as the stuff we contrived?

And there you have the reason why no sensible writer who dreams of writing for posterity, will ever think twice of engaging in this ephemeral but amusing art, the fiction of prophecy—on which I have spent so much of my time.

NOTES

1 Preceding *The Time Machine* (1895) were a *Text-Book of Biology* and *Honours Physiography* (both of which appeared in 1893).

On Science Fiction, Utopian Fiction, and Fantasy

2 Wells has deleted the words: 'Just before I left England I was finishing the proofs of a book about the Last of all the Dictators, who, you will probably like to hear, [is due to wind up about twenty years from now]'.
3 *When the Sleeper Wakes*, published in book form in 1899 and later (1910) retitled *The Sleeper Awakes*.
4 See the 'Preface to *The Sleeper Awakes*', n 2.
5 These remarks pertain especially to the penultimate chapter of *The Time Machine*, and imply (somewhat misleadingly—see EW, pp 89 and 112) that its apocalyptic vision derives primarily from the Second Law of Thermodynamics. In his foreword to an edition of *The Time Machine* issued in 1931 (Random House, New York; illus. W. A. Dwiggins), Wells claimed that he had predicated his cosmic pessimism on calculations (by Lord Kelvin) now recognized to be invalid.
6 This film, directed by William Cameron Menzies and starring Raymond Massey, was released in 1936.

Bibliography

Edel, Leon, and Ray, Gordon N., *Henry James and H. G. Wells* (Hart-Davis, London and University of Illinois Press, Urbana, 1958).
Gettmann, Royal A., ed., *George Gissing and H. G. Wells* (Hart-Davis, London and University of Illinois Press, Urbana, 1961).
Hammond, J. R., *Herbert George Wells: An Annotated Bibliography of his Works* (Garland Publishing, New York and London, 1977).
Mullen, R. D., 'The Books and Principal Pamphlets of H. G. Wells: A Chronological Survey', *Science-Fiction Studies*, 1 (1973), pp 114–35. (Revised as 'An Annotated Survey of Books and Pamphlets by H. G. Wells', in *H. G. Wells and Modern Science Fiction*, ed. Darko Suvin, with Robert M. Philmus (Bucknell University Press, Lewisburg, Pa and Associated University Presses, London, 1977).
Philmus, Robert M., 'H. G. Wells as Literary Critic for the *Saturday Review*', *Science-Fiction Studies*, 4 (1977), pp 166–93.
Ray, Gordon N., 'H. G. Wells Tries to be a Novelist', in *Edwardians and Late Victorians*, ed. Richard Ellmann (Columbia University Press, New York, 1960), pp 106–59.
Ray, Gordon N., 'H. G. Wells's Contributions to the *Saturday Review*', *The Library*, 5th series, 16 (1961), pp 29–36.
Timko, Michael, 'H. G. Wells's Dramatic Criticism for the *Pall Mall Gazette*', *The Library*, 5th series, 17 (1962), pp 138–45.
Wells, Geoffrey H., *The Works of H. G. Wells, 1887–1925: A Bibliography, Dictionary and Subject-Index* (Routledge, London, 1926).
West, Geoffrey (pseud. of Geoffrey H. Wells), *H. G. Wells: A Sketch for a Portrait* (Gerald Howe, London, 1930).
Wilson, Harris, ed., *Arnold Bennett and H. G. Wells* (Hart-Davis, London and University of Illinois Press, Urbana, 1960).

Index

of names, authors, and works cited in the text and notes (excluding bibliography)

Addison, Joseph, 110
Advertiser (Adelaide), 246
Aeschylus, *Prometheus Bound*, 218
Alexander, George, 27, 28, 29, 30, 31, 178
Allen, Grant, 33, 44, 51, 52, 59–62, 68, 225, 229; *British Barbarians, The*, 6, 59–62, 225; *Woman Who Did, The*, 6, 35, 44, 48, 59, 60, 61, 67, 71, 79, 82
Ally Sloper, 74
Alma-Tadema, Sir Lawrence, 121, 122
Altick, Richard D., *The English Common Reader*, 77, 93, 205
Amazing Stories, 224
Anrep, G. V., 176, 177
Answers, 74, 77
Apuleius, 222; *The Golden Ass*, 240, 245
Archer, William, *The Theatrical 'World' of 1895*, 39
Aristophanes, 78
Arnold, Matthew, 12, 17, 52
Atlantic Monthly, 179
Austen, Jane, 145, 150, 159
Author, The, 133
Aynesworth, Allan, 29, 30

Bacon, Francis, 4
Balzac, Honoré de, 5, 136, 145, 180, 187, 188
Barbellion, W. N. P., 2; *Journal of a Disappointed Man*, 18
Barnardo, Dr., 115, 118
Barrett, Wilson, 50, 119–23; *The Sign of the Cross*, 119–23
Barrie, J. M., 67, 71, 118, 173, 175;
Sentimental Tommy, 115, 118
Beckford, William, *Vathek*, 4
Beerbohm, Max, 184, 188; *A Christmas Garland*, 188
Bellamy, Edward, 111, 113; *Looking Backward*, 113
Belloc, Hilaire, 238, 239
Bennett, Arnold, 1, 8, 10, 15, 53, 138, 175, 180, 183, 185, 187, 196, 199, 205–6, 221, 222, 225, 244, 245; *Card, The*, 205; *Clayhanger*, 196; *Fame and Fiction*, 53; 'Herbert George Wells and His Work', 225, 228, 229; *Old Wives' Tale, The*, 196; *Regent, The*, 206
Benson, E. F., *The Babe, B.A.*, 188
Bentham, Jeremy, 236, 237
Berryman, John, *Stephen Crane*, 170
Besant, Sir Walter, 76, 78, 82, 129, 133; *Beyond the Dreams of Avarice*, 78
Blake, William, 4, 186
Blanchamp, H., 48, 49, 54
Boyesen, H. H., 157, 160
British Weekly, 205
Bronte, Charlotte, 43; *Jane Eyre*, 45, 74
Brooke, Emma Francis, *A Superfluous Woman*, 75, 78
Brooke, Sarah, 38
Brough, Fanny, 26
Buchan, John, 1, 83–7; 'Captain of Salvation, A', 87; *Sir Quixote of the Moors*, 83–7; *Thirty-Nine Steps, The*, 83
Burke, Thomas, *Limehouse Nights*, 172

Index

Burnett, Frances Hodgson, 50, 104–10; *Haworth's*, 104; *Lady of Quality, A*, 104–10; *Little Lord Fauntleroy*, 104, 105, 106; *That Lass o' Lowrie's*, 104; *Through One Administration*, 104–5
Byron, Lord, 207

Caine, Hall, 44, 47, 57, 58, 97, 99; *The Christian*, 58
Calendar of Modern Letters, 11
Calhoun, Eleanor, 35
Campbell, Mrs Patrick, 35
Cannan, Gilbert, 182, 196
Canninge, Mrs George, 29
Carlyle, Thomas, 4, 12, 17, 30
Carpaccio, Vittore, 212, 215
Carr, J. W. Comyns, 36, 37, 38
Casanova, Giovanni, 203, 205
Cellini, Benvenuto, 203, 205
Cervantes, Miguel de, 112
Chamberlain, Joseph, 130, 133
Chamisso, Adalbert von, *Peter Schlemil*, 240, 242, 245
Charles I, 143
Clark, Barrett H., *Intimate Portraits*, 175
Clodd, Edward, 215
Cody, Sherwin, 137, 156–60; *In the Heart of the Hills*, 156–60
Collins, Wilkie, 145; *The Woman in White*, 74, 77
Colvin, Sidney, 99
Conrad, Joseph, 1, 2, 8, 9, 13, 16, 50, 54, 88–93, 94, 118, 139, 174, 180, 182, 187, 198, 216; *Almayer's Folly*, 88, 90, 192, 205; *Heart of Darkness*, 88; *Lord Jim*, 175, 198; *Outcast of the Islands, An*, 50, 88–93, 94, 116, 205; *Secret Agent, The*, 8
Contemporary Review, 57, 144
Corelli, Marie, 78, 131, 132; *The Sorrows of Satan*, 74, 78, 133
Cosmopolitan Magazine, 229
Craigie, Pearl Teresa, *see* 'Hobbes, John Oliver'
'Craik, Mrs', *John Halifax, Gentleman*, 81, 82
Crane, Cora, 8, 137
Crane, Stephen, 1, 2, 7, 8, 54, 118, 134, 137–8, 140, 156–70, 187; *Black Riders, The*, 168; 'Death and the Child', 163, 166; 'Flanagan', 165, 166; *George's Mother*, 137, 156–60, 164, 170; *Maggie*, 137, 164; *On Active Service*, 164, 168; 'Open Boat, The', 165–7; *Open Boat and Other Stories, The*, 163, 166, 170; *Red Badge of Courage, The*, 137, 157, 160, 162–4, 165, 170, *Third Violet, The*, 164, 167, 169; *War is Kind*, 168; 'Wise Men, The', 166
Crane, Walter, 112
Criterion, 11
Crockett, S. R., 57, 58, 82, 85, 97, 104, 118; *Cleg Kelly*, 58, 115
Cromie, Robert, *A Plunge into Space*, 228
Cust, Harry, 5, 19

Daiches, David, *Max*, 188
Daily Chronicle, 88, 100, 103, 129, 130
Daily News, 84
Daily Telegraph (Sydney), 246
D'Arcy, Ella, 189, 191; *Monochromes*, 189
Darwin, Charles, 7
Davidson, John, *The Pilgrimage of Strongsoul*, 229
Defoe, Daniel, 217
Dickens, Charles, 6, 52, 53, 54, 136, 137, 145, 159, 175, 180, 186, 187, 195, 205; *Barnaby Rudge*, 145, 247; *Bleak House*, 155, 187, 194; *David Copperfield*, 205; *Martin Chuzzlewit*, 205; *Master Humphrey's Clock*, 195; *Old Curiosity Shop, The*, 205; *Oliver Twist*, 201
Disraeli, Benjamin, *Sybil*, 146
Dorr, Dorothy, 37
Drake, Joseph R., 160
Dryden, John, 122
Dumas, Alexandre, *fils*, 87; *père*,

254

Index

102, 103
Du Maurier, George, *Trilby*, 67, 70, 74, 78
Du Maurier, Gerald, 35
Dure, Michael, *An Impression . . .*, 68, 71
Dunne, Mary Chavelita, *see* 'Egerton, George'

Edel, Leon, and Ray, Gordon N., *Henry James and H. G. Wells*, 178–88
Educational Times, 5
'Egerton, George', 67, 70–1, 189, 191
Egoist, 188
Eliot, George, 5, 146
Eliot, T. S., 186, 187
Ellmann, Richard, *James Joyce*, 175, 177
Emerson, R. W., 17
English Association, 11
English Review, 9, 11
Evans, Caradoc, *Capel Sion*, 172; *My People*, 172
Eye-Witness, 13, 18

Fabian Society, 8
Family Herald, 106, 190, 191
Farrar, Dean, 119, 122; *Darkness and Dawn*, 119; *Eric; or, Little by Little*, 119
Field, Samuel, 113
Fielding, Henry, 33, 35, 159, 180, 186, 200, 205; *Tom Jones*, 144, 188, 194, 195, 200
Figaro, Le, 76
Flaubert, Gustave, 180, 187, 196; *Bouvard et Pécuchet*, 180, 196; *Madame Bovary*, 180
Fleury, Gabrielle, 134
Forbes-Robertson, Ian, 35
Forbes-Robertson, Johnston, 35
Ford, Ford Madox, *see* Hueffer, Ford Madox
Fortnightly Review, 5, 57, 179, 206
Futurism, 10, 172

Galsworthy, John, 10, 138, 198, 221
Garnett, Constance, 1, 67, 71
Garnett, David, 71, 240, 245; *Lady into Fox*, 240
Garnett, Edward, 69, 71, 216
Garnett, Richard, 71
Gaskell, Elizabeth, 159
George, Henry, 111, 113; *Progress and Poverty*, 113
Gernsback, Hugo, 224–5, 229
Gibbs, Philip, 171, 175
Gilbert, W. S., 19, 29
Gissing, George, 2, 6, 8, 16, 36, 51, 58, 67, 134–7, 140, 141–55, 156, 159, 187; *Demos*, 147; *Emancipated, The*, 146–7, 151, 153; *Eve's Ransom*, 39, 134, 141, 150, 151; *In the Year of Jubilee*, 147; *Life's Morning, A*, 147; *Nether World, The*, 135, 147–8, 149, 151; *New Grub Street*, 135, 150, 151–2; *Paying Guest, The*, 134, 135, 141–3, 149; *Sleeping Fires*, 72; *Thyrza*, 147, 149, 151; *Unclassed, The*, 147, 149, 150; *Veranilda*, 136; *Whirlpool, The*, 1, 135, 144, 146–55; *Workers in the Dawn*, 148, 155
Goldsmith, Oliver, 159, 205; *The Vicar of Wakefield*, 194
Gollancz, Victor, 240, 244
Gordon, Frederick C., 95
Gosse, Edmund, 13, 181, 207–8, 215
Graham's Magazine, 155, 205
'Grand, Sarah', *The Heavenly Twins*, 75, 78
Granville-Baker, Harley, 21
Green, Arthur, *Story of a Prisoner of War, The*, 171
Green, R. L., *Andrew Lang*, 57, 103
Gribble, Herbert, 123
Griffith, George C., 230, 231; *Outlaws of the Air*, 231

Haggard, H. Rider, 55–7, 98, 101, 103, 133, 230, 231; *Heart of the World*, 98; *Joan Haste*, 49, 55–7,

Index

Haggard, H. Rider (contd) 85; *King Solomon's Mines*, 55, 57, 103; *She*, 55, 131
Halleck, Fitz Greene, 160
Hardy, Thomas, 6, 44, 49, 52, 54, 68, 79–82, 102, 124, 145, 187; *Hand of Ethelberta, The*, 155; *Jude the Obscure*, 1, 8, 49, 52, 68, 77, 79–82, 155; *Return of the Native, The*, 128
Hare, John, 35
Harland, Henry, *Grey Roses*, 189–91
Harmsworth, Alfred, 77
Harris, Frank, 19, 48, 59, 160, 223
Hawkins, Sir Anthony, *see* 'Hope, Anthony'
Hawthorne, Nathaniel, 180; *Twice-Told Tales*, 205
Hawtrey, Charles H., 25
Heine, Heinrich, 124, 128; *Die Harzreise*, 128
Henley, W. E., 5, 57, 83, 172; *Macaire*, 86
Henry VIII, 237
Herrick, Robert, 112
Hichens, Robert, 51, 129–33, 179; *Flames*, 129–33; *Green Carnation, The*, 129
Hitler, Adolf, 244
'Hobbes, John Oliver', 63–4, 65, 197, 205; *The Gods, Some Mortals and Lord Wickenham*, 65
Hogarth, William, 212, 215
'Hope, Anthony', 49, 74–8, 90; *Change of Air, A*, 76; *Chronicles of Count Antonio, The*, 76; *Father Stafford*, 77; *God in the Car, The*, 77; *Half a Hero*, 77; *Indiscretion of the Duchess, The*, 76, 92; *Man of Mark, A*, 76; *Mr Witt's Widow*, 76; *Prisoner of Zenda, The*, 76
How to Write Fiction, 65
Howells, William Dean, 160
Hueffer, Ford Madox, 8, 9, 11, 16, 88, 216
Hughes, David Y., 62, 229
Hugo, Victor, 145, 163; *Notre Dame*, 247
Hutchinson, Horatio G., 85, 87
Huxley, Aldous, *Brave New World*, 248
Huxley, T. H., 4, 12
Huysmans, J.-K., 131, 133; *En Route*, 133
Hyde's Drapery Emporium, 4

Ibsen, Henrik, 32, 33, 35, 156; *Ghosts*, 32
Idler, 49
Illinois, University of (Wells Collection), 1, 54, 229, 246
International P.E.N. Clubs, 9

James, Henry, 2–3, 6, 8, 9, 12, 13, 14, 15, 16, 17, 53, 115, 138, 178–91, 207–15, 216; 'Altar of the Dead, The', 190, 191, 214; 'Coxon Fund, The', 190; 'Death of the Lion, The', 190; *Golden Bowl, The*, 212; *Guy Domville*, 1, 23, 29, 31, 178; *Hawthorne*, 188; *Notes on Novelists*, 188, 212; *Terminations*, 178, 189–91; 'Younger Generation, The', 182–3, 184
James, M. R., 159, 160
Jean-Aubry, G., *Joseph Conrad*, 92
Jeffries, Ellis, 35
Jerome, J. K., 48–9, 54
Job, Book of, 10, 217
Johnson, Samuel, *Rasselas*, 4
Jokái, Mór, *The Green Book*, 129–33
Jones, Wood, *Arboreal Man*, 171
Joyce, James, 134, 138–40, 171–7, 187; *Finnegans Wake*, 139; *Portrait of the Artist, A*, 2, 138–9, 171–5; *Ulysses*, 139; *Work in Progress*, 139, 176–7
Judd, Professor, 4

Kant, Immanuel, 210
Kelvin, Lord, 251
Kingsley, Charles, *Alton Locke*, 43
Kipling, Rudyard, 162, 167, 216; *The Second Jungle Book*, 77

Index

Knight, Damon, *In Search of Wonder*, 229
Knopf, Alfred, 244

Lane, John, 189
Lang, Andrew, 50, 55, 57, 71, 83–7, 103, 157, 160; *A Monk of Fife*, 83–7
Laurence, George A., *Guy Livingstone*, 47
Lawrence, D. H., 182
Leader (Melbourne), 246
Leavis, F. R., 11
Lecky, W. E. H., 150, 155
Leclerq, Rose, 29, 31, 36
Le Gallienne, Richard, 51, 124–8, 130, 133, 142, 159, 179; *Prose Fancies*, 124; *Quest of the Golden Girl, The*, 124–8; *Religion of a Literary Man, The*, 125
Le Queux, William, 230, 231; *Stolen Souls*, 231
Lewis, C. S., 224, 229, 232
Lie, Jonas, *One of Life's Slaves*, 71
Linnaeus, 216
Lodge, David, *The Novelist at the Crossroads*, 18
London County Council, 80, 82
Long, Edwin, 120, 122
Longman's Magazine, 157, 160
Loüys, Pierre, *Aphrodite*, 121, 122
Lucian, 222; *True History*, 240, 245

Macaulay, Lord, 4
MacDonald, George, 223, 232–3; *Lilith*, 71, 223, 232–3; *Phantastes*, 233
McDougall, Sir John, 82
MacFall, Frances E., see 'Grand, Sarah'
Machen, Arthur, 72–3; *Great God Pan, The*, 72; *Three Impostors, The*, 72–3
Machiavelli, Niccolo, *The Prince*, 10
Mackenzie, Compton, 182
Mackenzie, Henry, *The Man of Feeling*, 124, 126, 128

Mackenzie, Norman and Jeanne, *H. G. Wells*, 215
Mackintosh, Mr, 37
'Maclaren, Ian', 50, 67, 71, 82, 94–7, 104; *A Doctor of the Old School*, 94–7
Mallock, W. H., 11, 218; *The New Republic*, 12, 207, 214–15
Malory, Sir Thomas, 112–13, 114; *Morte d'Arthur*, 114
Maskelyne, J. N., 84, 86
Massey, Ramond, 251
Maude, Cyril, 36, 38
Meek, George, 2; *George Meek . . . by Himself*, 18
Menzies, William C., 251
Meredith, George, 6, 7, 44, 49, 51, 54, 63–6, 70, 82, 102, 136, 145–6, 159, 187; *Amazing Marriage, The*, 1, 63–6; *Diana of the Crossways*, 155; *Egoist, The*, 63, 155; *Lord Ormont and his Aminta*, 63
Midhurst Grammar School, 4
Mill, J. S., 12
Millard, Evelyn, 29, 31
Millett, Maud, 26
Milton, John, 169; *Paradise Lost*, 3, 55
Moore, George, 137, 142, 156, 175, 207–9, 211, 216; *Confessions of a Young Man*, 175; *Esther Waters*, 49, 177
More, Sir Thomas, 234–7; *Utopia*, 10, 234, 235–7
Morley, John, *Life of Gladstone*, 203, 206
Morley, Thomas, 3
Morris, William, 17, 50, 111–14; *News from Nowhere*, 18; *Well at the World's End, The*, 50, 111–14
Morrison, Arthur, 7–8, 52, 115–18, 138; *Child of the Jago, A*, 1, 8, 52, 115–18; 'Lizerunt', 115; *Martin Hewitt, Investigator*, 118; *Tales of Mean Streets*, 118
Mudie, Charles E., 91, 92
Mulock, Dinah M., see 'Craik, Mrs'

Index

Nation, 171
National Observer, 5
Neilson, Julia, 25
New Age, 209, 215
New Republic, 171
Newman, J. H., 12
Newnes, George, 77
Nietzsche, Friedrich, 127
Normal School of Science, 4
North American Review, 161

Omar Khayyam Club, 6
Orage, A. R., 215
'Ouida', 110; *Othmar*, 108, 110

Paine, Tom, 4
Pair of Spectacles, A, 22
Pall Mall Gazette, 1, 5, 19–47
Pall Mall Magazine, 245
Parsons, Albert, 113
Pavlov, Ivan, 139, 177; *Conditioned Reflexes*, 177
Peacock, Thomas Love, 207, 218
Pearson, Cyril, 77
Pearson's Weekly, 74, 77
Pemberton, Max, 230–1; *Impregnable City, The*, 223–4, 230–1; *Little Huguenot, The*, 230, 231
Pevsner, Sir Nikolaus, 123
Pinero, Sir Arthur Wing, 20–1, 32–5; *Notorious Mrs Ebbsmith, The*, 20–1, 32–5; *Second Mrs Tanqueray, The*, 32
Plato, 5, 11, 217, 234–7; *Republic*, 4, 234
Poe, Edgar Allan, 145, 155, 159, 160, 194, 205, 233
Pound, Ezra, 138, 139, 171
Pugh, Edwin, 115

Rabelais, François, 112
Raife, Raymond, *The Sheik's White Slave*, 98
Ramée, Louise de la, *see* 'Ouida'
Raphael, 142, 143
Ray, Gordon N., 1, 18, 54, 71; *H. G. Wells and Rebecca West*, 205; and *see* Edel, Leon, and Ray, Gordon N.
Read, Forrest, *Pound/Joyce*, 140
Reade, Charles, *It Is Never Too Late to Mend*, 74, 77
Rhythm, 140
Richards, I. A., 11
Richardson, Dorothy, 6, 8, 20, 171–2, 175, 200, 221; *Backwater*, 172, 175; *Pilgrimage*, 6, 9, 18; *Pointed Roofs*, 172, 175
Richardson, Samuel, 106, 110, 199, 200; *Pamela*, 110, 144
Ridge, William Pett, 115
Roberts, Morley, *The Private Life of Henry Maitland*, 136
Robinson, Ralph, 234
Rodin, Auguste, 167
Rolland, Romain, 180, 195; *Jean Christophe*, 195, 196
Royal Society of Literature, Academic Committee of, 13, 181
Ruskin, John, 17, 167, 170; *Fors Clavigera*, 170
Russell, Elizabeth Mary, 205; *Elizabeth and her German Garden*, 198; *Elizabeth in Rügen*, 198

Sardou, Victorien, 21–2, 36; *Delia Harding*, 21–2, 36–9, 134; *Woman's Silence, A*, 39
Saturday Evening Post, 110
Saturday Review, 1, 5, 7, 19, 20, 22, 40, 48–133, 137, 141–3, 178, 189–91, 192, 230–3
Scheick, William J., 188
Science Schools Journal, 4, 5
Scott, Sir Walter, 83, 86, 99, 102, 103, 156, 205
Scribe, Eugène, 36
Scrutiny, 11
Shadwell, Thomas, 119
Shakespeare, William, 3, 10, 43, 195, 205; *Hamlet*, 218; *Julius Caesar*, 120, 218; *Merry Wives of Windsor, The*, 205
Shaw, George Bernard, 1, 13, 19–22, 23, 32, 49, 69, 86, 112, 127, 173, 202, 218; *Unsocial Socialist*,

Index

An, 69, 70
Shelley, Mary, *Frankenstein,* 240, 241, 245
Shelley, P. B., 4, 207
Sherard, Robert H., 'Jules Verne Revisited', 222, 228
Smith, C. Aubrey, 35
Smollett, Tobias, 33, 35, 159
Society of Authors, 63
Socrates, 4–5, 217
Southern Literary Messenger, 160
Spectator, 206
Spenser, Edmund, *The Faerie Queene,* 113
Spies, August, 113
Standard, 77
Steele, Sir Richard, 106, 110
Sterne, Laurence, 10, 124, 126, 128, 135, 139, 142, 159, 173, 180, 186, 196, 217; *Sentimental Journey, A,* 128; *Tristram Shandy,* 180, 195
Stevenson, Robert Louis, 50, 51, 64, 65, 84, 86, 99–103, 126, 145, 155, 173, 175, 187, 216, 230; *Dr Jekyll and Mr Hyde,* 99; *Familiar Studies of Men and Books,* 155; *Inland Voyage, An,* 65; 'Isle of Voices, The', 99; *Kidnapped,* 86; *Macaire, see* Henley, W. E.; *Master of Ballantrae, The,* 101; *New Arabian Nights,* 73; *Prince Otto,* 99, 102, 103; *Treasure Island,* 101, 102, 103; *Weir of Hermiston,* 1, 99–103; *Wrecker, The,* 103
Struwwelpeter, 3
Sullivan, Sir Arthur, 19
Suvin, Darko, 229
Swift, Jonathan, 10, 110, 139, 172, 186, 225, 242–3; *Gulliver's Travels,* 4, 172, 242
Swinnerton, Frank, 2, 136; *George Gissing,* 136; *Nocturne,* 18

T.P.'s Weekly, 222, 228
Tatler, 110
Taylor, Tom, *The Ticket-of-Leave Man,* 104, 109
Tennyson, Alfred, 4, 63, 110, 113;

Idylls of the King, 108, 114
Terry, Ellen, 31
Terry, Fred, 20, 29, 31, 38
Terry, Marion, 36
Thackeray, W. M., 5, 6, 10, 52, 53, 54, 135, 142, 159, 180, 186, 197–8, 205; *The Shabby-Genteel Story,* 194
Thorne, Fred, 35
Times, The, 67, 71
Times Literary Supplement, 181, 188
Tirebuck, William E., 70, 71; *Grace of All Souls,* 71
Tit-Bits, 74, 77
Tolkien, J. R. R., 232
Tolstoi, Leo, 33, 35, 52, 67, 136, 137, 138, 145, 156–9, 162, 186, 187; *Anna Karenina,* 67; *War and Peace,* 145, 247
transition, 176
Truro, Bishop of, 123
Tupper, Martin, *Stephen Langton,* 85
Turgenev, Ivan, 49, 52, 54, 67–71, 135–6, 137, 145, 146, 156–7, 159, 160, 186, 187, 196; *Fathers and Children,* 1, 52, 67–71; *On the Eve,* 70, 71; *Rudin,* 70; *Smoke,* 145; *Sportsman's Sketches, A,* 67, 71; *Spring Floods,* 67–71; *Virgin Soil,* 145

University Correspondent, 5

Vanbrugh, Irene, 29, 31
Verne, Jules, 222–4, 225, 228–9, 230, 231, 240, 244; *Autour de la lune,* 222, 245; *De la terre à la lune,* 222, 245
Vincent, H. H., 30
Voltaire, 4

Waller, Lewis, 25
Walpole, Hugh, 182, 183
Ward, Charles, *A Leader of Men,* 20
Ward, Mrs Humphry, 67, 70, 71, 146, 199; *Sir George Tressady,* 71
Watson, John, *see* 'Maclaren, Ian'

Index

Wells, Amy Catherine ('Jane'), 5, 6
WELLS, HERBERT GEORGE
'About Sir Thomas More', 186, 228, 234–7; 'Academic Committee, The', 18; 'Adelphi Romance, An', 50, 119–23; *After Democracy*, 244; *Anatomy of Frustration, The*, 10; *Ann Veronica*, 13, 179, 206, 218; *Anticipations*, 11, 238–9, 243, 246, 249; *Apropos of Dolores*, 219, 227; *Autocracy of Mr Parham, The*, 244; *Babes in the Darkling Wood*, 188, 216, 227; 'Beyond Criticism', 57; *Boon*, 2, 12, 15–16, 183–4, 186, 207–15; *Brynhild*, 219; *Bulpington of Blup, The*, 227; 'Certain Critical Opinions', 18, 86; *Certain Personal Matters*, 40; 'Chronic Argonauts, The', 5; 'Contemporary Novel, The', 14, 179–80, 186, 192–206; 'Correspondence: "The Island of Dr Moreau"', 229; *Country of the Blind and Other Stories, The*, 13–14, 18; *Crux Ansata*, 140; 'Decay of the Novel, The', 18; '"Delia Harding"', 36–9, 134, 141; 'Depressed School, The', 39, 134, 141; *Desert Daisy, The*, 3, 18; *Englishman Looks at the World, An*, 192, 234; *Experiment in Autobiography*, 3, 4, 8–9, 10, 14, 16, 19, 31, 59, 113, 136, 178–9, 185, 186, 188, 226, 228; 'Fiction about the Future', 224, 227, 246–51; *First Men in the Moon, The*, 222, 228, 243, 244; 'Flickers of Imagination and a Flare', 50–1, 78, 129–33, 179; *Food of the Gods, The*, 224, 243, 244; '"Guy Domville", at the St James's', 23, 31; *History of Mr Polly, The*, 10, 53; *Holy Terror, The*, 219, 246; *Honours Physiography*, 250; 'Ideal Husband, An', 24–6, 31, 122; 'Immature Fantastic, The', 229; 'Importance of Being Earnest, The', 27–31, 178; *In the Days of the Comet*, 111, 244, 245; *Invisible Man, The*, 1, 48, 88, 223, 240; *Island of Dr Moreau, The*, 1, 48, 224, 240, 243; 'James Joyce', 171–5, 221; *Joan and Peter*, 14, 219; 'Joan Haste', 49, 55–7, 86, 97, 103, 109, 118, 133, 231; 'Jude the Obscure', 71, 78, 79–82, 103; *Kipps*, 10, 53; *Lady Frankland's Companion*, 43; '"Leader of Men, A"', 23; 'Limits of Individual Plasticity, The', 229; 'Lost Quest, The', 51, 124–8, 133, 143, 160, 179; 'Lost Stevenson, The', 50, 51, 99–103, 231; *Love and Mr Lewisham*, 48, 49, 53, 136; 'Making of Men at Cambridge, The', 188; *Mankind in the Making*, 11–13, 18, 210–11, 215; 'Margaret Ogilvy', 175; *Marriage*, 182; *Men Like Gods*, 17, 111, 242, 243, 244, 245; 'Method of Mr George Meredith, The', 51, 63–5, 103, 205; *Mind at the End of Its Tether*, 15, 16; *Modern Utopia, A*, 10; *Mr Blettsworthy on Rampole Island*, 244; *Mr Britling Sees It Through*, 16, 219; 'Mr Grant Allen's New Novel', 35, 44, 47, 51, 59–62, 70, 82, 225, 229; 'Mr Wells Explains Himself', 229; 'New American Novelists, The', 52, 86, 137, 156–60, 170, 180; *New Machiavelli, The*, 10, 13, 14, 179; 'Notorious Mrs Ebbsmith, The', 19, 32–5; 'Novel of Ideas, The', 16, 188, 216–21; 'Novel of Types, The', 52, 67–71, 77, 79, 135–6, 137, 155, 191, 227; 'Novels of Mr George Gissing, The', 67, 71, 135–6, 144–55; 'On George MacDonald', 128, 223, 232–3; 'On Lang and Buchan', 50, 83–7, 92, 103, 175, 231; 'On Max Pemberton', 223–4, 230–1; 'Original Farcical Comedy, An', 23; 'Outcast of the Islands, An', 48, 50, 88–92, 97; *Outline of History, The*, 14, 16;

260

Index

'"Pair of Spectacles, A"', 23; '"Passport, The"', 23; 'Paying Guest, The', 51, 134, 137, 141–3, 160, 180, 205; 'Popular Writers and Press Critics', 49, 74–8, 92, 133, 186; 'Pose Novel, The', 19, 40–3; 'Rediscovery of the Unique, The', 7; *Research Magnificent, The*, 14; 'Sawdust Doll, The', 22, 44–7, 58, 103; 'Scepticism of the Instrument', 12; *Scientific Romances of H. G. Wells, The*, 15, 71, 222–8, 240–5; 'Scope of the Novel, The', *see* 'Contemporary Novel, The'; 'Secrets of the Short Story, The', 18, 65–6; 'Servants' Hall Vision, A', 50, 104–10, 191; *Seven Famous Novels*, *see Scientific Romances of H. G. Wells, The*; *Shape of Things to Come, The*, 227, 246; 'Simple Art of Popular Pathos, The', 50, 71, 94–7, 109; *Sleeper Awakes, The*, 224, 225, 238–9, 246, 251; 'Slip under the Microscope, A', 87; 'Slum Novel, A', 115–18; 'Socrates', 4; 'Stephen Crane. From an English Standpoint', 137, 161–70; *Things to Come*, 249–50; *Text-Book of Biology, A*, 250; 'Three Impostors, The', 72–3, 223; 'Three Yellow-Book Story Tellers', 183–4, 189–91, 215; *Time Machine, The*, 1, 5, 48, 86, 137, 178, 223, 224, 240, 243, 246, 247, 250; *Tono-Bungay*, 15, 53, 134, 136, 228, 239; *Undying Fire, The*, 10, 218; *War in the Air, The*, 238, 246; *War of the Worlds, The*, 223, 240, 243; 'Well at the World's End, The', 48, 50, 111–14; *Wheels of Chance, The*, 48; *When the Sleeper Wakes*, *see Sleeper Awakes, The*; 'Woman Who Did, The', 44, 48, 59; *Wonderful Visit, The*, 48, 59, 71; *Work, Wealth and Happiness of Mankind, The*, 17–18, 244; *World Set Free, The*, 238, 246; *You Can't Be Too Careful*, 216

West, Florence, 25
West, Geoffrey, *H. G. Wells*, 2, 140, 229
West, Rebecca, 188; *Henry James*, 188; *Strange Necessity, The*, 177
Westminster Gazette, 194, 196, 206
Weyman, Stanley, 86, 87, 90, 92, 230, 231
Wharton, Edith, 182
Whistler, J. M., 138, 162, 167, 170; *Gentle Art of Making Enemies, The*, 170
White, Barton, *Margate*, 23
Whiteing, Richard, 115
Wilde, Oscar, 20, 24–31; *Ideal Husband, An*, 20, 24–6, 31; *Importance of Being Earnest, The*, 20, 22, 23, 27–31; *Lady Windermere's Fan*, 26; *Woman of No Importance, A*, 24, 26
Williams, Charles, 232
Wilson, F. S., 57
Wilson, Harris, *Arnold Bennett and H. G. Wells*, 15, 53, 185, 187, 229, 245
Woman Who Didn't, The, 82
Woman Who Wouldn't, The, 82
Woolf, Virginia, 220, 221; *Jacob's Room*, 221; 'Modern Fiction', 221
Wyndham, George, 163

Yeats, W. B., 13
Yellow Book, 87, 189–91
Young Man, 13, 18

Zamyatin, Yevgeny, 225, 229
Zangwill, Israel, 242, 245
Zola, Emile, 6, 136, 145; *Lourdes*, 145; *Rome*, 145